The
Conspiracy

- the Real Story of the Cameo Cinema Murders.

by

GEORGE SKELLY

a n

publication

Further copies of this book are available from:-
Avid Publications
Garth Boulevard, Higher Bebington,
Wirral, Merseyside L63 5LS
United Kingdom.
Tel/Fax : 0151 645 2047
e-mail : avid@publications.freeserve.co.uk

Other publications from Avid are detailed at the rear of this book.
The Cameo Conspiracy - the Real Story of the Cameo Cinema Murders
ISBN 0 9521020 9 6

Editing and cover design by William David Roberts - Avid Publications.

Cover Photos:
Front: The Cameo Cinema and from the top:-
George Kelly, Lord Goddard, Charles Connolly,
Det. Chief Inspector Herbert Balmer.
Rear: Street plan of central Liverpool including the numerous
pubs and locations mentioned in the investigation.

The Author

Born in Liverpool the youngest of eleven children, *George Skelly* left school at 15 and was later educated at Ruskin College, Oxford and Liverpool University. Before then he worked variously as a butcher's assistant, shipyard labourer, waiter, barman and fitter's mate. In the 1997 General Election he stood for the Referendum Party in Liverpool's Riverside Constituency.

With several short stories and book reviews published and broadcast on radio, and a novel awaiting publication, *The Cameo Conspiracy* is his first published full-length work.

Acknowledgements

I should like to gratefully acknowledge the following persons and organisations without whose kind help, support, advice and assistance this book would never have happened:-
Lord Alton of Mossley Hill, Brian Aspinall, Robert ("Plumb Bob") Barlow, Alan Brown, Charlie Butterworth, Paddy Collingwood, the late Charles Connolly, Eileen Connolly, Stephen Connolly, the late Thomas ("Birkenhead Tommy") Conway, Jackie Corrigan, Thomas Gill Jnr., His Honour Judge Richard Hamilton, Ronald Harrison, Audrey Harrison, Kathleen Hughes, Harold Jones, Hilda Kelly, Peter Kelly, Agnes Kelly, Professor Mike McConville (Warwick University), Jean Warburton (University of Liverpool - Faculty of Law.), David Marsden, Tony Mossman - Curator: Merseyside Police Museum, Chris Mullin MP, Craig Nuttall, Iris O'Brien, Wally O'Brien, Vera Patterson, Doris Siner, Bridget Skelly, Neville Skelly, my brothers, Christopher Skelly, and the late James Skelly and John Skelly, Colin Stebbing, Frederick Thomella Jnr, Elvyn Thompson.
I am also greatly indebted to the helpful and hard-working staff of the following: Liverpool Crown Court, Liverpool Central Library, Liverpool Coroner's Office, Liverpool Daily Post, Merseyside Public Record Office, Merseyside Police, News of the World Library, The Public Record Office (Chancery Lane & Colindale, London), the Home Office.
There are of course many, many more individuals who provided valuable help and information but for understandable reasons wish to remain anonymous. To those persons I am equally indebted and immensely grateful.

George Skelly 1998

Photographs & illustrations courtesy of:- The author, I.L.N. PLC, Snapscene Ltd., Syndication International, Michael Rains of Newcastle - upon -Tyne, Liverpool Daily Post & Echo, the private collections of Eileen and Stephen Connolly, David Roberts, Ian Boumphrey, Gina Cummings, Mrs. Eilleen Jones, Ronald Harrison, Lou Santangeli and Mr. George Simms.

Introduction

On the Saturday evening of March 19th 1949, the manager of the Cameo cinema in Liverpool, forty four year-old Leonard Thomas, and his thirty year-old assistant, John Bernard Catterall, were brutally gunned down in a botched armed hold-up whilst counting the evenings takings of just £50.08d.

One year and nine days later on March 28th 1950, George Kelly, a 27-year-old unemployed labourer, was hanged for this crime. His co-accused, 26 years-old Charles Connolly had earlier been sentenced, in a separate trial, to ten years imprisonment after pleading guilty to Robbery and Conspiracy to Rob the Cameo cinema manager on that tragic night.

Originally Kelly and Connolly had sat in the dock together at Liverpool Assizes for thirteen days. However, when the jury returned to court after a mere four hours deliberation, to ask for further information about a prosecution witness, it was promptly dismissed by the Judge, Mr. Justice Oliver, and separate trials were ordered. This had never occurred before, nor has it ever occurred since in a case of two persons jointly charged with murder.

At his second trial, which lasted five days, Kelly was found guilty and sentenced to death on February 8th. Five days later on February 13th Connolly was tried and, in order to avoid a similar fate, was urged by his Counsel to plead guilty to the lesser charge of robbery.

This tragic conclusion to the Cameo Cinema case - at that time the longest murder trial in British criminal history - came about despite there not being a shred of forensic or material evidence against either man: no murder weapon, no bloodstains, no fingerprints and no eyewitnesses.

Despite both men steadfastly maintaining throughout that they did not even know each other, they were convicted on the evidence of a prostitute, her pimp, and a mentally ill convicted con-man.. To all intents and purposes however, public feeling at the time was that this was the correct legal and moral outcome to the case. The verdicts were fully in keeping with the prosecution evidence and Connolly's eventual guilty plea.

Public opinion was reassured by this apparent victory of law and order over the postwar tide of gangsterism and thuggery - widely regarded as a legacy of the wartime American influence and the spate of 1940's gangster movies. Indeed, Kelly was described rather melodramatically in the *Daily Mail,* as the, "Little Caesar of Lime Street." And the *Daily Express,* in an editorial following his execution, proclaimed, "Kelly richly deserved to hang and the world is the better for his removal."

Most of all, the verdicts were regarded as an affirmation of the impeccability of British Justice. "These two dangerous criminals" had got their just deserts. Indeed, the public mood was summed-up in that well-worn phrase: "Good riddance to bad rubbish".

After Kelly's execution there was an atmosphere of unashamed triumphalism in the Liverpool C.I.D. - particularly among the Murder Squad, who received eulogies and commendations galore from the city's Watch Committee. In this euphoric climate a senior detective involved in the case admitted to a well-known criminal lawyer that Kelly and Connolly had been fitted-up, telling him, "they were only scum anyway".

Two years later in Manchester, the prosecution's star witness, the 23 year old prostitute who had allegedly been racked with disease during the two trials, was sentenced, in the company of her latest pimp, to two years imprisonment for Robbery with Violence .

The families and friends of the two men had been virtually the only ones to assert their innocence. But the general feeling was that they would say that wouldn't they? Predictably their desperate pleas fell on deaf ears. The Court of Public Opinion was totally unsympathetic. After all, hadn't the two villains had not one, but two trials? What could be more fair? And did anyone for one moment, in 1950, believe the police would tell lies? Hadn't the two main prosecution witnesses been publicly complimented and financially rewarded by the trial judge for their public-spirited action? And weren't Connolly's guilty pleas to Robbery and Conspiracy to Rob, a virtual admission of the rightness of the convictions? Confirmation, surely, that the pair were rightly convicted?

Both families, bereft of any influence or resources, finally came to accept the injustice. The odds were insurmountable. Yet throughout every minute of his ten year prison sentence Charles Connolly had to control a burning sense of outrage. He *knew* he was innocent. But why should anybody listen to him? Hadn't he after all, pleaded guilty to plotting the crime with Kelly, and to robbery at the cinema?

Another man, Kelly's friend, *knew* that Kelly was also innocent. He knew this with the utmost certainty because Kelly was actually elsewhere with him on the evening of March 19th when he was alleged to have been plotting the crime with Connolly and the two prosecution witnesses. But why should anybody take his word? After all, didn't he too, like Kelly and Connolly, have a criminal record? It didn't seem to matter that the three main prosecution witnesses also had criminal records.

When Kelly was hanged in Liverpool's Walton prison another "murderer" had been judicially despatched in similar fashion two weeks earlier in Pentonville. His name was Timothy Evans, the young illiterate lodger of serial killer John Christie.

Evans was ultimately granted a posthumous pardon. But at the time, among the mass of law-abiding folk, there was no doubt about his guilt. Nor was there, in 1950, a Derek Bentley, a James Hanratty, a Birmingham Six, a Guildford Four, a Maguire Family, a Luton Three, a Bridgewater Three, a Cardiff Three, a Judith Ward or a Stefan Kiszko. In 1950 there was nothing to indicate the extent or even the existence of police corruption, nor of just how stubbornly incompetent and biased the judiciary could be.

Kelly's friend, over the course of many years repeatedly insisted Kelly's innocence to me. He was an alibi witness but little value was attached to his testimony. Indeed, the judge at the first trial made a point of discrediting his evidence solely because of his record. So much so that at the second trial Kelly's counsel declined to call him.

That man was my eldest brother James.

Charles Connolly, over the years, repeatedly protested his

innocence but nobody ever listened, apart from Lou Santangeli, a retired Liverpool businessman whom he met in 1990.

Becoming convinced of his innocence, Santangeli advised and encouraged him to make a final attempt to clear his name and used his own time and resources in order to try to establish his innocence. This resulted in a radio play in 1995.

At the time Santangeli, a respectable and hard-working member of the community, commented to the press:- *"In common with most people at the time of the Cameo trials, I always believed the verdict of the courts. It was the honesty and integrity of Charles Connolly, whom I met completely by chance some 40 years later, that inspired me to research the true facts of the case".*

My brother, aware that I was researching this book, provided me with invaluable information. And since his death in 1993 much of what he told me has been independently borne out by others in recorded interviews and confirmed in official documents hitherto unavailable.

When I first met Charles Connolly in 1993 and told him I was writing this book he and Santangeli were initially apprehensive, fearful that I was yet another sensation-seeking journalist. But after finally accepting my credentials as genuine, Connolly agreed to co-operate with me to tell for the first time the full true story of the Cameo case. During the next three years he not only provided me with invaluable information and abundant factual detail but also became a man whom I grew to admire and respect. During his wartime service in the Royal Navy he had an impeccable record, serving in the Pacific and on decoy duty at the Normandy landings.

Although 73, Connolly, an ex-amateur boxer, was a sociable, active and clean living man, whose appearance belied his years. It therefore came as a great personal shock when he collapsed and died of a heart attack in April 1997. Right up till his death however, he steadfastly maintained his innocence, swearing on his children's and grandchildren's lives that he had never known Kelly before the Cameo murders. Sadly however, he was tortured to the very end by his unshakeable conviction that his guilty plea had been responsible for the other man's execution..

Contrary to the usual form of books about miscarriages of justice, I have used a "faction"- style narrative to cover the movements and interaction of most of the principal characters, leading up to and during the actual trials. Where there is obviously no official record of these, they have been portrayed from information given to me in confidence and /or in a manner which, on a careful balance of probability, seemed to me the most likely - given the circumstances and context at any particular juncture. In addition I have drawn extensively on my personal knowledge of the milieu of which Kelly, my brother and their associates were part.

As for the absurdly tragic nature of the trials and the compounded wickedness of the false testimony against the two men, this will become self evident through the reader's familiarity with the earlier chapters depicting what really happened. The entire fabricated case against Kelly and Connolly will thus speak for itself.

In his closing speech to the jury at the first trial, Connolly's Counsel, Mr. Basil Neild KC., had this to say *"I ask you to use this test: would it be right in the years ahead when you look back to the Cameo murder trial to be able to say, 'I know what I did was right' Then your verdict is right. If you looked back and said, 'I think', and 'I hope', then your verdict will not be right."*

After the passage of so many years it is doubtful whether the two men's innocence can now be proved conclusively. For although I was allowed by the Home Office, "privileged access" to one file (which had been previously vetted), other files were to remain closed for fifty years, with a possible extension to a hundred years. Requests to both Conservative and Labour Home Secretaries to open them, have met with identically-worded refusals - on the grounds that public disclosure may affect the privacy of some person or persons. This "privacy" is apparently regarded by the Home Office as more important than the probability that an innocent man was hanged.

Today, when the Government in the public interest regularly opens previously classified state papers, *after a mere thirty years*, on such matters of national security as germ warfare, civil insurrection and armed nuclear strategy, one cannot begin to imagine what awesome threat to our national security the files on a fifty year-old provincial murder trial must hold! It would thus appear that the conspiracy continues.

Despite these obstacles however, what can now be established are such grave doubts about the safety of Kelly's conviction, that it must be reviewed. For no jury today would ever convict on the evidence as it stood then. And even the strongly influenced 1950 jury could not have reached their guilty verdict had they known all of the facts which are revealed in this book for the first time.

By exposing the police and judicial conspiracy against Kelly and Connolly in the Cameo case, it is hoped that Kelly's conviction and execution, even after all this time, will cause such anxiety in the public consciousness - which is now so much more worldly about our criminal justice system - that never again in such a case will a jury member be able to look back and say, "I know what I did was right."

And in the case of Charles Connolly, that never again will an innocent man become so cruelly entangled in such a finely woven web of police corruption, and the vagaries of British justice, that he is forced to wrongly condemn himself.

The Cameo Conspiracy

Georgie and Jimmy leaving the *Midland* pub en-route to *Tracey's*. 1949.

George Kelly (left) James Skelly (right).

Prologue

9.00 am. March 28th. 1950

"They hanged him as a beast is hanged:
They did not even toll
A requiem that might have brought
Rest to his startled soul,
But hurriedly they took him out
And hid him in a hole."
Oscar Wilde.

"I didn't do it yer know. I didn't. I didn't do it, straight up. Honest, I didn't do it". The plea had been constantly made by Georgie to all of the prison officers taking it in shifts to guard him in the condemned cell at Walton Gaol, Liverpool.

He'd been telling them this for weeks now but since his Appeal had been turned down a few days ago, the pleas had become more regular and insistent. And as always they were made out of sheer indignation and incredulity rather than for mercy. Georgie wasn't going to beg anyone for anything. Why should he? He'd done nothing wrong. Two trials he'd had at the Assizes. And he'd told them minute after minute, hour after hour, day after day, that he was innocent. God! How maddening! Why won't they fuckin-well believe me?

Suddenly the cell door flew open. At the same time a tall cabinet against the left-hand wall was shoved aside to reveal two open yellow doors. Georgie jumped up from the table and spun around to face the cell door. A smallish, neatly-dressed man was coming towards him with a leather strap in his hand. He had a cold, no-nonsense, business-like look about him. He was Albert Pierrepoint, the Public Executioner.

Georgie knew who the man was and why he was here. But his reaction was what it would have been in *any* situation of simply being taken by surprise. He'd never been in a situation like this before in his whole twenty-seven years.

"Oh, alright", he said, as if simply greeting an unexpected visitor. There was no reply as his arms were pulled behind his back and his wrists quickly strapped together.

"I didn't do it yer know. Straight up, I didn't do..."

"Follow me", interrupted Pierrepoint as he strode purposefully through the yellow doors. Flanked as he was by two prison officers, Georgie didn't have much choice. But, unable to comprehend what was happening, he almost hurried after the Hangman, calling out to him with increasing urgency, "Honest to God, straight up, on me mother's life, I didn't do it!"

It was as though he hadn't realised he was walking straight into the Execution Chamber; as if he hadn't even noticed the noosed rope hanging directly in front of him. His overriding concern was to convince him he had nothing to do with the murders. Even when he felt his ankles being strapped behind him it didn't really register.

Aware now of several other men in civvies standing around in the Chamber, he frantically thought, surely *these* people will understand? *These* people look educated. He appealed directly to them. "Honest to God, I didn't do this. Th..."

Suddenly, Pierrepoint put something over his head and everything went black. He then felt the noose being fixed under his left jaw. Before he could finish the sentence he felt himself falling and heard a loud crashing bang. Then everything went *completely* black. Georgie never spoke anymore.

Pierrepoint, followed by the prison Medical Officer, immediately went to the steps at the side of the Gallows and walked briskly down into the Pit where the body hung motionless. Tearing open the freshly laundered white shirt, he exposed Georgie's chest for the doctor's stethoscope, then stood down from the small set of wooden steps.

The Medical Officer ascended the steps, and after a few seconds said in a professional tone, "Good. Everything's fine."

Hangman and Medical Officer then walked back up into the Chamber to rejoin the Governor, Father Lane, the Catholic chaplain,, the Under Sheriff and other officials. After a few more seconds they all left and a prison officer locked the doors to the Execution Chamber and the Condemned Cell.

An hour later at 10.00am, Pierrepoint and his Assistant, Harry Allen, returned to the Chamber with two prison officers. Georgie's hooded body was still hanging in mid-air, suspended solely by his jaw-bone.

Pierrepoint quickly took out a tape measure and, with the assistance of Allen down below, measured the height from Georgie's feet to the scaffold floor. It was considerably longer than the drop he had given him. But not to worry, he thought, it was probably due to the neck being stretched for the past hour.

Allen, now up top, rigged up a second rope to the lifting tackle on the Gallows main beam, whilst Pierrepoint, now in the pit, removed the straps from Georgie's ankles and wrists and began stripping the body.

The brown patent leather shoes were the first. But since the newly dead man had not been allowed shoelaces these came off quite easily. He then began removing the trousers of Georgie's immaculate grey suit. But as these were being peeled off, he suddenly shouted out in exasperation, "Oh no! Bloody hell!" Allen up above asked, "What's up Albert?"

"What's up?, mimicked Pierrepoint, ignoring the grim-faced prison officers. "What's up? The bugger's only shit himself that's what's up! Let's bloody-well hurry up and get it over with."

Clearly annoyed, Pierrepoint quickly went about stripping the remaining clothes from the body as it swung to his touch. Finally, as an afterthought, he tied Georgie's shirt around his naked body at the waist.

Allen was now lowering the second rope, which Pierrepoint quickly looped in a sling under Georgie's arms, tightening it, as he did so, around his bare chest so that it would not slip. Then, whilst Allen and the two prison officers hauled up the corpse, he quickly dashed back up into the Chamber.

Georgie's hooded head was now slightly above the level of the open trap doors. And the slack now gained in the hanging rope enabled Pierrepoint, who was kneeling on the gallows floor, to remove the noose and the hood. Then, clasping the lolling head with both hands, he rolled it from side to side, almost in an embrace and proudly whispered to his assistant, "Good. Instantaneous. A clean break. The third vertebra!"

As the body was slowly lowered back down into the Pit,

Pierrepoint was waiting with open arms and screwed-up nose to receive it. Then, easing it into the plain unvarnished coffin lying nearby, he undid the rope from under the limp arms and roughly pulled it away, causing the lifeless body to slowly roll from side to side.

When Georgie's soiled, naked body was at last reposed in the wooden box, Pierrepoint shouted up to Allen, "Righty O, that's it. Tea up!" He and his Assistant then left the Execution Chamber as quickly as possible, leaving the two prison officers to guard the body until the inquest and burial later on that morning.

The Inquest was held an hour later by the aptly named Liverpool Coroner, Mr. Cecil Mort, along with a coroner's jury. The prison Governor, Mr. Alfred Coombe Wall Richards, and the Medical Officer, Dr. Francis Brisby, testified that, "the arrangements went without a hitch and the Execution was carried out in a skilful, humane and decorous manner."

At lunchtime Georgie was buried in grave number 54, under the east wall behind the prison hospital. By that time the phlegmatic Pierrepoint was already on his way to Birmingham's Winson Green prison to hang another condemned man - a Pole named Piotr Maksimowski.

It was March the 28th 1950 - one year and nine days since the double murder of the manager and assistant manager of the Cameo Cinema in Wavertree Liverpool. And with the execution of Georgie Kelly everyone was satisfied that justice had been done. But had it?

Chapter One

Saturday March 19th 1949. 1.15pm.

"We're off to see the Wizard"

It was a sunny but blustery day in Liverpool city centre. Georgie Kelly and Jimmy Skelly were leaving the *Midland* pub, opposite Central Station, on their way to *Harry Tracey's* in Hanover Street. Today they were going to make a day of it on the ale.

Georgie as usual, was immaculately dressed in a brown bird's-eye double breasted suit, cream shirt and tie, and well polished brown shoes. At five foot seven and almost as broad as tall, everyone said he was a dead ringer for the film star John Garfield. Jimmy was smartly dressed in similar fashion At five foot eight he was as broad as Georgie but of stockier build.

Striding jauntily across busy tram-lined Ranelagh Street in the Spring sunshine , the two men spotted street photographer and spiv Johnnie Costello giving out phoney receipts to passers-by for the photos he'd pretended to take of them. "Hey John!", shouted Georgie, "What about us two like?"

Georgie and Jimmy were well known down the town. And although likeable, they could "have a go" when the occasion arose. A few months earlier Jimmy had been involved in an epic fist-fight in the *Midland* with Paddy McGrath, an ex-professional boxer and big wheel in the Seamen's Union. And only just over a week ago in broad daylight, the two friends had been in a fight with two policemen at the bottom of Brownlow Hill outside the *Adelphi* Hotel. So far they had been lucky enough to evade arrest.

"Okay Georgie, you're on", said Costello, his camera clicking, this time for real. "Be ready Monday. All right?" Georgie nodded agreement and turned to Jimmy with a satisfied grin: "All right there eh Jim? More free smudges on Monday?"

"Bet there's no film in the fuckin' thing if I know him", said Jimmy. "Better had be", he replied.

Jimmy thought Costello was probably giving copies to the police. "He took me old fella last week walkin' down here", he said. "How come all the smudges are always taken in the same spot. And", he went on, "how come he always takes our smudges when *we* never pay him?"

"Aw, come on Jim", said Georgie, "that's his normal pitch outside the Station. An' he knows he's got no chance of getting any dough out of us - especially *your* old fella." "All I know", insisted Jimmy, "is I don't fuckin' trust him".

Tracey's was pretty crowded, as it usually was on a Saturday afternoon. Sitting under the window drinking a glass of beer was Black Sheila, a middle-aged, cadaverous-looking prostitute, who wore too much make-up and suffered from Tuberculosis.

"Hello Georgie.", she greeted. Gonna get us a drink darling?" "Sure what yer havin' kid?"

"A Gin and tonic if you don't mind pet", she replied." But before he could respond, Jimmy told her to fuck off. "Go `an ask your fuckin' ponce", he hissed. Who d'yer think we are?" At this, Sheila slowly bowed her head in defeat, and pointing two fingers upwards at them, whispered into her glass, "Fuck yiz then".

"Cheek of her", said Georgie lightly. "I wouldn't mind but she was only drinking a glass of bitter". "Fuck her," said Jimmy dismissively, "Get a bad name talkin' to that one. Bad enough being a whore but I believe she's a fuckin' stoolie as well".

"Yer don't think I was really gonna get her a bevvy do yer?" said Georgie with a smile. Then across the crowded bar he shouted, "Hey Harry". are yer serving or what?. We're bleedin' parched here". "All right boys. Keep yer shirts on," said the approaching Harry Tracey.

"What are you two cowboys up to now?", he chided with mock reproof. "Heard yiz got shut of those clothing coupons the other day? 'Bout time *I* got a bleedin' bevvy off you two!"

"Turn it in Harry", said Jimmy light - heartedly. "Give us two pints... and give that whore a bucket of water...over her head!" Harry smiled tolerantly. "Listen", he said, "as long as they don't pull any mushes in here I don't mind. Live and let live, that's what I say boys." "You're jokin' aren't yer", said Georgie. "She got Johnny-One a five stretch last week just cos he didn't pay her for a short time. Swore his bleedin' life away. Lying bastard said he tried to rape her". "You what!" he exclaimed. "I didn't know that!"

With a determined expression he quickly moved towards Sheila, still sitting dejectedly clasping her near-empty glass. "Come on you", he ordered. "Drink that and get out!" I don't want no stool-pigeons in here. Johnny-One Cunningham was a bloody nice fella". "What's up with you"? she indignantly cried, "I don't know what you're fuckin' talking about". "You know full well what I'm talking about", he said menacingly. "Now Get out before I throw you out!"

Sheila slowly rose from her seat, and as she slunk out of the door muttered under her breath, "Bastard! They're all fuckin crazy in this town."

The two friends had been watching the incident with amusement. And as Harry made his way self-righteously back around the bar, Georgie mischievously whispered , "That's the competition knackered Jim".

"Too right", said the other indignantly. "Yer can't get a look-in with a Payoff with vultures like her always hanging around". Georgie, grinning, said, "I'll tell yer what, it'd be just our luck for Johnny One to walk in here any minute now and make a fuckin' liar of us!"

Tracey's was one of the few pubs in the city centre with a radiogram, which was why it was so popular. So Jimmy asked Harry to put on a record.

"Bloody'ell lads I've only got one pair of hands!", he responded, then called to the barmaid, "Hey Tessie put some bleedin' records on for these two will yer before I have a riot on me hands".

As they bit into their frothy pints of the renowned Walkers mild, the pub began to fill with the sound of Vera Lynn singing, *We'll Meet Again.*

"Ah hey Harry", Georgie moaned, "nark it will yer. Do us a favour. Not *her* !"

"Yeah", echoed Jimmy, "It's like a fuckin' mortuary in here listenin' to that one. "D'yer know what ", he lied, "there was more fellas than soft Joe done themselves in with depression during the war through her whingeing." At this Harry, who himself had seen active service, protested defensively, "Ah, come on lads you've gotta be jokin'? The Forces Sweetheart? She was the only bloody thing that kept us going during the war".

Tiring of the subject, Georgie pleaded, "Come on Harry", put a *decent* record on. Go on, give us a few Jolson's".

"Yeah, or a Fats Waller", added his friend.

Ignoring their requests, Harry said with a pained expresssion, "I suppose it'd be too much to ask yiz for the money for the pints?" But Georgie joked, "Yer wanna be careful Haitch, yer can get locked up for offensive language like that." Then, in more serious tone, he said, "Straight up we'll see yer all right later on. We've got a bit of gear to pick up tonight."

"Yeah, I know", he sighed wearily, "Tell it to the friggin marines George."

Moments later the sound of Al Jolson came booming out from the radiogram, drowning the steady hub of conversation. *"California Here I come, Right back where I started from..."*

"That's more like it", said Georgie as he began miming to the record, whilst Harry, pulling a pint, quietly murmured to himself, "He's a bleedin' character that lad."

The two friends were still larking about at the bar when a tall, well-built, craggy-faced man wearing a gabardine raincoat and trilby, entered the pub and stood in the passageway. With him was another less well built, slightly smaller man, similarly attired.

On seeing them Jimmy's expression changed immediately. "Nitto George", he whispered. "The Balmer fella's just come in." Unconcerned, Georgie calmly said, "Take no bread poultice. He's probably on the mooch looking for info."

"Who's the prick with him?"

"Don't yer know him?" said Georgie, surprised at his friend's ignorance. "That's the famous Detective Sergeant Farragher, the patron saint of stoolies and whores." Peeved at his own lack of knowledge, Jimmy grunted sarcastically, "Same thing aren't they, whores and stoolies?" "Ah yeah, but what about all the other stoolies; the taxi drivers and ale-house managers, he replied knowingly?"

Detective Chief Inspector Balmer and Detective Sergeant Farragher were standing by the large aperture of a serving hatch, which gave them an unrestricted view of the L-shaped bar and the open parlour behind them. They always drank in the passage and never stood in the public bar or sat down in the parlour. It was as if they regarded the ordinary drinkers in the bar as beneath them. And in the parlour your hearing and vision was too restricted. In the passage you saw and heard everyone and everything.

As Harry served their drinks Balmer mouthed something to him, indicating Georgie and Jimmy, and as they caught his eye he gave a silent nod of recognition. Moments later two pints appeared in front of them and Harry gave them a sideways glance in Balmer's direction. Without saying anything they both contented themselves with a mere nod of acknowledgement across the bar . It didn't do your reputation any good in the town to be seen talking to detectives, much less taking drinks off them - especially Balmer.

By now, *California...* had been followed by *April Showers, Swanee* and *Ma Blushin' Rosie* , and Georgie and Jimmy still hadn't had to pay for a drink. They were glad Black Sheila had been thrown out, for as popular as they both were, most pay-offs, especially those just paid-off a ship, would much rather treat a whore than them.

Balmer and Farragher were still drinking in the passage but had now been joined by two other detectives, both wearing the familiar belted raincoats and trilbies. Whilst they were quaffing their glasses of draught bass and laughing dutifully at one of Balmer's jokes, Georgie beckoned Harry over and whispered. "How are yer fixed for a Oncer till tonight?".

"Aw come on George", he pleaded in a hushed tone, "you've just had two buckshee pints and you already owe me two pound from last week. D'yer think I'm fuckin' made of the stuff?"

"Honest to god", Georgie lied, "We've got loads of nylons lined up later on, straight up, no messing. Haven't we Jim?"

"That's straight that Harry" said Jimmy, "It's money in the bank".

Harry considered the proposal for a moment then pulled out a pound note. "There! Now no more George. That's the last, d'yer hear!" Slipping the money unobtrusively into his pocket, Georgie whispered, "You're a real pal Harry". Then glancing across at Balmer, he said, "Don't let that bastard know anything".

Fearing that once the pound was spent they would be after more,

Harry decided it was time they both left. "By the way", he lied, "Flat-Nose" Barney was in earlier on. Loaded he was. Just paid off I believe". "Go away!", they both exclaimed. "Well, believe it or believe it not", He went on convincingly. "Throwing his dosh around like confetti, he was. Just finished a three-month South African trip I believe".

"Flat-Nose", a Bosun with the Union Castle Line, was noted for his generosity whenever he came home from sea. And although he'd earned his nickname through being an ex-pugilist, he was a generous, convivial man who liked nothing more than to have a good time.

"Did he say where he was off to?", asked Georgie. "Nah, didn't say", replied a straight-faced Harry. "Did mention though, he'd probably end up in Renee Brown's, probably looking for a whore after three months away, I should imagine."

Renee's, an illicit club in the South End of the city, was open every day after the pubs closed. Providing you had the cash you could get anything there, from black market clothing coupons, cigarettes and whisky, to a woman, or even a car.

On hearing the good news about "Flat-Nose", the two friends quickly finished their pints and hurriedly bade farewell to Harry. As they were leaving a Fats Waller record - *My Very Good Friend the Milkman* - came on the radiogram, and a smiling Harry called out, "Hey Jimmy aren't yer gonna listen to yer request?"
"Nah, yer alright Harry", he shouted back, "It's ale we're after it, not milk. See yer."

Once outside the two young men made their way briskly back up Ranelagh street, past the *Midland* and the *Central* pubs, towards the bombed site opposite *Lewis's* department store where Georgie's mother was selling fruit and flowers from her barrow.

Unlike the other Liverpool barrows, which were merely glorified handcarts, the barrow was a genuine Cockney one. It had been a parting gift to Georgie from Jacky-the Greek, the owner of the Primrose Cafe in nearby Cases Street.

Up till a few months ago, Georgie had been the doorman at the Primrose and Jacky's general factotum but had left to run the barrow. But soon becoming bored with selling fruit he'd passed it on to his mother, who had been a fruit hawker all her life.

Passing Central Station, Jimmy mentioned how uneasy he'd felt with Balmer in the pub. "I can't stand the bastard either" said Georgie. "Or that fuckin' Farragher. But what can yer do Jim when they send you a bevvy over?"

"Yeah, but I don't like taking ale off bizzies. Get a fuckin' bad name."

"Don't worry about it," said Georgie dismissively. Then, rubbing his hands in anticipation, he said, "Let's concentrate on Flat Nose. But I wanna tap me old-lady first for a few more bob so's we can get up there and catch him."

Jimmy however wouldn't drop the subject of Balmer. "Did yer notice", he mused, "never threw any money across the bar for our ale. Or his own. Or anyone else's for that matter...did yer notice that?"

"Too right", said Georgie. "Would you, if you had the whole fuckin' town sewn up? Got all the whores and the ale-house managers in his pocket hasn't he? Probably got a bit of black on Harry as well, if the truth's known. Don't play ball with him", he went on, "and' yer can say ta-ra to your fuckin' licence for a start."

Jimmy quickly changed the subject, for although he would never admit it, he was always impressed with Georgie's superior knowledge of the C.I.D. "I'll tell yer what", he laughed, "If they knew it was us who stretched those two coppers the other week, they'd have been throwin' fuckin' handcuffs at us instead of pints!" Not wishing to be reminded of the incident, Georgie said, "Aw nitto will yer Jimmy, that's history. Say no more".

Georgie's mother, a slightly built woman in her mid-fifties, was sitting on an up-ended orange box beside her barrow. "Here we are", she was shouting, "five for a shillin' the oranges. Tenpence a bunch, the daffs!"

"Alright Mam", said Georgie, "how's tricks?" Well used to her son's approach when he wanted anything from her, she said, "I hope yer not after money again, cos I've got none." She then asked Jimmy how his mother was. "She's all right Mrs. Kelly", he replied.

"Ah, hey Mam", Georgie began, "I only need a pound. We've got a bit of gear to pick up in a club later on but we haven't got the entrance fee. Isn't that right Jim?" Jimmy nodded. "Oh, Jesus, Mary and Saint Joseph", she moaned wearily, "God forgive yer, the tales yer come out with."

"Honest to god Mam", he insisted, "I'll give yer it back later. Honest. Only a pound that's all"

Finally, with a sigh of resignation, his mother dug deeply into the large black pocket tied around her waist and counted out a pound in half crowns. Then, handing him the money, she moaned, "You'll have me in the bleedin' Workhouse before yer finished."

Giving her a hug, he said, "Yer the best in the world". Then mimicking Jolson, he started singing the first few bars of *Mammy*. But Jimmy, growing impatient, interrupted, "Are we off then, George?", then added quietly, "If we don't fuckin'-well hurry up someone else is gonna capture Flat-Nose"

"Yeah okay", said Georgie, quickly taking the point and bidding his mother a hasty farewell.

Crossing the road en-route to the tram stop in Renshaw Street, they spotted "Irish Paddy", the store detective from *Lewis's*, coming down Ranelagh street on his way back to the store.

In keeping with the nature of his job, 'Paddy' was a thin, medium sized, unobtrusive, shabbily dressed man. Georgie often got money off him because he knew - and Irish Paddy knew he knew - that instead of calling the police and having the female shoplifters arrested, he would frequently frogmarch them to the store's staff toilets and demand sex. Some of the persistent offenders, the professional "hoisters" with long records, who otherwise would have faced a long gaol term, were only too willing to comply with his demands. Nobody knew his real name so they all called him 'Irish Paddy' because he was supposed to have originated from Northern Ireland.

As 'Paddy' got nearer, Georgie, whispered, "Must be my lucky day Jim, Look who's walking straight into me bleedin' arms!" On seeing them, 'Paddy' tried to pass un-noticed among the Saturday shopping crowds but Georgie blocked his way. "Hello me old friend", he said. "Just the fella I wanna see." Looking sheepish but anticipating Georgie's request, he murmured, "Before you ask, I've got no money."

"Ah, come on Paddy", he cajoled, "all we need is half-a quid. We're trying to get in the club but we need the entrance fee. Come on", he pleaded, "ten shillin' won't break the bank."

Knowing how persuasive Georgie could be and the futility of arguing with him, 'Paddy' rummaged in the pockets of his shabby mac and pulled out a handful of coins and some notes. Then without saying another word, he begrudgingly thrust a ten-shilling note into his outstretched hand and quickly scurried away into *Lewis's*.

Pocketing the money, Georgie casually said, "I believe he fucked the arse off one of the McKay sisters last week. Caught Mary red-handed with a load of kids socks and shirts. Mind you", he continued, "she had no choice, know what I mean? She's got form for the Hoist as long as yer arm."

"Dirty little bastard!", said Jimmy angrily. "Yer know what, if I was her fella I'd kick his fuckin' bollocks in". "Well", he said, "she's not likely to tell her fella is she? Anyway", he laughed, "never mind his bollocks, kick his *pocket* in like I do. That's the best way to do a tight fisted bastard like him. He fuckin' hates parting with money."

As the two friends confidently strode up Ranelagh street and around *Lewis's* corner to the tram-stop, Georgie slipped Jimmy the pound note from Harry Tracey and they both began singing, *"We're off to see the Wizard, the wonderful Wizard of Oz. He must be a wonderful Wizard cos look at the things that he does..."*.

Chapter Two

Saturday March 19th 1949. 2.00pm.

"Oh! How We Danced"

Charlie Connolly, his wife Mary and three-year-old baby Tina were enjoying tea and cakes in Littlewood's cafe on the corner of Cases Street and Clayton Square in the city centre - less than two hundred yards from *Tracey's* pub.

Charlie felt happy for a change. What with the problems with his in-laws and the shift working at Bibby's flour mill, things hadn't been too good lately. But he was really enjoying today, alone with Mary and Tina at last.

He'd finished his last shift of the week at ten-o'clock last night. And was he glad! Now he could relax. Glancing at Mary wiping some cake crumbs from around his little daughter's mouth, he felt proud and protective towards them.

As they finished their tea and cakes, Charlie spotted, sitting at another table, a young prostitute he'd occasionally seen parading up and down Lime Street. And although she seemed to have dyed her hair blonde since he'd last seen her, she still looked dirty and scruffy. She always looked dirty and scruffy. He'd even seen her a few times picking up dog-ends out of the gutters in Lime Street.

She had a bandage around her head, which wasn't unusual, he thought, because every time he saw her she always seemed to have a dirty bandage either around her leg or on her head. He didn't know her personally, or even to speak to, but he'd heard a fellow named "Bobby" Woolerton, who knocked around Lime Street, had done six months for poncing off her. He'd heard her name was Jackie Dickson but he couldn't remember who he'd heard it from.

Charlie had no time at all for women like her. She disgusted him. So when he saw little Tina, who was now becoming restless, going over to her table, he quickly nipped over and, grabbing her up in his arms, brought her back to their own table. He didn't want his innocent little daughter endangered in any way. You never knew what she might catch from the dirty whore!

Quite handsome in a rugged sort of way, Charlie, who came from around the city centre's Park Lane area, was nearly six foot tall and had been a successful amateur boxer.

At the age of twelve he'd represented his school, St. Peter's in Seel street, and become English Schoolboy champion. Later, during the war, whilst serving in the Indian ocean with the Royal Navy he'd become Welterweight Champion of South-East Asia Command, never having lost a fight. One of his victories had been against Randolph Turpin who, ten years later, would go on to defeat the great Sugar Ray Robinson for the World Middleweight title.

Charlie didn't like bullies. One day, just before joining the Navy, he was having a football kick-about with some youngsters in the square of St. Oswalds tenements near his mother's house in Old Swan. A group of policemen, going on duty at Derby Lane police station, were taking a short-cut through the square when one of them ordered the children to stop playing. Charlie shouted over, "Ah leave them alone. There's nowhere else for them to play around here." But the officer, piqued at this apparent challenge to his authority, tried to arrest him by grabbing him in an armlock. Charlie retaliated by punching him on the chin. The other officers then pounced on him with their batons and proceeded to kick and drag him through the busy Old Swan shopping area, all the way to the police station.

The following day he was fined forty shillings for Disorderly Behaviour and Assault on the Police. He was sixteen at the time.

Nowadays though, Charlie did his best to avoid trouble. In fact he was trying to start a new life with Mary and Tina in Australia. He'd actually signed the forms three months ago but had still not heard anything tangible. This was his second application. His brother Billy, who had emigrated to Sydney in 1945, had offered to sponsor him two years ago, but nothing had come of that either.

Charlie put these delays down to government red tape so he wasn't unduly worried. He knew things would turn out right in the end. And meanwhile the thought of going to live in the new land of Australia was really something to look forward to.

On their shopping list today was a new coat for Tina. They thought

Lewis's would be the best bet because they sold good stuff. Tina wasn't going to wear any old rubbish. She deserved the best. And Mary knew *Lewis's* was a quality shop because she'd worked there last year as a waitress in the basement restaurant - where Charlie would often call in for something to eat before catching the bus in Lime Street, to work. .

Although originating from Dickinson Street off Upper Frederick Street, Charlie and his small family were now living up on the new Huyton estate. But though the house was nice and had all the modern conveniences it was a very long way from town. - and it wasn't even their own home. It was Mary's parents. And they were so overcrowded that there always seemed to be friction. Any sort of privacy for Charlie and Mary was simply out of the question. And the area itself was so soul-less and barren. A born city dweller, he'd rather have the hustle and bustle of town any day.

After they'd bought Tina's coat they crossed over the road to the *Adelphi* Hotel and caught the No 6A tram at the bottom of Brownlow Hill up to Charlie's mother's, who still lived in Old Swan.

Trundling up Edge Lane past Botanic Park and the Littlewood's Pools building, the tram finally stopped directly across the road from St. Mark's Church.

Charlie and Mary were hoping to go to the Dance there tonight. They'd gone last Saturday night and Mary had won two half price admission tickets and a nice bracelet for winning the crooning contest, singing *"Sorrento"*. Charlie too had won a spot prize - a half-price admission ticket. They'd also had their photos taken and were looking forward to picking them up.

His younger sisters, Doris and Irene, would be going tonight as well. They went to St. Marks every Saturday night without fail. It was almost a ritual for them. Indeed, the main reason for him going last week was to make sure his sisters were safe. Because two weeks ago a fracas had broken out and Doris, an innocent party, had ended up with a black eye.

Charlie, Mary and little Tina got off the tram at the next stop and arrived at his mother's around 6.45pm.

Doris, at nineteen the elder of the two sisters by a year, was just finishing her Tea. Irene, having already finished her meal, was reading the evening paper. Their mother had a raging toothache. But although they were all sympathetic, Charlie and Mary couldn't help feeling disappointed, for they knew that they couldn't now expect her to baby-sit whilst they went to the dance.

As Mrs. Connolly prepared something to eat for her son and daughter-in-law, the girls began to get washed and dressed and made-up. Charlie watched with amusement as the girls put on leg-tan and drew for each other a line down the backs of each leg with a pencil, to make it look as though they were wearing nylons.

When they were finally ready, Doris said she was going around to call for her friend and would see Irene in the Dance. About ten minutes later, at 8.15pm, Irene's friend, Betty Dixon, called and they too left for the dance.

Charlie and Mary had now finished their meal and Charlie told his mother he was still worried about the girls going to St. Mark's without any protection. She replied that, since he had the half price ticket from last week he might as well go too. "That's what you'd originally intended to do anyway, wasn't it?", she said. So after being assured that Mary didn't mind, he quickly washed, grabbed his coat from the back of the chair, and, putting on his trilby, said, "I'll go around and make sure they're all right".

Although still in pain, Mrs. Connolly felt sorry for Mary, so after about ten minutes she told her, "You might as well go too. I'll keep an eye on the baby".

"Are you sure?"

"Yes, go on. You'd better start getting ready".

Mary was thrilled. And feeling both gratitude and sympathy towards her mother-in-law, she went to the bathroom to get ready.

Irene, Doris and their friends, Betty Dixon, Frances Roberts and Frances Cairns, who were all a bit younger than Charlie, were full of joy and laughter. But Charlie, feeling out of place without Mary, couldn't *really* enjoy himself. Shortly after nine-o-clock however she appeared. His face suddenly lit up at the sight of her This truly made his night. Now he could really enjoy himself.

At a quarter to ten the Compere announced there would be a

Rumba competition. So after a brief conference between Charlie, Mary, Doris and Irene, it was decided that Charlie would partner Doris because it was acknowledged they were the best at the Rumba. That way they'd have a better chance of winning one of the spot prizes.

Mary didn't take umbrage. After all, so long as the winners were among the family, that was the main thing. She was enjoying herself regardless. And so was Charlie, as he suavely swept Doris across the dance floor to the Latin- American beat of the saucy Carmen Miranda number, *"Aye, Aye, I Like You Very Much"*.

As they danced , Doris who had been a fan of Carmen Miranda's since childhood, lightly remarked that the dance was really a Samba because the singer was known as the "Queen of the Samba". Charlie laughingly replied, "I don't know the difference so, I'll tell yer what, let's call it the Sumba!"

"Or," Doris laughed, "the Ramba!"

In the event it was the two Frances', Cairns and Roberts, who won. The "grand prize" was ten cigarettes! And they all laughed as Frances Cairns opened the packet and offered the cigarettes around among them.

At about ten thirty the photographer Tommy Milligan, came in with his partner. He came in every Saturday around about this time, after the pubs closed. Charlie, having already paid him the two shillings deposit last week, paid the remainder to Milligan's partner, who was dealing with the cash, and got the two prints off him.

Mary liked the photographs but Charlie wasn't too keen. He always felt he took a lousy photo but his wife assured him he looked great.

Later, at around 10-45, the Dance was ending and Charlie asked for his trilby from the cloakroom girl. But no sooner had he put it on when he felt Irene grabbing at his arm, and pulling him back onto the dance floor for the Last Waltz. He reluctantly obliged but as it turned out it wasn't *the* last waltz. The *actual* Last Waltz was *The Anniversary Song,* so he stayed on the dance floor and partnered Mary for this special last number.

As they danced Mary, feeling happy and relaxed, began to quietly sing to the music, *"Oh, how we danced on the night we were wed... "*

Charlie was quite oblivious to his faintly eccentric appearance as he innocently waltzed around the dance floor still wearing his trilby But Mary wasn't. "Ah, hey Charlie", she said , "get the hat off *in here*". But, although embarrassed, he just mumbled that it didn't matter as they'd be leaving in a few minutes anyway.

Although Charlie had enjoyed the evening and didn't wish to spoil anyone's enjoyment, he was worried about his mother being in so much pain, and couldn't wait to get home to see how she was.

After they had all stood for the national anthem, Charlie and his crowd left and walked together the short distance up Edge Lane and around the corner to his mother's, where Betty Dixon and the two Frances's said goodnight and carried on home.

Despite her toothache, Mrs. Connolly had made them all tea and spam sandwiches and asked if they'd enjoyed themselves. Irene and Doris told her about the two Frances' winning the Rumba competition and Mary showed her the photographs. Charlie asked his mother if the toothache was any better and she replied that she had taken some Aspro's and it had gone a lot easier.

At twenty-to-twelve , whilst Mary began dressing Tina, Charlie said, "Well Mam, we'd better be getting off now. We don't wanna miss the last bus."

He didn't relish the prospect of returning to his in-laws house. Things hadn't been going too well lately. There had been quite a bit of friction between him and them. But until such time as the Corporation offered him a house of their own, he had no choice but to put up with it.

They were just in time to catch the last Number 10 bus at the corner of St. Oswald's Street and Prescot Road and were home in Huyton in about twenty minutes.

When they arrived the house was in darkness with Mary's parents already in bed. So not wishing to disturb them Charlie carried Tina, who was now asleep, upstairs to the one bedroom they shared, with Mary following on tip toe.

His wife and baby daughter had been fast asleep for hours but Charlie still lay awake worrying about all sorts of things. Would he really ever be able to make a new life for them in Australia? He'd been trying now for two years but didn't seem to be making any progress. He'd actually filled the latest set of forms in three months ago but nothing seemed to be happening. What if it all fell through? What sort of future could he provide for his wife and little daughter?

Mary might be starting a new job in *Maison Lyons* on Monday, but that place was self-service. Waitresses money wasn't all that great as it was but now she wouldn't even be getting any tips. In any case, it was his place to be the breadwinner. He didn't want to be sponging off his wife. So how was he going to tell her he'd already given his notice in at Bibby's? The thought of *that* filled him with dread In two weeks time he'd be out of work and on the Dole. What were they going to do then?

Chapter Three

Saturday March 19th 1949. 4.30pm.

"We are the Brothers Malone"

Georgie and Jimmy were having a great time in Renee Brown's. The shebeen, which had legally been known as the Ludo Club before losing its licence, was jumping. Never mind a radiogram, there was actually a big Wurlitzer jukebox in here!

If you wanted to attract the American servicemen from Burtonwood you just had to have a jukebox. And if Renee was nothing else, she was a good businesswoman. Although very astute she nevertheless had a heart of gold. She liked people to have a good time and she was always good for a loan.

The place was packed with uniformed Americans, both black and white, and West Indians and Nigerians and some Liverpool blacks. The latter were called 'half-castes' among the white Liverpudlians but they referred to each other as 'half chats'.

Most of the girls off the town were also here: Red Betty, Scotch Esther, Taxi Annie, Irish Pat, Red Rita, Blonde Peggy, Welsh Margaret, Norwegian Margie, Deaf Dolly, The Widow, and several more. They, like Renee, were good business women: they knew where the mushes and the money were.

Georgie and Jimmy had still not spotted 'Flat-Nose Barney' but they weren't too worried. They were well known and well-liked in here - mostly by the half-castes who had been in gaol or Borstal with them.

As couples danced the Rumba to the Andrews Sisters *Rum and Coca Cola* on the jukebox, Jimmy went to the toilet, whilst Georgie got into conversation with an American Army sergeant who said he worked in the PX Stores at the Burtonwood Army base.

Georgie had been involved in the black market business with Americans in the past on behalf of Jacky-The-Greek: Whisky, cigarettes, nylons, that kind of stuff. Inspector Balmer had known about it and used to get the occasional case of *Dimple* whisky or carton of *Lucky Strike* off Jacky to keep him quiet. But he suddenly put a stop to it, telling him things were getting too hot. But Jacky said the real reason was because Balmer had become involved with bigger fish and didn't want anybody rocking the boat.

The bigger fish, said Jacky, had been running a large scale operation on the docks, involving American PX supplies like cigarettes, spirits, watches, jewellery and even army jeeps. And Balmer had taken his cut by acting as the discreet middleman between the gang and selected cafe and club owners, and pub licensees.

Because of his position he was able to ensure that the pillaged goods were sold to them at rock bottom prices. But when the gang decided to cut Balmer out and get better prices from other buyers, he resorted to his official role and had them all arrested, claiming he had merely been posing as a buyer in order to smash the black market ring.

Jacky said Balmer had been very clever. He knew they couldn't expose him without admitting their own guilt - which would have been suicidal. So when they were all found guilty and sentenced, Balmer not only received a judge's commendation for his brilliant detective work, he also ensured that in future nobody would deal through anyone else but him.

When Georgie mentioned Balmer's name the sergeant's attitude quickly changed. "Well buddy it's been nice knowing you", he said nervously, as he picked up his drink and moved slowly away.

Surprised and disappointed at the American's sudden departure, Georgie looked around the crowded room for Jimmy. Suddenly he heard a familiar voice. "Alright George, how's it going me old cocker?" It was Paddy "Banjo" O'Hara.

Banjo, a brilliant musician, was always bumming drinks off people on the promise that he would play their favourite tune. The instrument was almost like a bodily appendage. He never went anywhere without it but hardly ever played other than for his own enjoyment or if forced to by an indignant benefactor. His regular excuse, after he had obtained his free drinks, was that a string was broken or that it needed tuning. So despite him being a talented performer, the banjo was utilised more as a gimmick than anything else.

Georgie got in first. "Before you start Banjo", he asserted, "I'm skint, so don't start playin' that fuckin' thing. Yer know I can't stand that George Formby fella. Anyway", he went on, "we've only come in to see if we can see Flat-Nose-Barney. Believe he's just paid off a ship".

"That's okay Georgie", said Banjo, patting him on the shoulder. "What are yer worrying about. No bother. You can have a bevvy off me. And by the way", he added, "don't class me with that Formby clown. Imposter that fella. Strums, that's all he can do. Gets away with fuckin' murder, he does." Then, proudly sticking out his chest, he said, "Bet yer he can't play the fuckin' *Warsaw Concerto* like me. That takes real talent".

Ignoring Banjo's hurt artistic feelings, Georgie light-heartedly remarked that he must have plenty of money to be offering drinks. "Where did yer touch?" He asked.

Looking furtively around under the grimy peak of his flat cap, Banjo rolled up his coat sleeve to reveal a bare arm straddled from wrist to elbow with a line of cheap, flashy, gold-coloured watches. Then, with a sly wink he whispered, "Say nothin'. They're going like hot cakes in here. These Yanks don't know the fuckin' difference. They think they're the real McCoy". Georgie laughed. "Yer crafty old bastard"

"Hey, d'yer mind", he protested. "Less of the old. I might have lost most of me hair but I'm still only forty-one yer know".

Through the strains of Tommy Dorsey's *On The Sunny Side of The Street,* Georgie shouted through the dense throng to his friend, who was talking at the far end of the bar. "Hey Jimmy get over here quick, a bleedin' miracle's happened. Banjo's getting the ale in!".

"Ah, eh George, yer don't have to make a show of me", said Banjo with a hurt expression.

As Jimmy approached he cried, "Hello! Hello! Hello! What's goin' on here Paddy? Won the pools have yer?" Still looking hurt, Banjo said, "Yer know what George, I'll ignore that from him 'cos he's a gentleman Jimmy is. He's the only fucker in this town who calls me by my *real* name. Anyway what are yiz havin' lads?" Renee's didn't sell draught ale so they both ordered bottles of Blue Bass - the strongest drink in the club.

After paying for the drinks Banjo haughtily exclaimed, "Well I can't waste valuable time talking to you fellas. I've got business to do".

And as he drifted off into the crowded club Georgie told his friend about the watches. "He'd better be careful", warned Jimmy. "These yanks don't like being conned yer know. They'd put a fuckin' knife in him as soon as look at him, no messin'".

"Don't worry about him ", said Georgie, " Yer know him. He can talk his way out of a jigger of shite."

Georgie wanted to borrow a few pounds off Renee but she was busily serving at the bar so whilst he awaited his opportunity, Jimmy began telling him the latest news he'd just heard from an acquaintance in the toilet.

Marty McManus, whom they both knew, had received five years last week at the Assizes. "Fuckin' ell!. What for?", exclaimed Georgie. "Some whore I believe", said Jimmy. "Seems she short-changed him so he gave her a smack. Danny Mills was just tellin' me. Said this fuckin' Brass swore Marty's life away."

"Who was she?"

"Dunno, never heard of her", said Jimmy. "Some whore from Manchester I believe - name of Jackie Dickson. D'yer know her?" "Never heard of her", replied Georgie, "she must be a ruthless cunt whoever she is, getting him five penn'orth just 'cos he wasn't mug enough to let her con him". "I believe it was a bit of a frame-up" said Jimmy, "How d'yer mean?"

"Well," he explained, "it seems this Dickson one is well in with that Busy who was with Balmer in *Traceys*. What's his name, Farragher? Anyhow it seems she takes the half-a quid off Marty for a short time - down in Hanover Street on an 'oller it was. But then she won't come across and tries to sneak off. Anyway, he catches her and asks for his money back but she starts calling him all kinds of names and starts screaming 'Police!' So he gives her a smack. Well", he continued, "Marty realises with his form, its gettin' a bit dodgy. So he spots a copper and goes over to explain what's happened. In the meantime it seems this fuckin' Dickson Brass was half bevvied and she'd fell over on the 'oller and cut her head and scraped her face on the bricks and rubble. So she tells the copper that Marty done her with half-a-brick. But the copper doesn't believe her. So after taking Marty's name and address he tells him he can go. Anyway, to cut a long story short", he continued, "this Dickson one goes the Royal in an ambulance, gets a few stitches and sends for Farragher. Farragher orders the rookie copper to go to the Sally Army Kip-house in Norton Street, and arrest Marty for Attempted Murder!"

"Fuckin' ell", exclaimed Georgie, "I don't believe it. He was only staying in the Sally Army cos' he'd split up with his missus. That's terrible that, Jimmy. What a bastard!"

"Well", said Jimmy shrugging his shoulders, "that's the score. That's what Danny was tellin' me in the piss-house. It seems the Farragher prick got the rookie to change his story to say he'd seen Marty attackin' her and that he'd ran after him and arrested him, and that Marty had admitted hitting her on the head with the half-a-brick a few times to try and kill her. Problem was, he had a bit of form for violence didn't he? And that's why he got the five-stretch"

"Oh yeah, but not for smacking whores" said Georgie. "Only for fair fights. *You* knew Marty. He could have a Go couldn't he? The twat must have asked for it."

"Well, yer know the bizzies," said Jimmy shrugging his shoulders. "Gotta look after their stoolies haven't they?"

"How d'yer know she's a stoolie? Yer don't even know her do yer?"

"Come on", said Jimmy with a cynical shrug. " I told yer, Danny said she was well in with the Farragher fella. And it was you who said he had a fuckin' army of stoolies and whores, didn't yer?"

As they talked, Norwegian Margie approached. A beautiful brunette of twenty-seven, Margaret Hanley had a strange melancholy air about her. She was originally from Stockport, where as a child she had gone to Grammar School. But during the war, whilst still a teenager, she'd married a petty officer in the navy, a Norwegian named Kjeld Taanevig. The marriage hadn't lasted. And when he left her she'd drifted into prostitution around Lime Street. Nowadays she was always slightly tipsy and noticeably always wore too much make-up.

Georgie liked Margie a lot. He even used to visit her occasionally when she'd lived over the surgical outfitters shop at the bottom of Mount Pleasant. But he was very discreet about it. He didn't want it known that he was seeing a whore or even fond of one. That was why he kept Doris O'Malley, the woman he now lived with, in the background as much as he could, even though *she* was no longer on the game.

Embracing Georgie, a somewhat tipsy Margie asked him to dance. He reluctantly obliged - more to save himself from embarrassment in front of Jimmy than anything else.

Dick Haymes was singing *You'll Never Know* on the Wurlitzer, and as they slowly danced to the music, tears appeared in Margie's eyes. "You know I love you", she whispered, "but you don't want to know me do you? I know what it is though", she went on, "You don't think I'm good enough for you?"

Feeling uncomfortable, he said, "Ah, come on, nark it will yer, it's the ale that's talking now. Yer know I think a lot of yer Marge". And to reassure her he held her closer and kissed her neck. But she went on, "I'd pack the game in tomorrow if you'd only say you love me. Don't you understand, I think the world of you but you hardly ever come and see me these days." No, and I'm not likely to, he thought. He'd heard she was now living in a furnished room around Grove Street, with some pimp posing as her husband.

When the music ended, Georgie said he'd like to buy her a drink but lied that he had no money. "I'm waitin' to tap Renee for a few quid", he said.

Telling him not to be stupid, Margie said she had plenty of money. "You don't have to bum off her," she said. "You can have what you want off me." But, without letting on he knew she was living with a ponce, he simply said that he couldn't take money off her. And as he returned to his friend at the bar, she drifted tearfully back to her seat...and, as usual, began re-applying her make-up.

Meanwhile the jukebox had broken down and the customers were becoming agitated. Clicker Clarke, a cheeky little half-caste, and a regular in Renee's, was kicking the front of it and telling everybody that this remedy always worked. But this time it didn't, and Renee was getting worried. Discontent was spreading and some customers were beginning to leave.

Spotting his opportunity, and pointing to the banjo slung across his shoulder, Banjo O'Hara shouted, "Hey Renee there's *real* music here if the price is right. What d'yer say?" Renee quickly agreed to pay him two pounds before any more customers left, whereupon he immediately started up with a Dixieland medley that soon had the Americans happily dancing and clapping their hands.

Clicker, very black and handsome, with slicked-back wavy hair parted down the middle, came over to Georgie and Jimmy. "Hard luck there lads", he complained. "A kick usually works. Can't understand it. If I'd got it going I'd a been alright for a few bob off Renee. Still", he sighed philosophically, nodding in Banjo's direction, "I guess one man's loss is another man's gain".

The two friends knew Clicker well. A real character who always joking, he was known as 'a personality'. Flashing a straight row of brilliant white teeth and chuckling throatily in his own inimitable way, he had the most captivating smile. Some people called him a bum and a ponce. He certainly had loads of charisma and could charm men or women. But as far as Georgie and Jimmy knew, he was a genuine fellow who simply lived on his wits like them.

With an impish aspect to him, Clicker was a witty and humorous raconteur who got free drinks off people on the strength of his personality and entertaining company. But he never *asked* anybody for a drink. So in that sense he was not a bum.

"Well, Mr.Kelly and Mr.Skelly, sirs", he declared with mock formality and a twinkle in his eye, "Nothing would delight me more than to ask you'se to partake of some alcoholic refreshment with me. Unfortunately however, we have a temporary problem of insufficient funds".

Familiar with his patter, Jimmy good-naturedly said, "Pack it in Clicker. What are yer havin'...apart from a bad time?" Unruffled, he replied, "Well, since you are kind enough to ask sir, I shall have a bottle of Guinness with you and your esteemed friend." And as Jimmy ordered the drink, Clicker, reverting to his streetwise persona, said, "Hey lads, I've got a nice little bit of philosophy for you'se two. Learned it in the Nick a few weeks ago. Listen":-

My days of youth are ended, my torch of life is out. What used to be my sex-appeal, is now my water-spout. Off-times of its own accord, it would from my trousers spring. Now I've got a full time

job, to find the fuckin' thing. It used to be embarrassing the way it
would behave. For every single morning it stood and watched me
shave. But as old age approaches it sure gives me the blues, To see
it hang its weary head and watch me clean my shoes."

The two friends burst out laughing, and before they could recover
he quickly asked, "Have yiz ever heard of the famous poet Longfellow."
They hadn't. "Well", said Clicker, "he's heard of you two. He even
wrote a poem about yiz".

"About us ?", asked a puzzled Georgie. "Yeah, you'se two", he said
with a straight face "Listen":-

*"Between the dark and the daylight, When the night is beginning
to lower, Comes a pause in the day's occupation, That is known as
the burglars hour. From my study I see in the lamplight, descending
the broad hall stairs, Georgie Kelly and Jimmy Skelly. Dial 999!"*
"Get it?", he laughed throatily at his own parodying of *The Childrens
Hour*. "You'se two screwing a posh gaff." But this time, instead of
laughing, they simply stared deadpan at him.

Clicker could have gone on all day with his quick-fire repartee but
Georgie, observing that Renee was at last available, said politely,
"Excuse me a minute will yer Click, got a bit of business on with
Renee. You know the score". Taking the hint, Clicker nodded knowingly
and drifted away still flashing his white teeth and smiling to himself.

Renee willingly obliged with the loan of two pounds. She knew
who to lend and who not to lend to. Georgie always paid her back.
And if he didn't pay with money, he would pay with gear such as
nylons or cigarettes or clothing coupons.

Banjo, sitting down in front of the defunct jukebox, was giving a
plaintive rendition of *La Paloma* to a hushed appreciative house when
suddenly, a burly, drunken GI staggered over towards him, grabbed
him by the throat and called him a "goddamned fuckin' shyster".

Banjo had sold one of the fake watches to the G.I.'s friend.
Unfortunately for him, it seemed the G.I.'s father owned a watch
repair business back in the States!

The huge American now had Banjo pushed up against the wall and
was throttling him whilst demanding his friend's money back. Seeing
this Georgie and Jimmy raced over and whilst Georgie stood facing

the crowd with clenched fists, Jimmy dragged the American off Banjo and butted him several times full in the face.

As Banjo staggered forward into the jukebox it started playing again, bringing forth the racy rhythm of The Andrews Sisters, *Boogie Woogie Boy Of Company B*.

The American, with an ugly gash suddenly appearing down his nose, swung a punch at Jimmy, but he slipped it and began throwing rapid hard lefts and rights to the G.I.'s head. Finally, under the pressure and speed of this assault, the American, his entire face now a mask of blood, slowly crumbled and finally collapsed over a chair.

It was all over so quickly that the two friends were away out of the club before anyone had fully realised what had happened.

Once outside in the tree-lined Princes Avenue, they whistled down a passing taxi but it sailed past without stopping. Cursing the driver, they ran up towards the taxi rank outside the *Rialto* cinema at the junction of Princes Avenue and Upper Parliament Street. But again they were out of luck. The rank was empty.

After a few anxious moments they spotted a No. 25 tram slowly turning the main junction from Princes Avenue into Upper Parliament Street. This tram, which went across the city from Aigburth to Walton, didn't go near town but so long as it got them away from the scene it would have to do.

As they jumped aboard, the over-zealous conductor was immediately upon them, demanding their fares. Already annoyed at having to jump this tram instead of one going to town, they glared at him and with one voice told him to "fuck off". Smelling the drink on them, he discreetly disappeared upstairs without another word.

"Talking about money", said Jimmy, "where's my cut of the two quid off Renee?" Georgie dug into his trouser pocket and handed him a pound note as Jimmy gave him a mock reproving glance. Slightly annoyed at this he said, with a hurt expression, "Fuckin' ell Jimmy, what am I supposed to do? Run over and stick the money into your fuckin' hand while you're battering the Yank?" Jimmy smiled knowingly but said nothing more.

Just before leaving the tram at the end of Crown Street they asked the conductor for the time. Very subserviently he told them it was six o'clock. They then walked the few yards to *The Royal William* pub at the major junction where Crown Street, Elizabeth Street, Pembroke Place, West Derby Street, Boundary Place, Hardwicke Street and Fairclough Lane all converged.

Waiting outside they saw Yorkie Bob, shivering with the cold. Yorkie, was a pint-sized ex-seaman of sixty-five who had sailed with Jimmy's father as a Trimmer on the White Star and Cunard ships. He had always been noted for his generosity when he'd paid off from a trip. And although originally from Sheffield he had long ago lost his Yorkshire accent and now spoke with a full Scouse brogue. Wearing a flat cap, greasy with dirt, and a scruffy overcoat, he looked really down-at-heel.

"Hey up!", greeted Jimmy, and Georgie cried, "All right, Yorkie pal, What yer doing out here?" And before he could reply they invited him to have a drink.

Yorkie explained that he wasn't waiting for someone to take him in. He had a few bob, he said. He'd just been waiting for the pub to open. "Why? Aren't they open yet?, asked Georgie. "Should have been open at half-fuckin'-five", said Jimmy, rubbing a slight graze on his forehead where he had butted the G.I.

"What happened to you Jimmy?", asked Yorkie, "Been in a bit of lumber, have yiz?" Georgie answered for him: "Yeah. Some big Yank tried to work out on Banjo O'Hara in Renee Brown's so he filled him in".

"Fuckin' hell!", exclaimed Yorkie, "Yer don't say". Then turning to Jimmy he said, "Yer wanna watch it yer know in case the bizzies come looking for yer. Yer know what that place's like? Full of whores and stool-pigeons. And the coppers like to keep in with the yanks yer know". Jimmy, still rubbing his forehead said, "Fuck them. I'm not worried". Then turning to his friend he said, "Anyway, it was a fair fight wasn't it George?"

"Oh aye yeah. Too right" agreed the other. "And he was *big* enough wasn't he Jim? Yer know what I mean like Yorkie", he went on, "it's not as though he picked on a little mug or something". Anyway Jim", he said, "there's no chance of Renee calling the coppers. She's not gonna blow her own goldmine up."

Curious about what they were doing around here, Yorkie, who lived in nearby Moon Street, said, "Never seen yiz around this area before lads". Georgie explained that they had jumped the first tram that came otherwise they would have gone down the town.

The three men continued talking outside the pub for about thirty minutes before the doors were finally opened by the Manager, who gave no explanation nor made any apology as he hurried inside to start serving. "About fuckin' time", grumbled Yorkie. "Talk about brass monkeys! The balls are frozen off me. Been standing here since half fuckin` five, I have!"

Several other customers who had also been waiting outside followed them in through the open door.

As Georgie ordered three pints Jimmy remarked what a miserable looking bastard the Manager was. To humour him Yorkie began telling them about an incident the previous day with Jimmy's dad in the *Caledonian* in Lime Street.

"Hey Jimmy", he said, smiling. "He's a fuckin' case, yer owld fella. Yer know what, when I went in he was with this Payoff and every time the Payoff called for a round yer owld fella put me on a drink. Anyway", he went on, "when the Payoff goes the piss-house, he says to me, 'I've gotta nurse this mush good-style Yorkie, 'cos those whores in the corner are waiting like vultures to snatch him off me'.

"Yer know what a mean like," continued Yorkie, "cos there was three whores sitting in the wing giving this Payoff mush the eye. Anyway, when the Payoff comes back from the piss-stone, he starts looking around at the Brasses, getting interested like, yer know what I mean? So yer owld fella puts his arm around him, real friendly like, and whispers in his ear:- 'Be careful pal, them whores are *all* dosed up. "Not only that, they fart like men...only louder."

At this they all broke into laughter. "Anyway", went on Yorkie, chuckling between each sentence, "the mush wasn't put off. He just said to yer owld fella, `That's disgusting that is!' "Well, yer owld fella isn't put off that easy either. So the next thing is, he winks at me and tells the Payoff he's just going to the piss-stone."

"Well," he went on, "I didn't know what Johnny was up to at the time. Anyway he comes back and then some of the whores start going for a piss. By this time the ale's coming up good-style from the Payoff. And like I say, Johnny keeps putting me on every round."

"Anyway", continued Yorkie, "me and Johnny are slowly getting bevvied but the Payoff seems to be getting randier and starts looking around at the brasses again. I'll tell yer who they were", he interjected. "Red Betty was there and Taxi Annie. Don't know the other one's name."

"Well, all of a sudden, they start pullin' funny faces and squirming in their seats and rubbing their arses. Next thing yer know is they're all fuckin' off out of the alehouse in a hurry like they were in agony. Well the Payoff's blimping all of this carry-on, and he looks real puzzled. So yer owld fella says to him, `I told yer didn't I? They're all dosed to the eyeballs with the pox'".

"Anyway," laughed Yorkie, "the mush turns round to yer owld fella and says, `Thanks for marking me card Johnny. Could've caught a dose of syphilis there'. Then he goes for another piss. When he's gone, yer owld fella pulls a tube of ointment or liniment or something out of his pocket and says, `That's the answer to the whores Yorkie. They can't beat that. Strongest stuff on the market. Burns like fuck!'."

Georgie and Jimmy by now were almost doubled up with laughter. "Anyway", Yorkie continued, "I'm still no wiser so I asks him what had happened. Ah, well, I'm not kiddin' yer lads, I was in fuckin' stitches when he told me".

Yorkie again burst out laughing and after finally catching his breath , he went on, "Yer know what he'd done? He'd only gone into the ladies lavatory and smeared this stuff all over the lavatory seat. The best thing about it, never once did he laugh or even smile. Me? I'm not tellin' yiz a word of a lie, I was fuckin' doubled-up!"

Standing by the bar and listening to all of this was another acquaintance of Jimmy's dad. And as all three were roaring with laughter, he shouted over with a deadpan expression, "That's fuck all. The other week I saw him clean all the whores out've Fat Johnnie's club in ten minutes with a jar of Epsom Salts". At that, Georgie, Jimmy and Yorkie again burst out laughing.

After another round of drinks and the swapping of several more ribald tales, Yorkie left, saying he was going down to Feeney's pub in

Myrtle Street to see if he could see his brother-in-law. It was now 7.35pm and Georgie and Jimmy were beginning to get tipsy.

Despite the fun they'd had, *The Royal William*, wasn't a lively pub. It had no music. And when they attempted to have a song a distinct scowl of disapproval appeared on the Manager's face. But mindful of the earlier fight in Renee's, they didn't want any trouble in case he called the police so they decided to go across the road to *The Liverpool Arms* at the bottom of Fairclough Lane and West Derby Street.

This pub was much bigger and livelier than *The Royal William*. It was known as a "singing house". Indeed, it was one of the few pubs in Liverpool to actually have live music on Saturday nights, with a compere and a piano.

The Public Bar was about a quarter full, and from a record player behind the bar came the sound of the Mills Brothers singing, *You Always Hurt The One You Love*. Ordering two pints of Mild, the two friends began singing along with the record but were given an apprehensive look by the barman.

Looking around for any sign of food, Georgie said, "Yer know what Jim I'm fuckin' starvin' are you?"

"I was earlier on but it's gone off me now", said Jimmy. "Can't understand these alehouses" said Georgie irritably. "Never see a fuckin' pie or a sarny do yer?".

They didn't usually drink in this pub. It was on the fringes of the city centre and although it had a sort of cosmopolitan atmosphere when it became crowded on a Saturday night, it was still regarded as their *local* by the inhabitants of the cramped terraced houses in the densely-packed surrounding streets.

Whilst Georgie was ordering another two pints, Perry Como came on the record player singing the sentimental ballad, *When I Lost You*. This prompted Jimmy to matter-of-factly say, "Wouldn't he put years on yer?" But Georgie retorted, "Ah, nark it Jim. Me mam loves him singing that song. It's her favourite." And to emphasise his approval, he began singing along with the record, *"I lost the sunshine and roses, I lost the heaven so blue..."* But the Manager quickly interrupted him, saying there was no singing allowed. "Yer jokin' aren't

yer pal", he cried indignantly. "I thought this was a singing house?"
"It is, at nine-o'clock when the *live* music starts, but not this early,"
he piously replied.

Nothing further was said. They both knew they couldn't afford
to have any more trouble tonight so they didn't pursue the matter.

The record had now changed to Frank Sinatra singing, *Begin The
Beguine*, and Jimmy, feeling himself getting drunker, wanted to get
nearer to home. Suddenly he muttered in the direction of the officious
manager, "Fuck him and his alehouse. Not a pie or a sarney anywhere.
May as well be on fuckin' chokey in the Nick!" Then attacking Sinatra,
he went on, "And havin' to put up with that skinny little bastard trying
to sing. Fuck it George, let's get off the side. Come on, let's go up the
`Coach?"

"Hang on Jim", said Georgie, burping, "let's finish our ale first".

As they gulped down their pints another Sinatra record came
on. This time it was *Whispering*. The Manager had by now gone
down through the trapdoor to the cellar so Georgie started singing
again. This time Jimmy joined in. But as they didn't know the proper
words, they sang a parodied version:
*"I'd like to sleep with Daddy Christmas. I'd smack his arse and
pull his whiskers..."*

Suddenly emerging from the cellar, the Manager prudishly declared,
"Aye aye, we'll have less of that!" But having drank up by this time,
they told him to fuck off, before making their way up Fairclough Lane
to the *Coach & Horses*.

Fairclough Lane, a steep hill, ran diagonally with Prescot Street up
to Low Hill and *The Coach and Horses*.
The pub straddled the corners of Low Hill, Holborn Street and
Kensington at another busy junction with Prescot Street and Hall Lane.

A few yards down Prescot Street, in the direction of the city centre,
was the police station, which housed B Division of Liverpool City
Police. Many of the detectives drank, after hours, in the adjacent *Blue
Ball* pub and in the '*Coach*.
The managers of both pubs liked to keep in their good books. A few
free drinks after hours was a good insurance policy. You had to rely
on the police for your licence. If they objected to that you were out of

a job! So it paid to keep them sweet.

Jimmy was relieved to be in the '*Coach* at last for he lived only a few yards away in Holborn Street, a thickly populated, cobble-stoned street of tightly-knit terraced houses down both sides.

The pub was quite full. And as the pair entered, several of Jimmy's neighbours showed out to him. One of them, Taffy Roberts, who was standing by the bar, offered them a drink and told them that Liz, the Manager's wife, was in charge tonight because her husband was having a night off. Another neighbour then sent two pints over for them

The licensee's wife was quite easy going so Jimmy told Georgie they'd be all right for a sing-song.

Georgie didn't know anyone in the pub and nobody knew him, but they reckoned that if he was with Jimmy he must be all right.

The *Coach*' didn't have any music. Nevertheless the two friends began to sing quietly. And before long "Not-Guilty-Billy", sitting in the corner, pulled out his mouth organ and began accompanying them.

Billy, with a neatly trimmed moustache and a thin, faded aristocratic appearance, had been a pickpocket at the racecourses in his younger days. But he'd been retired for several years after getting severe arthritis in his fingers. His nickname had been acquired through him always pleading not guilty whenever he was arrested - even when caught red-handed. But these days he could just about grasp the mouth organ in one hand.

Georgie and Jimmy were by now singing in close harmony, a parodied chorus of an old Irish song:-
"*We are the Brothers Malone. We come from the County Tyrone. We are two dandies and we are two swells. And to the ladies, we raise our straw cadies. We've a beautiful style of our own. You can tell by our hats, we're a right pair of twats. We're the brothers Malone from Tyrone...*"

Liz, who was busy serving customers in the lounge didn't seem to object to their singing so they gradually got bolder and louder. Then, two grey-haired old market women sitting in the corner, dressed in black *Mary Ellen* "uniforms" of blouses, long skirts, shawls and lace-up boots, got up and started dancing.

To earn a few shillings the women occasionally sold parsley and celery outside St. Johns Market down town. The combination of their appearance and their dancing prompted the two friends to break into another, more appropriate song:-

"All me life I've wanted to be a barrow boy. A barrow boy I've always wanted to be. Now I've got me title, I'll stick to it with pride. I'm a Coster, a Coster, From good old Merseyside. I turned me back upon the old society. Just take me where the ripe bananas grow. Ten for a shillin'. That's how I earn me livin'. I ought to 'ave been a barrow boy years ago..."

Their singing was however abrubtly interrupted by the entrance of a police sergeant and a constable, at which a hushed silence descended over the entire pub. The sergeant, wearing a grim expression, tapped his truncheon lightly on the floor as he and his colleague strolled silently around the bar and into the lounge.

This sort of patrol was a regular occurrence in the pubs at weekends. The police hoped it would re-assure licensees and keep the drinkers under control. But most customers simply viewed it as an occupational hazard. Usually, it had no effect other than ensuring a temporary silence until they'd left.

When the uniformed duo emerged from the lounge the Sergeant asked the Manager's wife if everything was all right. She nodded agreement, but as soon as they had left she told Jimmy to quieten it down.

"They're early aren't they Jim," said Georgie. "Don't usually go on their rounds till about quarter to ten". Hearing this, Not-Guilty-Billy, in a feeble attempt to be funny, said to Jimmy, "They must've known you two were in here". The two friends ignored the remark and Georgie told Jimmy he was leaving. The policemen's visit seemed to have broken up the happy atmosphere.

"Ah, don't be like that George," cried Jimmy with a mixture of surprise and disappointment, "What are yer going for? It's only early yet. Lets have another bevvy and a song".

"Yer know the score Jim", he replied with a slight slur. He then explained that he wanted to get to *The Leigh Arms* to spend the last hour of drinking with "Dolly" - his nickname for girlfriend Doris O'Malley.

Urging him to stay, Jimmy explained that the pub clock was twenty-minutes fast and that it was really only twenty-to-nine. But Georgie couldn't be persuaded. "Nah, I'm getting off the side now Jim", he insisted. "Alright then," said the other shrugging his shoulders. "Its up to you. Yer know yer own score George. I'll see yer when I see yer then".

"Yeah, okay. Might see yer tomorrow Jim".

Apart from exchanging a brief pleasantry with the manager's wife Georgie left quietly without any further ado. It was all right for Jimmy, he thought. He was already home.

Although beginning to feel the effects of the day's drinking, once outside in the fresh air he nevertheless, stepped lively across Kensington and walked briskly along Hall Lane to Wavertree Road, where he jumped a tramcar down past Edge Hill railway station and Botanic park, to *The Leigh Arms*.

Chapter Four

Saturday March 19th 1949. 1.15pm.

"Man, being reasonable, must get drunk;
The best of life is but intoxication."
Lord George Byron

The Leigh Arms was on Picton Road, almost facing Cambridge Street where Georgie lived, on and off, with Doris.

Entering the public bar, he glanced around but, unable to see Doris, he ordered a pint for himself. Harry Harrison, a 35 -year-old street Bookie, from nearby Cecil Street, was drinking with his brother Ted. They both liked Georgie because, apart from his friendliness, he'd often send them a drink over.

When Harry asked him to have a drink, he replied, "No, yer all right, I've just ordered a pint". He then asked Fred Thomella, the Manager, if Doris had been in. Fred hadn't seen her but said she might be in the *Bramleys* pub across the road. The Harrison's chimed in that they had just left the *Bridge* and she wasn't in there. Harry again invited him to have a drink but he declined, saying he was only having one because he wanted to go and find Doris.

Georgie and Harry Harrison had one thing in common: they both hated Chief Inspector Balmer. But Harry's hatred, unlike Georgie's, was based on fear. He ran an illegal network of street runners to collect his bets. And to stay in business he had to meet Balmer every week, outside St. Hugh's Church in Lawrence Road, to pay him off. The worst thing though, was that Balmer, in order to cover himself, would occasionally "forget" to warn him of an impending street raid. And when that occurred he would have to pay a hefty fine in addition to Balmer's bribes.

Knowing his intense dislike of Balmer, Georgie teasingly told him he had seen him in *Tracey's* earlier on in the day and that Balmer had actually bought him and his mate a drink. "Don't talk to me about that bastard!" Said Harry. "He's got me fuckin' skint. I pay the prick protection and I still get turned over every month!" When Georgie laughed, Harry said, "Don't laugh lad, it might be your turn one day.

"Take my advice. Don't have fuck all to do with that bastard. He's a bad man".

"I know," he replied, "He's tried to stitch me up a few times but I'm too sharp for him".

The pub clock said 9-20 pm but Georgie knew it was always ten minutes fast. So thinking that Doris, although unlikely, might be still at home, he told the two brothers that he was going to look there first. Then quickly finishing his pint he walked the few yards across Picton Road down to 67 Cambridge Street.

There was nobody in the house. Not Doris, not her twelve-year-old daughter Doreen nor her eighteen-year-old son, Charlie, who was home on leave from the Army. So he decided to go next door to Hilda and Bowie Kelly's house to see if they knew where she was.

Although unrelated to Georgie, Hilda and Bowie, were good neighbours to Doris, obliging her with anything if she was short. They also thought quite a lot of him. Whenever he'd see them in the *Cambridge*, on the corner of the street, or in the '*Leigh*' he'd always buy them a drink.

Hilda, invited him into the front parlour where her daughter, little Hilda, was lying on the couch covered with a blanket. When he asked what was wrong with her, Hilda said she didn't know but thought it might be Pneumonia. "She hasn't half been sweating", she said.

When Georgie asked where her husband was she replied with a look of resignation, "D'yer have to ask George? Down the town on the ale as usual."

He said he had called next door for Doris but there was nobody in. "D'yer know where she might be?", he asked. Hilda said she thought she was around the corner in *The Spofforth* pub. "Anyway, she said she was going to the *Bramleys*".

Georgie and Doris occasionally had a drink in *The Leigh Arms* with Hilda and Bowie - which was usually followed by getting "jars out" and having a sing-song in the house -so momentarily forgetting about the sick child, he asked Hilda if she would like to go with him to have a drink with Doris. "I would any other time", she replied, "but I'm waiting for the doctor to come out." Then glancing back at her daughter she sighed, "God, I hope it's not Pneumonia".

Georgie looking sheepish , said, "Oh Yeah, I'm sorry Hilda, I forgot." Then nodding towards the child, he said . "I hope she gets all right. Hope it's nothing serious. Anyway, I'd better be getting round there to *The Spofforth*."

Doris was not in *The Spofforth* but he ordered a pint anyway. He recognised the Manager, Eddie Ellis, from when he'd had a pub nearer town in Crown Street. But he'd never liked Ellis and Ellis had never liked him.

The pub was pretty quiet for this late on a Saturday night. Probably due to this miserable bastard, he thought. Looking around there was no sign of Doris. Reluctantly, he asked if a nice-looking blonde had been in. But, without bothering to answer, Ellis simply shook his head.

Quickly downing his pint, Georgie thought, what a miserable prick, as he headed back up to *The Leigh Arms*.

The clock in the '*Leigh* was nearing 9-40 pm and the public bar was now crowded. This time he accepted a drink from Harry Harrison and told him he was browned off with Dolly for fucking him about. "Never mind," said Harry, "she'll probably be there when you get home. That's the main thing".

It was now 9.50pm on the clock, and since they would soon be shouting "last orders", Georgie decided he could now let himself go. But as he tried to order a round of drinks, Ted Harrison, who was standing nearer the counter in the densely packed public bar, shouted across to him, "Don't worry about it George, I'll get these in cos' I'm going in a minute."

By 9.55pm on the clock. Ted had left, and although Harry was enjoyable company, the crowded bar was beginning to irritate Georgie. He was also getting drunker and becoming increasingly annoyed at not being able to find Doris.

Thinking she may have come in from the street and gone straight into the Buffet, he decided to have one last look in there. But as he began making his way down to the bottom end of the bar to go around into the Buffet, he decided that by the time he fought his way through the dense throng of customers it would probably be too late to get a drink. So he went out through the main Picton Road door into the vestibule and then through the other door into the Buffet.

As he entered he was relieved to see that, although it was pretty full it wasn't as jam-packed as the public bar; probably because they charged parlour prices in here.

Spotting Mrs. Butterworth, one of Doris's neighbours, sitting with a man friend, he said, "Hello Ma are yer havin' a drink?" But her male companion seemed resentful towards him. And, noticing that Georgie looked a little flushed, he asked sarcastically, "What's the do with you? Have you been in the sun?"
"No", he quickly replied, "I haven't been in the fuckin' sun. I've been having a go on the bevvy". Then, although he did not really know the man, he again offered them a drink.

Although Georgie was clearly the worse for wear the man had nonetheless been taken aback by his rapid response so, not wanting any trouble, he said they would have two halves of bitter.

In an attempt to jump the queue at the very busy bar, Georgie shouted out to Fred to have a drink on him. He'd always found this to be a successful ploy in a crowded pub. It did the trick! And when Fred came over to serve him, he ordered three glasses of Bitter and told him to treat himself and the staff to a drink. Last orders had already been shouted and the beer pumps were covered with a towel but, although declining the offer of drinks, Fred still served him.

Waiting for the drinks, Georgie leaned forward on the bar counter with his fists clenched. His stance, not intentionally aggressive, was adopted simply in order to prop himself up for he was getting drunker by the minute.

Taking the drinks over to Mrs. Butterworth and her male friend, Georgie, still sensing the man's hostility, decided not to bother asking Mrs. Butterworth about Doris's whereabouts. Indeed, after handing them the drinks he never spoke to them again. He noticed though, that the man had no trouble in obtaining more drinks from Fred. Must be well in, he thought, as the man, without uttering a word, came over and placed a glass of bitter on the counter before him. Independent bastard, he thought. Doesn't want to be under any obligation.

Fred was now shouting "Time Gentlemen Please" and gradually the Buffet was emptying. Georgie, still leaning on the bar counter, was trying to catch his eye in order to get a "deposit" off him on the promise of some black market cigarettes and whisky. Meanwhile, Mrs. Butterworth and the sarcastic man left without even saying goodnight. "Snobby bastards", he thought.

What Georgie didn't know was that the man, James Corrie, was a taxi cab owner and a very good friend and drinking partner of Inspector Balmer's.

Although he lived with Mrs. Butterworth as her husband, and stepfather to her children, Corrie had left his wife and his own children in the family home just a mile away in Smithdown Road.

Balmer had helped him to obtain a baggage pass for all the Elder Dempster Line ships. This gave him the exclusive right to enter the police guarded docks any time of the day or night unchallenged, to transport the luggage of disembarking ships officers. It was a privileged and very lucrative position to be in. Enjoying a virtual monopoly of taxi trade, he always carried a thick wad of notes. This however was kept secreted in the cab in case he got 'rolled' by a fare.

Balmer had told him there was a gang operating downtown who used prostitutes to lure taxi-drivers to a quiet back street on the promise of sex, then attacked them and robbed their takings. But when he'd be out on a drinking spree, touring all the Draught Bass pubs, with Balmer and his colleagues half drunk in the back of his cab, he wouldn't bother hiding his money. After all, he reasoned, you couldn't be in safer company.

In return for Balmer's favours - which extended to occasionally fixing him up with a particularly promiscuous policewoman - Corrie regularly provided him with information. And because he wasn't actually paid for this he didn't consider himself a police informer.

Eventually, when the pub was almost empty and Fred asked Georgie what he wanted, he put the proposition to him about the non - existent whisky and cigarettes.

Despite being an ex-policeman, Fred had often bought gear off him. Yes, he was interested but he refused his request for a cash deposit. He would pay on delivery, he said. Pretty drunk by now but still sociable, Georgie smiled at him. "Yer crafty old bastard", he said. Fred smiled back knowingly. He hadn't been a copper for twenty three years for nothing!

As Georgie finished his beer and half stumbled through the door on his way back down to Doris's, Fred called after him, "Goodnight George. Mind how you go now."

Chapter Five

Saturday March 19th 1949. 2.30pm.

"Smart Girl, Wise Guy"
(News of the World)

Jackie Dickson was chilled to the bone as she stood sipping a hot cup of tea outside the City Caterers stall at the Pier Head. For although the sun was shining, there was a bitter wind blowing down the Mersey from the Irish Sea. The only thing that cheered her up was the prospect of her impending reunion with Jimmy Northam. He was coming out of Durham prison today after doing three months for receiving when they were both up in Cumberland in January.

Due any minute now, she was really looking forward to seeing him again. But somehow her excitement was marred by this constant feeling of dread.

A lot had happened since Jimmy had been put away. She'd often thought that maybe she'd have been better off getting three months with him instead of the two months she'd received. That way they would have come out of gaol together and all of the bad things wouldn't have happened to her. "Bobby" Woolerton for one: that bastard! As if the six months he'd got last year for pimping off her wasn't enough, he'd again tried to take over from Jimmy as her ponce.

It was bad enough last year, just before he'd got the six months, when he'd gone over to Jimmy's parents house in Birkenhead, beaten Jimmy and his dad up, and dragged her back to Lime Street. Now he'd started beating her up again because she refused to hustle for him anymore. She couldn't even go down the town because she was so scared of him. The other girls had told her he was now gunning for her.

After the attack on Jimmy and his dad she'd got "George" Kelly to frighten him off. And it had worked for a while. But when he'd come out of prison after doing the six months, Kelly had already left her and gone back to his wife, so he'd started threatening her again. That's why she and Jimmy had left town and ended up in the Lake District. That was also why she'd had to arrange to meet Jimmy down here at the Pier Head today - well away from Lime Street. She'd ran the risk of going into *Littlewoods'* cafe on the way down here because she'd been really dying for a cup of tea, and, she had to admit, she'd always liked the idea of courting danger.

And that Austy O'Toole, the bouncer on the Billiards Hall in Lime Street, he was as bad. She'd only gone to him because she'd heard he was a hard case. She'd been so desperate for protection she even tried to kid him that she was in love with him. But he wasn't interested. He'd told her he couldn't care less about prostitutes or ponces like Woolerton. Why should he fall out with people in the town and make enemies because of a "tanner -a- wank", cheap Brass like her? That's what he'd said, the insulting bastard!

Out of all of them, it was Jimmy she really loved. She would do anything for him. When she gave him the money from the mushes it made her feel good. She actually got pleasure from it. It made her feel motherly towards him; made her feel needed. That was what appealed to her about Jimmy Northam: he was like a gentle little boy. He really *cared* about her, not like that "George" Kelly. And he wasn't a cruel bastard like Woolerton or hard and insulting like Austy O'Toole. He was just nice and kind. That's why she always felt sorry for him when people called him "Stutty".

He couldn't help his stuttering. Strangely, she thought, he himself never seemed to mind the nickname. She did though. And when she'd catch anyone calling him by it, she would immediately reprove them in her most respectable voice: "Do you mind but his name is James Phillip, not Stutty." She wanted to be proud of Jimmy because if she could be proud of him she could also be proud of herself for being his girl.

Jackie had not been out on the game for over a week. The Cystitis was far too painful. And as if that wasn't bad enough, Bobby Woolerton had given her a few black eyes that were only now beginning to clear up. And to make matters even worse, her chest had been killing her for weeks: she just couldn't stop coughing. The pain was almost unbearable at times. She'd really would have to stop smoking those dog-ends out of the gutter, she thought determinedly.

What, with all of this and the cold weather too, she'd had to forget any notion of taking any more mushes up the back alleys off

Lime Street... for the time being anyway.

The cough was so bad at times that she thought she might have Tuberculosis but she was terrified of going to the doctor. If she did have TB she didn't want to know - not at twenty three years of age. To be told she had *that* would have completely destroyed her.

Not being able to carry on her trade, Jackie had become almost destitute. And knowing that Jimmy, just coming out of prison, wouldn't have any money either, she felt desperate. She needed money, not only for herself but also to impress Jimmy; to celebrate his release and to give him a good time.

Standing here, shivering in the March wind, cold hands clasping the warm mug of tea, she began thinking more and more about that fellow she'd met in the *Boundary* pub last week, and the cinema job he'd been telling her about. Johnny, he said his name was. He'd said it would be dead easy. Just wait for the cashier to take the money up to the Manager's office, then stick him up with a gun and take the money.

He'd told her he'd been weighing it up for weeks. It was a piece of cake, he'd said. And he reckoned the best night to do it would be a Saturday. The place would be full and all that, and they'd get about two hundred quid out of it. The only problem was that he needed someone to go in with him to keep douse in case anyone came up the stairs. He'd asked her if she was game but she'd told him she was too scared. But Jimmy, she'd thought. If Jimmy was out I'd go with *him*. I wouldn't be scared with Jimmy.

They had done quite a few jobs together, her and Jimmy. Breaking into houses and shops, that sort of thing. She'd always got a huge thrill from the danger of it. It was so adventurous and daring.

Usually they just drifted aimlessly around the country. But in the case of Brampton, where they'd been caught, they'd deliberately gone there because Jimmy knew the place from when he'd been in the Army up there in Carlisle.

When they'd done the job in January Jimmy had been caught but she had got away. But a week later she'd robbed a woman's handbag in the market at Chester and unfortunately for her the woman happened to be an off-duty police officer. When she'd appeared in Court, they said she was already wanted for more serious offences in Carlisle, so she was discharged and sent up there to face trial with Jimmy.

She'd told the Johnny fellow in *The Boundary* about Jimmy being in Durham gaol for receiving. She'd also told him that Jimmy was a good shop-breaker and that she would put the proposition to him when he came out. At the time, she'd only said that to get rid of him. She'd no intention of asking Jimmy any such thing. But standing here now shivering, without a penny to her name and expecting him any moment, the prospect of getting some money quickly, seemed more and more attractive.

The Pier Head was crowded with people and, being the tram and bus terminus, the clanging tramcars shunting to and fro only added to the noise and confusion. Perhaps that was why she didn't see Jimmy alight from any particular tram. But suddenly he was there standing in front of her, his face beaming with his wide boyish smile.

"Alright J..jackie love", he stammered as he clasped her in his arms. Taken by surprise, she was speechless for a moment. Then she threw her arms around him and clung to him as hard as she could. The two months they'd been apart had seemed like two years, but now he was here with her at last!

When he asked about the bandage around her head she said dismissively, "Oh, it's nothing love, I slipped getting off a tram a few days ago". She was afraid to tell him about Woolerton beating her up. He might not want anything more to do with her, she thought, because he was as scared of Woolerton as she was.

The ships sirens wailed intermittently and passers-by sneaked curious glances as they kissed passionately. But they were oblivious to everything around them. Finally pulling themselves apart, Jackie told him how much she had missed him and how a friend of his mother's had got her a bedsit in Upper Parliament Street. "It's not much like", she said apologetically, "but it's okay for the time being".

"Pparliament Ssstreet!", he stammered . "What happened to mme Mmam's in Bbirkenhead. I thought you wwere alright in me Mmam's?"

"Well", she replied, "things were gettin' a little bit strained in your mother's. I mean, I couldn't really do any business in Liverpool while

I was living in Birkenhead. I mean it was too awkward, know what I mean like?"

"I ddon't llike the idea of that Jackie," he said with a frown. "Rough area that Ttoxteth. Full of blackies around there".

"No Love", she tried to reassure him, "it's not that part of Parly. Not the Rialto area. More up the top end by Smithdown Road and Lodge Lane. You know, the *white* part. Anyway", she added, " it can't be that bad if your mother recommended it."

"Oh tthat's alright tthen", he stuttered. "Well llet's get up tthere and have a ggander at home ssweet home eh?"

"Well to tell you the truth love", she said softly, "I've been having a bit of a bad time lately. There's no food in and it's quite cold and bare up there really."

Although that was true, the real reason was that she was terrified of Woolerton calling and giving her - an maybe him too - another hiding.

Surprisingly, Jimmy never asked her how business was. Nor did she mention it, except to tell him she was suffering from Cystitis - hoping he would get the message without her having to be explicit. But boyish as she thought he was, he could also be crude and insensitive.

"Ddon't tell me you've ccaught a ffuckin' ddose?" He cried. And before she could answer, he continued with growing annoyance, "Ddon't llike the idea of this Pparliament Sstreet lark Jjackie. How ddo I know yer haven't bbeen ffuckin' around with them bblackies and ccaught a ddose?"

His annoyance now blossoming into outright anger, he stammered on, "I'm wwarning yer Jjackie. "You knnow I've nnever allowed nno bblackies. It's just nnot ffuckin' on! Anyway," he continued, "I tthought you'd hhad enough of tthose bastards after the wway tthat ffuckin' husband of yours ttreated yer in Manchester?"

Reassuring rather than protesting at this outburst, Jackie murmured soothingly: "Of course I haven't caught a dose. And you know I promised I'd never go with a coloured bloke again after that cruel bastard. You know I wouldn't do that love". Then, in an attempt to lighten the mood, she added, "Jesus! I haven't even bloody-well been with a *white* fella for the past fortnight! A woman's problem", she went on, "Cystitis. That's all it is love. It'll be cleared up in a day or two".

Her soothing tone, together with a peck on the cheek, seemed to calm him. "I'm sorry love", he whispered. "Its just that I still ffeel a bit ffunny and nervous bbeing on the outside aggain." Then, brightening up, he said, "Ccome on. lets ggo over to me Mmam's and get something to eat. I'm bbleedin' sstarvin`."

Feeling happier and more relaxed now, they strolled leisurely down the gangway to catch the ferry boat to Birkenhead with Jackie linking her arm in his and stopping occasionally to give him a kiss,

As the *Royal Daffodill* ploughed across the Mersey, Jackie, aware there would be no privacy once they reached Jimmy's parents house, began to tell him about Johnny and his plan to rob a cinema . "Ffuckin'-ell Jackie", he exclaimed in a hurt tone, "I've only just come out this morning!"

"I know that love", she replied. "It's just that I remember him saying the best time to do it was a Saturday night. So if you were interested, we could go over and see him tonight. He's always in *The Boundary*."

"Yeah okay then", he conceded, "we'll go over llater and see what the sscore is. Jesus knows I ccould do with a few bob, I'm ffuckin' sskint".

Jackie hugged him appreciatively. She'd feel a lot more secure if Jimmy done the job. She had confidence in him. *He* knew what he was doing. That Johnny fella seemed to be all talk.

The biting March wind was blowing even more wildly across the Mersey as the ferry boat rode the swell, so they went inside the crowded saloon and huddled close together. And, nibbling his ear, Jackie whispered what Johnny had said about a gun being needed in order to frighten the cinema manager. "Mind you", she went on, " I don't know whether *he's* got one".

"Whhat are yer ttrying to say Jjack", he asked testily. "Well love", she replied, I just thought that if you took your one with us when we go over tonight it'll save any problems in case he doesn't have one himself. Know what I mean?"

"Wwhat d'yer mean?" He said indignantly. "Who says *I've* ggot a ggun"?

"Honey, remember this is me", she gently reminded him. "You told me all about it ages ago. Remember? The one you said you'd taken off that dead German when you were in the army?"

He knew about the gun all right. He'd hidden it ages ago up the bedroom chimney in his mother's. But he hadn't taken it off any dead German. He'd only told her that out of bravado. The truth was he had won it, and the bullets, off a Lance-jack in a card game when he was in the army. The Lance-jack had brought it home as a souvenir from Italy or Germany or somewhere so he wasn't worried about him opening his mouth. But Jackie might if they ever split up. He'd thought she'd forgotten about it. But what the hell! He thought. If this job's worth it the gun will come in handy, if only as a frightener. And if Jackie comes with me on the job she won't ever be able to open her mouth anyway.

Jimmy's parents lived in a small two-bedroomed terraced house in Wood Street in central Birkenhead. It had no bathroom or running hot water or inside toilet. The rear bedroom was Jimmy's, and his parents had kept it nice and clean for him since Jackie had moved out.

They'd been glad when she'd had finally left. She was so untidy and dirty. And her personal hygiene had been disgusting. That was the main reason for Mrs. Northam asking her friend in Liverpool to give her a room.

The Northams' would be nice to her today. But only for Jimmy's sake. Mrs. Northam didn't forget that she was the cause of Jimmy and his Dad being attacked by that Liverpool fella last year. And in their own house too!

When they'd finished the evening meal served by his mother, Jimmy went upstairs and made straight for the open fireplace in his parents bedroom. With its broken, empty, cast-iron grate and its two cracked hobs, the fireplace was usually covered in dust but he was alarmed to see it had been recently cleaned. Apprehensively stretching one hand up the chimney he felt around on the soot-laden ledge and was relieved to find the gun and bullets still there. Both were wrapped separately in two small flannel tea-towels. He knew the chimney would be a good hiding place because his Dad never lit the fire in this bedroom on account of the decrepit grate.

Stuffing the gun and the bullets into the two inside pockets of his jacket, he sneaked down into the back yard and threw the dirty towels in the bin before washing his hands and face in the back kitchen sink.

It was now 7.30pm. Jimmy borrowed two pounds off his dad, telling him that he and Jackie wanted to go to the pub to celebrate his release from gaol. Jackie had meanwhile freshened up in the back kitchen but was still wearing the scruffy bandage on her head. Jimmy told her to take it off and brush her hair. When she had done so they both set off on the return journey to Liverpool and their meeting with Johnny.

The Boundary was a large Victorian pub, situated on the corner of Lodge Lane and Smithdown Road at the busy junction with Earle Road, Tunnel Road, Smithdown Lane and Upper Parliament Street. About two miles southeast from the city centre, it was one of Liverpool's main suburban focal points. Every New Year's Eve, for example, crowds would congregate outside *The Boundary*, bringing traffic to a standstill as they sang and danced and generally caroused in the roadways. The area was similar to London's Shepherds Bush or The Angel. And the equivalent of the *Shepherds Bush Empire* or *Collins Music Hall*, was the *Pavilion Theatre,* which was just across the road from *The Boundary* in Lodge Lane.

The sensational American singing group, The Four Aces, were topping the bill on the "Pivvy" tonight. And the crowds were already queuing up outside for the Second House, as the No 8 tram deposited Jackie and Jimmy at the top of Upper Parliament Street.

Just as Jackie had said, Johnny was there in the passageway in *The Boundary*. But he was with another man. This man, whom she'd never seen before, was about the same age as Johnny. He was drinking a half of bitter and Johnny was drinking a Rum and Pep - probably, she thought, to give himself some guts.

Johnny's friend was wearing a brown , loosely belted overcoat which was obviously too big for him. And although he was trying to look like a gangster, Jackie thought he just looked ridiculous. The outfit didn't suit him at all.

Ignoring the unknown man, Jackie introduced Jimmy Northam to Johnny, who immediately began telling him about the cinema job. She then spotted Norwegian Margie sitting on a stool a few feet away along the passage.

She knew Margie quite well, from when she'd lived in Oxford Street last year and Margie had lived around the corner in Grove Street. They also knew each other from the town. So, feeling a little out of place at the unexpected presence of Johnny's unknown friend , she went over and asked Margie how she was keeping and where she was now living. Telling Jackie she still lived in Grove street, Margie, who as usual was putting on make-up, mumbled, "You'll have to excuse me love, I've had a few drinks...been in the club all day, know what I mean."

In truth Margie was more depressed than drunk. She hardly ever got drunk.

"I see you're back with Stutty eh", she said. "I thought he was in gaol.?"

"Ah, don't call him Stutty", said Jackie defensively, "his name's Jimmy. He only came out this morning."

"I'm sorry luv, but I didn't know his real name", said Margie. "I've always known him as Stutty."

Feeling the need to confide in somebody, Margie put the lipstick back in her coat pocket and began telling Jackie about seeing Georgie Kelly earlier on in Renee Brown's club. But before she could tell of her feelings for him Jackie interrupted. "Oh him", she said, "I used to knock around with him last year, but he went back to his wife."

"His wife!", exclaimed Margie. "What d'you mean his wife? Are you sure it's the same fellow. He's been separated from his wife for years. It couldn't have been him you knocked around with".

"Yeah, of course I am", she replied . "It's the same fella alright. Dark features, not bad-looking. Lives down Brownlow Hill?"

"Yes, that's right!" cried Margie. Then, shaking her head in disbelief she quietly murmured, "Well, the dirty sly bastard."

The two women however were unknowingly talking at cross-purposes. It was Kelly's brother Joey, whom Jackie had been associating with. But, fearing any repercussions from his wife, he'd told her his name was George.

Although Joey was slightly older, the two brothers did look alike and both lived off Brownlow Hill: George, with his mother in the Trowbridge Street tenements, (when he wasn't staying with Doris O'Malley) and Joey, across the road in Pleasant Street.

The conversation between the two prostitutes was abruptly ended when Northam called Jackie over and asked if she would go on the job with them to keep "douse" outside. Unable to resist the adventure of it, she readily agreed.

Discussing the robbery plan, the three men made no attempt to lower their voices. Margie could hear everything.

Johnny was vehemently protesting, "Fuck that! I'm not goin' on any job with a *loaded* shooter!" And Jackie was whispering "Hush" whilst Northam and the other man were trying to calm him.

When Johnny had quietened down and the conversation became more subdued, Margie noticed the other man quickly slipping a gun into his overcoat pocket.

Several minutes later, Jackie called out, "ta-ra" to Margie and left with Northam and Johnny's friend, leaving Johnny alone in the passageway. It was 9.15pm, although the pub clock, which was fast as usual, said 9.25pm.

About ten minutes later, Johnny left the pub, went across the road to the Pavilion and bunked in through the side door in Beaumont Street.

Margie didn't know who he or the other man was. She'd never seen either of them before.

Shortly afterwards she decided to get a taxi downtown to one of her favourite haunts, the *Spanish House* in Whitechapel, to see if she could pick up a mush before closing time.

Chapter Six

Saturday March 19th 1949. 9.20pm.

"Calling all Cars!"

The two young men paid to go in the best seats, the one-and sixes. The young blonde stayed outside but she didn't make herself conspicuous; didn't hang around. She walked up Webster Road, then around the corner and up Bird Street at the side of the cinema. Then walked down Bird Street again, this time on the other side of the street. It was necessary to keep on the move so as not to arouse suspicion because there was a man from the cinema sticking up posters on the wall for next week's features.

It was a bit inconvenient but she knew she wouldn't have to wait long. The cashier would be closing the pay box and cashing up in about five minutes.

Inside, one of the men had the gun in the left hand pocket of his brown belted overcoat, and, stuffed into the other pocket, a black silk scarf and squashed up trilby The second man carried only a pair of pliers.

The big picture had just started as they walked up the aisle and took their seats at the end of a row of the rear stalls. When the time came they needed to be near to the aisle without being too noticeable.

·The film , a British thriller called *Bond Street* , starred Jean Kent and Roland Young, and there were two murders in it. As it turned out that would be no bad thing.

Spot on 9-30, the cashier came strolling leisurely up the aisle carrying the blue cash bag. Sitting where they were, in the two end seats , she passed close enough to touch them .

If the crime had been planned differently, they were near enough, and she was relaxed and unsuspecting enough, for them to have simply snatched the bag out of her hand and run down the aisle and out into the safety of the dark night. If they'd done it that way, the terrible tragedy that was about to unfold would have been avoided.

The gunman's accomplice was becoming increasingly nervous. But he didn't want to show it. It was too late to back out now. Besides, he had a vital job to do.

They both knew where the cashier was going. She would go through the door leading into a vestibule and through another wooden spring-loaded door to the bottom of the spiral staircase. She would then climb the iron staircase and take the money a few paces along the passageway to the manager's office.

Outside the cinema the young blonde was still waiting. This time in front of the cinema entrance. She had nothing to worry about now: the bill poster had finished and had gone inside.

A young man named Donny McQuade was just leaving. He'd already seen the big picture in the First House and didn't feel like sitting through it again. "Hey lad," asked the blonde, "is the cashier still in there?" Donny hadn't even noticed. "I don't know love", he replied. "I'll go and have a look."

Donny thought the blonde was perhaps a friend of the cashier waiting for her to finish work, so quickly darting back up the marble steps, through the glass-panelled doors to the foyer, he saw that the three-sided pay kiosk was now empty and unlit. Returning down the steps, he told the blonde, "No, There's no-one there. It's locked up. She must have gone up to the office, girl. " Thinking no more of it, he continued his short journey down Webster Road to his home in nearby Earle Road.

Knowing it would happen any minute now, the blonde moved up Bird street to the emergency exit, ready, according to the plan, to receive the cash bag as her two companions came running out.

Three minutes after the cashier had disappeared through the vestibule door the gunman whispered to the other, "Right, lets go!" Both men quietly left their seats and swiftly followed her.

Once in this closed area out of view of anybody, the gunman, quickly masking his face with the black scarf and donning the trilby, nodded to the second man in the direction of the telephone on the wall. The second man then pulled out the pliers and severed the telephone wires. If anybody else came through those doors, his next job was to shout up a warning to the first man, who was now stealthily ascending the spiral staircase.

The cashier, Ellen Jackman, had by now delivered the takings to the manager's office and had gone further along the passageway to join the supervisor, Mona Watkins, in the staff room for a cup of tea.

Mrs. Jackman was in and out of the office so quickly because the money was mostly notes. The silver was never counted, she simply initialled the silver bags with the amount she said they contained. And there was hardly any small change because her practice was to send this out to nearby pubs, to be changed into notes, before she cashed up. The total amount in the bag was £50. 8s. 0d

In his office, the Manager, Mr. Leonard Thomas and the Assistant Manager, John Catterall, were still counting the confectionery takings with the help of ice-cream girl Valerie June Thornhill. Ellen Jackman's cash-bag was placed in the open safe for the time being until they'd finished counting.

Forty-four year-old Mr. Thomas had only been manager for three months. Invalided out of the army following a wartime Bren gun accident, the father of two - a nine year-old boy and five-month old baby daughter - first became a special constable. Then after a stint working in a large store, he joined Circuits Management Association in 1943, working his way up to become assistant manager of the Rialto cinema. He was such an outstanding employee that the company, upon the death of the Cameo's previous manager three months ago, had promoted to the post.

Mr. Catterall, a thirty-year-old married man, had been demobbed from the Royal Navy just two months ago. A native of Grimsby, he had served during the war as a signaller and was torpedoed three times. In 1944 he had been decorated with the Distinguished Service Medal by the King at Buckingham Palace for his part in the sinking of the German battleship, the *Scharnhorst*.

Valerie Thornhill had now also left the office and the two men were sitting chatting when the door quietly opened. Thinking it must be Valerie or Mrs. Jackman coming back for something or other, they didn't take any particular notice at first. But suddenly they were confronted by the masked man brandishing the gun in his left hand.

"Okay, give us the money" he demanded. The startled men simply stared open-mouthed in bewilderment and shock for a few seconds.

Then Thomas, with a nervous half grin, asked the gunman,, "Is this some sort of joke or something?"

"Its no fuckin' joke", came the stern reply. "Give us the fuckin' money!"

Thomas rose carefully from his chair and went to the open safe, taking out the cash-bag. He then moved toward the gunman. "Look," he said, "don't be silly..." But the gunman, moving nervously backwards, halted him in his tracks with a menacing gesture. "Shut your fuckin' mouth", he said. Then, angrily pointing the gun straight at him, again demanded, "Give us the fuckin' money!" At this sudden threatening movement Thomas, fearing for his life, instinctively threw the cash bag at the gunman. There was a loud report, and in a flash the 9mm bullet traced a rapid path along the underside of his outstretched arm and through the side of his chest, shattering both lungs.

As the stricken Manager slumped to the floor, his life blood draining out of him, a shocked Catterall, who had earlier moved to the door to block any escape, cried out, "What the bloody 'ell did you do that for!" The immediate reply was another shot which hit Catterall in his right hand , the bullet going straight through it. But amazingly, he moved toward the gunman, shouting, "You bastard!" The gunman then fired again. This time the bullet went through Catterall's right shoulder and sent him reeling backwards.

Tearing at his shirt in agony, he fell to his knees by the office door, but once again, began to slowly drag himself up and bravely tried to grab the door handle to shout outside for help. The gunman, by now in total panic, rushed over and fired a third shot into his back.

Now bleeding heavily from his wounds, Catterall finally collapsed onto the floor. Thomas was lying nearby, his head half under the table, quietly moaning as his life ebbed away.

Ignoring the cash, which had spilled onto the floor, the gunman tried desperately to push open the office door. By now he could hear voices outside but the door would not budge. In panic he fired at the lock and tried again to push it open but it still would not budge.

Mrs. Watkins and Mrs. Jackman had heard the gunshots and both ran out of the staff room to see what was happening. At first they had raced to the Projection room but saw nothing amiss. They then ran to another room and again saw nothing unusual. But upon reaching the manager's office, they heard the moans and screams of the dying men and saw the closed door and the whole wooden partition in which it was set, rattling violently as the gunman desperately tried to get out of the office.

Inside, the gunman by now wildly desperate, stood back and again fired at the lock, thinking that somehow Catterall must have managed to lock him in. He then went over and pushed the door again but it still would not open. Only then did it occur to him to *pull* the door! As he did so it finally sprung open and he was confronted by Mrs. Watkins, Mrs. Jackman and Patrick Griffin, the young cinema fireman. "Stand back!", he ordered waving the gun at them. Mrs. Watkins, who was facing him, hesitated for a moment. The gunman shrieked, "Get out of my way or I'll let you have it". And as they stood back, he dashed past them towards the spiral staircase.

Quickly recovering from the initial shock, Mrs. Watkins gamely chased the gunman and tried to grab him by the shoulder as he raced down the spiral stairs. Unable to hold onto him, she quickly returned to tend to Mr. Thomas and Mr. Catterall, leaving the young Griffin to give chase.

In the vestibule downstairs, it only took the first shot for the gunman's accomplice to realise what had happened. He didn't wait to hear the second shot. Panicking, he raced down the aisle, through the foyer and out into Webster Road, where he veered sharply right up Bird Street, then left into Garrick Street and away towards Smithdown Road. A young usherette, nineteen-year-old Edna Ashley, seeing him race past her, ran after him as far as the cinema entrance but did not pursue him any further.

Seconds earlier, Miss Ashley had been sitting in the end seat of the front row stalls talking to her colleague, Phyllis Stevens, when they had heard the gunshots. And as the accomplice dashed out of the cinema, Mrs. Stevens ran through the auditorium to the vestibule to investigate.

Opening the vestibule door she saw the masked gunman struggling with the push bar on the emergency exit door. He was having difficulty opening it. She knew why. This was her duty station. It was her job to position herself here each evening until the pay desk closed, in case anyone tried to "bunk in" without paying. And she knew the door had been stiff all week.

Transfixed and uncomprehending, she stood watching the gunman for what seemed like an eternity but was actually about six or seven seconds. Strangely, she noticed that, despite his desperation to get the emergency door opened, he never once took his left hand out of his overcoat pocket.

With the cinema fireman and the projectionist, Leslie Preston, now racing down the spiral staircase after him, the killer, with only seconds to spare, finally managed to open the door. Then running along the same route as his accomplice minutes before, he was spotted by Percy Evans and his wife Elinor of 31 Garrick Street. They thought there must have been a row in the cinema and that he was running for the police, until they saw Griffin close behind shouting ,"Stop him, we've been robbed".

But the fireman could not keep up with the killer as he raced towards busy Smithdown Road. Quickly returning to the cinema, he tried to dial 999 but Mr. Preston told him the telephone wires had been cut.

Mr. Simpson and his wife, whose house in Garrick Street backed on to the cinema, had heard the gunshots and ,thinking it was somebody banging on their back yard door, had gone out into the back entry to see what the commotion was about. There they met Griffin who told them what had happened and asked if they had a telephone.

By now the Simpson's neighbour, Elsie Jones, had emerged from her house and told him she had a telephone. "Quick", cried Griffin, "ring 999 and get the police . Tell them to come to the Cameo. We've been robbed... the boss has been shot!".

There was no sign of the blonde. She had vanished as if into thin air.

As soon as the 999 call was received at 9-45 pm, the urgent message in the clipped, stentorian tones of the police radio operator, was booming out over the air: "Calling all cars! Calling all cars! About 9.45pm, a man, twenty to thirty, dressed in brown tweed overcoat, brown trilby hat, pulled down, with black silk scarf, used as a mask, entered Cameo cinema, Webster Road, Wavertree, and shot two men in armed hold-up! Repeat. Calling all cars! Calling all cars!..."

When the ambulance arrived at the nearby Sefton General Hospital shortly afterward, it was obvious that the manager, Mr. Thomas, was already dead. The surgeons then battled for several hours to save the life of John Catterall, but it was useless. He died on the operating table at 12-20 am.

By 10.00pm Webster Road was blocked with police cars and the surrounding streets were swarming with police. The cinemagoers inside the Cameo were questioned but each and every one said they hadn't heard any gun shots. People outside were also stopped and questioned to see if anybody had seen the gunman as he made his escape. But nobody, apart from the Evans's, had seen anything.

Within half an hour Detective Chief Superintendent Tom Smith was on the scene, and soon afterwards set up the Murder hunt headquarters at nearby Lawrence Road police station.

Despite being the Head of Liverpool C.I.D. Smith was no great detective. Besides he was due for retirement in a few months. He'd had enough of all this excitement. He didn't really fancy playing Sherlock Holmes anymore. But he knew somebody who would. He knew precisely the man for this job. Somebody who would really relish it - Bert Balmer. If anyone could sort this out it was Bert.

Balmer was the head of Central Division C.I.D. based in the city centre's Dale Street Headquarters. But Smith quickly decided he would give him a much wider roving commission. This was a case that just had to be cracked. Bert knew everyone and everything that went on in the city. He was a born copper. He could sniff anything out. And his network of informers was legendary in the force. But, Smith wondered, where the hell was he? Probably whoring again or out on the draught Bass as usual, he thought.

Balmer could not be found at home and nobody knew where he was. Eventually in response to a message he telephoned Smith at Lawrence Road at 2.00am. He had indeed been out on the tiles and had been drinking, But what the hell! Thought Smith. "Get down here Bert as soon as you can . We've got a double murder on our hands."

At 2.15am a telephone call was received at Dale Street. The caller said, "I have just seen a man in the convenience (toilets) at the Pier

'Smart Girl' - Jackie Dickson as a brunette.

'Wise Guy' - Jimmy 'Stutty' Northam.

Charles Connolly

Det. Chief Inspector Balmer - 'The Exterminator'.

The killers escape route. (Kelly lived in the opposite direction).

Tracey's (now 'Scruffy Murphy's'), corner Hanover Street and Wood Street.

The derelict *Royal William*, Crown Street, today.

The Liverpool Arms, **West Derby Street. Now demolished.**

The Coach & Horses **today, Low Hill.**

The Leigh Arms **today, Picton Road.**

The Spofforth **today: scene of Kelly's fateful visit.**

The Midland **today, unchanged since 1949.**

The Boundary **today: The real scene of the plot.**

The Beehive - **Mount Pleasant, today; unchanged since 1949.
The *alleged* scene of the plot,**

Head with a black mask and he has a gun. I have rubber soles on my shoes and he did not hear me come in".

When asked for his name, the man gave a name which later proved to be that of a businessman who was in hospital. When police arrived at the empty Pier Head telephone box, from which the call was made, they noticed that the businessman's name appeared at the top of an opened page of the telephone directory.

The police had asked the caller to wait at the phone box until officers could be sent in a squad car but he said he would walk to the Dale Street Headquarters. He then hung up.

Superintendent Smith later told a *Liverpool Daily Post* reporter, "We immediately went to the Pier Head but there was nobody about and we have heard nothing since from the mysterious caller".

Liverpool C.I.D. were puzzled as to how the caller knew that a masked man was wanted. There had been no reports of the shootings by 2.15am and nothing had been broadcast on the radio.

Later that day, with Webster Road and the surrounding streets still awash with police on house-to-house enquiries, Donny McQuade approached a police officer and told him about the blonde waiting outside the Cameo the previous evening, and what she had asked him. The policeman listened attentively and wrote down his name and address but Donny was never again contacted by the police.

On Monday the 21st March Dr. W. H. Grace The Home Office pathologist, having carried out postmortems on the two dead men, presented Smith with his report.

Thomas had died almost instantly through the bullet entering the left side of his chest and shattering both lungs. The bullet which had killed Catterall had struck him in the chest at the back on the right side and had travelled in a downward trajectory hitting a rib, passing through his liver, and had been found lodged in the pelvic cavity. It appeared, said the report, that this fatal shot was probably delivered when Catterall was on his hands and knees.

On the same day, Albert Louis Allen, a ballistics expert from the North Western Forensic Science Laboratory at Preston completed his report. It stated that the empty cartridge cases found in the managers office had been fired from a self-loading pistol and from a magazine.

A damaged copper casing and three bullet cores were from ammunition of 9 millimetre diameter and were consistent with having come from ammunition of the same type and manufacture as the cartridge cases. The bullets removed from the bodies of Thomas and Catterall were also of 9 millimetre. All of the ammunition was of German origin. The bullets appeared to have been fired from a P38 automatic pistol which had been standard issue to German Officers during the war.

Copies of Grace's and Allen's reports were immediately handed to Balmer. As the officer in charge of the case, they would greatly assist him in attempting to reconstruct what had actually happened in the Manager's office.

Chapter Seven

Saturday March 20th 1949. 11.00 am.

"An Inspector Calls"

Georgie Kelly had a bad hangover. He couldn't even look at the breakfast of fried kippers Doris put in front of him. Instead he asked, "And where were you all last night?"

"Oh don't be like that George", she said placatingly. "Don't you remember? I told you when you came in. *I* was in the *Bramleys*." Telling her to fuck off, he hissed. "I was in the *Bramleys*, *The Spofforth*". Then added sarcastically, "You know, the one where you told Hilda next door you'd be".

Hilda must have misunderstood, she said. She hadn't meant *The Spofforth*, she'd meant the other *Bramleys* pub, *The Bridge*, on the corner of Alfred Street and Picton Road opposite the *Leigh*.

When Georgie had arrived home last night, Doris and little Bowie Kelly were in the front parlour with a few quarts of ale. But after he'd told Bowie his daughter was sick next door he'd left and Georgie had gone to bed leaving Doris downstairs.

He didn't remember her saying anything about being in the *Bramleys* all night. But knowing the *Bridge* was where Bowie drank when he came up from the town, he'd assumed she must have been. He'd forgotten the Harrison's had told him at nine-o-clock that she *wasn't* in there. If he had known the truth he would have been flabbergasted. For she had actually been drinking for most of the evening in the *Royal Standard*, a "Bass House" in West Derby Road, with none other than Chief Inspector Balmer.

Having seen Georgie with Jimmy Skelly in *Tracey's* in the afternoon, Balmer guessed they were both out for an all day session on the booze. He knew Georgie's habits well, which is why he'd called up to Doris's at tea time. If Georgie wasn't in by then he knew he wouldn't be home till late, if at all. And if he got *very* drunk he'd probably stay overnight in his mother's in Trowbridge Street. But should he arrive unexpectedly, Balmer's excuse would be that he was making a social call. After all, he *was* a regular visitor to the house, so that would hardly arouse any suspicion.

Doris was a very attractive, thirty-three year old platinum blonde, with a voluptuous figure. But despite being besotted with her, Balmer was still keenly conscious of his status as a senior police officer. Discretion was essential.

After she'd agreed to have a drink with him, he'd driven ahead to the *Royal Standard*, a few miles away, telling her to follow him shortly afterwards. And in order to cover himself, he'd given her two pounds to show herself, *alone*, in *The Leigh Arms* before getting a taxi to the rendezvous near the *Hippodrome* cinema. That way he could refute anything she might subsequently say about being with him.

Doris had duly obliged by showing herself in the *Leigh* at about 8-30 pm, where she'd briefly spoken to Edna Bore, the barmaid, before leaving to meet him. She'd earlier told Hilda next door that if Georgie came home before ten, to tell him she'd be in the *Bramleys* - deliberately not specifying which *Bramleys*.

In the '*Standard*, Doris had told Balmer she'd have to be back in the *Bridge* before closing time, just in case Georgie checked. That was fine with him. He was content for now to simply impress the manager of the *Standard*, an acquaintance of his, by showing off such a stunning woman in his company. There had been convenient occasions when they'd been more intimate and there would no doubt be others in the future.

During the next hour, as she'd grown more loquacious with the whiskies he was plying her with, Doris had told Balmer about the latest fight she'd had with Georgie. He hadn't been surprised. He was aware of the tempestuous relationship between them. He'd seen her often enough during his visits to the house, with bruises and black eyes. She hadn't mentioned, of course, her constant taunting and provocation of Georgie, and having other men and drinking parties in the house when he wasn't around. But then she didn't have to. He knew about that too He'd known her from down the town when she was on the game, before she'd ever met Kelly.

Despite knowing that Doris could give as good as she got, he'd told her Georgie was nothing but a bum and a ne'r-do-well and that she would be better off getting away from him. What he was careful not to tell her of however was his determination to eventually put Georgie away for a long time. For as much as he'd always fancied her, he'd never forgotten that she was an ex-prostitute and couldn't be trusted to keep her mouth shut.

Neither did he tell her of his anger at Kelly's arrogance and disrespect; about his dislike of him always acting over familiarly and embarrassing him in public. He certainly didn't tell her about his humiliation the night Kelly was drunk in the *Globe* in Cases Street and soiled his trousers and of how he had helped him to put on the new pair he'd been carrying; and of how he'd taken him home to his mother's in the tenements, carrying his soiled trousers in the carrier bag, only to be ridiculed for his good turn.

He wouldn't have been capable of putting into words the deep hatred he'd felt for Kelly when he'd drunkenly shouted from the top landing to all the neighbours, "Look at the great Inspector Balmer, carrying Georgie Kelly's shitty kecks!" He was far too proud to tell Doris *that*. But that was the night his hatred was consolidated with a vengeance. From then on he was determined, despite the false bonhomie between them, to have Kelly the very first chance he got.

It was 9.45pm when the taxi dropped Doris outside the *Bridge*. She'd just been in time to meet Bowie and get some quarts out before "Time" was called.

Balmer hadn't bothered telling her to keep her mouth shut about the *Royal Standard*. It wasn't necessary. He knew she wouldn't tell him anything. Kelly being a bastard had its compensations after all!

Despite his hangover Georgie had now washed and shaved and was fastidiously dressed in the same brown bird's-eye suit of yesterday, which was now complemented by a fresh white shirt and grey tie. He always liked to look smart, especially of a Sunday. It was an ingrained habit from childhood when he'd been an altar boy in Holy Cross Church in Crosshall Street.

Today, he was going as usual, down Brownlow Hill to see his mother and his brother's. He went down there every Sunday. Then after a few pints in *Charlie Mathews* or *Back Bents*, he'd go with Joey (and Frankie when he was home from sea) across to the crowded Toss

School in the Bullring tenements, to try and win a few quid at Toss or Craps.

Calmer now, he apologised to Doris for his bad temper. With his hangover, a prolonged argument was the last thing he wanted. In any case Charlie and Doreen, her son and young daughter, were now up and about and he didn't want to cause a bad atmosphere in front of them. But, desperate for a "curer", he couldn't wait for twelve o'clock for the *Leigh* to open!

Combing his brylcreem-ed hair in the front parlour mirror for the third time, he caught a glance of the *News of the World* lying on the table. The double murder at the cinema was front page headlines.

"Hey Dolly", he shouted. "'Ere a minute. `Ave you seen this about the Cameo?"

Doris, who was serving breakfast to Doreen and Charlie, dashed in from the back kitchen. Taking the paper from him, she began reading the story aloud, then interrupting herself, she cried, "Bloody'ell Georgie, that's terrible isn't it. Jesus! it's only a few streets away."

"I'll tell you what Doll", he said, "its a dead cert we'll be getting a visit off the coppers".

"Why d'yer say that?"

"Can't yer read?", he replied, "It says they're carrying out house-house enquiries doesn't it?"

"Oh yeah".

Suddenly their conversation was interrupted by the sound of light knocking on the front door. And Doris, throwing down the newspaper, said, "Bloody 'ell, they're quick enough aren't they?"

"That's not the law", he said knowingly. "That's not a copper's knock".

He was right. It was only a neighbour, Mrs. Matthews, who'd come to borrow some margarine.

As the two women entered the parlour Georgie was now sitting in the easy chair, re-reading the newspaper account of the murders. An excitable Mrs. Matthews said, "What d' yiz think of that terrible do at the Cameo last night. Isn't it terrible Georgie? We were in there only the night before last, me and my fella and..."

"It's a bleedin' Yank whose done that", he interrupted. "Yer don't get English fellas doin' stick-ups with guns and all that palaver. I'll bet yer any money it's a Yank from Burtonwood or somewhere".

As they talked there was another knock. This time it was very loud and urgent, on the heavy cast iron door knocker. And as Doris went to answer it he knew that this time it *was* the police. Only the gasman or the landlord or the police knocked like that - and the gasman and the landlord never called on a Sunday.

"Hello Georgie," came the familiar voice. It was Balmer. With him was Farragher and Detective Chief Inspector Morris.

He'd thought that if he did get a visit it would be a routine one from the uniformed police. He hadn't expected Balmer and his friends. But quickly recovering, he responded cheerily, "Hello Mr. Balmer What can I do for yer?"

"I suppose you know why we're here George?", he said calmly. "Yeah", he replied, "we've just been reading about it in the paper." Then turning to Doris, he said, "What did I tell yer? I told yer they'd be here didn't I?" But Doris, stuck for words at seeing Balmer so soon after last night, simply nodded. "Now, now, George", said Balmer ignoring Doris, "no need to panic. It's only routine. We're calling on everyone in the immediate area."

With Charlie and young Doreen in the now crowded parlour, an embarrassed Georgie said, "Can you come into the back Mr. Balmer?" Then, glancing towards the others, he whispered, "Don't wanna talk here, know what I mean." The three detectives obligingly followed him into the small back kitchen. But because it was so cramped they all moved into the back yard.

"All right George", said Balmer, "what do yer know?"

"Only what I read in the *News of the World* this morning."

"Where were you yesterday?"

"I was on the ale all day, with Jimmy Skelly".

"Have you got a brown overcoat by any chance George?"

"Nah, haven't had one for years. I've only got a Mac".

"What about a gun?", he went on. "Have you got a gun?"

"A gun!" Georgie laughed at the suggestion. "A gun! Come on Mr. Balmer, yer know me. I wouldn't know what to do with one. Wouldn't know how to fire one never mind anything else. Nah", he said dismissively, "never had a gun in me life."

Balmer, who seemed to be only half-listening, told Farragher to go back in the house and have a look around. And although they didn't have a search warrant, Georgie made no objection. Balmer then said, "By the way, you've met Jimmy Morris before, haven't you?" "Yeah, I know Mr. Morris", he replied as the other Inspector gave a silent nod of recognition.

"Where were you last night George?", asked Balmer.

"I left Jimmy in *The Coach and Horses* in Low Hill, on the corner of his street. He was getting bevvied. So I caught a tram and made me way up home to see Dolly."

"What time?"

"About half eight, quarter to nine", he replied, adding,. "I went in *The Leigh Arms* as soon as I got off the tram, but I only had one pint there. I was looking for Dolly to have a drink with her but she wasn't there. So I came down to the house but she wasn't here either so I went down to *The Spofforth* and then...."

"*The Spofforth*", interrupted Balmer. "That's only five minutes from the Cameo."

"So what ? he replied indignantly. "I do live around here yer know. Anyway", he continued, "Dolly wasn't there either so I only had one pint and went back up to the *Leigh*. Like I said, I was on the ale."

Balmer asked him which *Coach & Horses* he had been in. " I told yer," he replied, "the one in Low Hill on the corner of Holborn Street by Jimmy's house. If yer give me a lift in the danny-marr I'll show yer. We'll go there if yer like. The manageress'll tell yer I was there."

"Not a bad idea that George", said Balmer. Then turning to Farragher, who had now finished his search, he asked, "Anything?" The sergeant simply shook his head.

Before they left the house Balmer agreed that, in order to save him any embarrassment in front of the neighbours, Georgie could leave by the back yard door and meet them at the top of the street.

This wasn't so unusual: most of the families in the area came and went this way. It saved their highly-polished brass front door knockers and letter-boxes, and their sandstone-scrubbed steps from getting dirty too quickly.

Walking briskly up the back entry Georgie passed Rosie Coyne, who was being helped by her young daughter Vera to brush up outside her back yard door.

Hiding his apprehension and trying to appear his usual friendly self he quipped, "Hey up Rosie girl, don't be workin' too hard now."
"Hey George", she joked, "I hope you had nothing to do with that do at the Cameo last night". Responding in similar vein, he said, "Yer must be kiddin' Rosie. Me Tommy-Gun's been in the pawn shop for months!" Then, more soberly, he added. "Nah, not *my* style Rose. Might've done a few little naughty strokes but a wouldn't dream of doing anything like that."

"I know that lad", she said reassuringly. " I'm only jestin'." And as he continued up the back entry, Rosie, still wearing the trace of a smile, said to her daughter, "Lovely fella, Georgie."

In the car Balmer told him, "When we go in Skelly's don't forget, I'll do the talking." He then added, "Meanwhile, how's about telling me exactly where you did go yesterday".
"Hang on, Mr. Balmer", he said, "What d'yer mean `Skelly's`? I thought we were going to the *Coach and Horses.*?"
"Never mind that . We'll see to that later. Where were you yesterday?" Georgie started to tell him about *Tracey's,* then suddenly remembering said, "Anyway, you saw us there yourself. Sent us a bevvy over didn't yer ?"
"That was earlier on. I'm talking about after that".
"Well," he said, " we went to a club in the South End. Then, about six o'clock we jumped a tram to a boozer along Crown Street, right at the end by Pembroke Place near the Royal Infirmary."

He purposely omitted the name of the club in case there had been a report about Jimmy attacking the American. And to his surprise, Balmer never asked.

"Then", he continued, "we went across the road to *The Liverpool Arms*, and then we went up to the *Coach & Horses*. By that time Jimmy was getting bevvied and I wanted to see Dolly, so I got off the side and caught a tram up to the *Leigh*."
"What time was that?", asked Balmer.
"Oooh, I'd say about half-eight, quarter to nine."
Apparently satisfied for the time being, Balmer then asked the number

of Jimmy's house. Georgie replied that he knew the street but didn't know the house. "Never mind", said the Inspector, "we'll call into Prescot Street and get it from the files."

Whilst Jimmy's record was being located in the police station, Farragher brought in cups of tea for everyone and Balmer told him he could stay at the station and that he and Morris would walk with Georgie to Skelly's. "It's only across the road", he said.

Shortly afterwards, when he'd obtained the house number, Balmer quickly drained his tea-cup and said, "Right let's get over there". And as the three men walked down Holborn Street, Balmer again warned, "Don't forget George, when we go in I'll do the talking."

Jimmy was still in bed, when his wife told him there were two C.I.D men downstairs with Georgie Kelly. Wearing only a vest and struggling into his trousers, he went down to see what they wanted. His head was banging. He had a worse hangover than Georgie

"Hello Jim", said Balmer disarmingly, "you know Mr. Morris here don't you?" Before Jimmy could reply, he added laughingly, "Bloody'ell Jim you're a hard man to find. We had to go to Prescot Street station to get your address. Couldn't remember the number for the life of me, could I George?" And as Georgie shook his head in agreement, Balmer asked, "Got a brown overcoat have yer Jim?"

His brain slowly clearing, Jimmy asked why he wanted to know. But after being told about the murders at the Cameo, he said, "Yeah, I've got a brown overcoat". Then, running his fingers through his tousled hair, he went on, "but I don't know nothing about any murders"

"Let's have a look at it then Jim", said the Inspector.

The rusty, almost orange coloured, overcoat looked very conspicuous. But after a cursory inspection, Balmer handed it back, saying, "Okay Jim, that's fine".

Although he didn't say anything, Jimmy was amazed at Balmer's casualness. It seemed that a brown overcoat was somehow involved in a murder yet here was the Inspector handing his brown overcoat back to him. Knowing how the police worked, he'd fully expected him to take it away to be examined. He was however, greatly relieved that Balmer hadn't, as he had originally feared, come about the fight with the American in Renee Brown's.

As the questioning continued, Georgie, heeding the Inspector's earlier warnings, simply leant against the living room door with his hands in his pockets, saying nothing.

"Now Jim," said Balmer maintaining his friendly tone, "Georgie says he was with you last night. Is that right?"

"Yeah, that's right".

"Which pub did you finish up in?"

"In *The Coach and Horses* at the top of the street."

"Where were you before that?"

Jimmy then confirmed Georgie's story by recounting their visits the previous day and evening to the club, the *Royal William* and *The Liverpool Arms* .

"What time did he leave you last night?" asked Balmer. "About nine-o'clock, quarter to nine, something like that", he replied. "In fact, I asked him to stay but he wanted to see Doris." Then turning to his friend, he said, "didn't yer?" Nodding his head in agreement, Georgie then spoke for the first time. "There yer are. I told yer that Mr. Balmer, didn't I?" But Balmer ignored him and asked, "And what about you Jim. Where did you go?"

" I didn't go anywhere. I stayed in the *Coach* till closing time. I ended up bevvied. A few of the neighbours helped me home at ten -o'clock. By that time I was rotten drunk."

"Can you prove that?"

"Prove what?", he said innocently, That I was bevvied?"

"No" laughed Balmer. "That the neighbours brought you home at closing time".

"Well," he replied, " I don't know about *prove*, but I remember one of the fellas was Taffy Roberts from over the road. Yer can ask him if yer like. They'll all tell yer in the *Coach,* I was there till closing time, singin' me head off."

Balmer seemed satisfied with Jimmy's story so Georgie, sensing the interview was at an end, asked if it was now all right to speak. And without waiting for an answer, he told his friend he was sorry he didn't stay with him in the '*Coach* because, as it turned out, he couldn't find Doris anywhere last night. "I told you that Mr. Balmer, didn't I?" Knowing only too well where Doris was last night, the Inspector made no reply. Instead, he rubbed his gloved hands together and said, "Right, George, do you want dropping off back at Doris's or what?"

Before answering him, Georgie asked Jimmy if he felt like going for a drink down Brownlow Hill. But when his friend declined, he said he might as well accept Balmer's offer of a lift. "If yer feel any better later on I might see yer in Charlie Mathews`'", he added. "Yeah ", said Jimmy "I'll probably feel a bit better later on."

In truth Jimmy had no intention of going to Charlie's or anywhere else, or even having any ale today. The strongest drink he'd be having would be a bottle of *Schofield's Cream Soda* out of the sweet shop up the street. He'd always found that to be the best cure for a hangover.

"Charlie Mathews" was a pub on the corner of Clarence Street and Brownlow Hill, almost opposite the Trowbridge Street tenements. A regular haunt of the two men, it's real name was the *White Star Vaults*, but everyone called it after it's manager, an easy-going laconic landlord who fenced black market and stolen property off all the local villains.

By now Balmer was growing impatient. "Come on George, if you want a lift", he grunted. "We haven't got all day."

Retracing their steps back to the police station, Georgie and the two detectives passed the *Coach & Horses* but Balmer and Morris didn't bother calling in to check the men's story. It wasn't all that important now. They seemed to have pretty well confirmed each other's account. Balmer was satisfied they had nothing to do with the murders. Nevertheless he decided for form's sake, he would check later on, when he'd dropped Georgie off... just to make sure.

The Chief Inspector' offer of a lift wasn't entirely altruistic. He had to restore some goodwill between himself and Georgie after showing - albeit in the course of his official duty - his suspicion of him as a possible murderer. After all, he might turn out to be a valuable source of information.

As the car cruised away from Prescot Street police station back to Picton Road, Balmer said in a determined tone, "Listen Georgie, this is one job that's got to be solved." Recognising the seriousness of the situation and grateful that he was no longer under suspicion, he replied, "Bloody'ell, yer can say that again Mr. Balmer!". He then added gravely,

"A double murder! What!"

"I'll tell you something George", he continued,, "Any good info on this one and there's no less than *fifty quid* in it for you! We've got to catch the bastard who done this. The quicker the better. So you know the score. Keep your bloody eyes and ears to the ground down the town. First thing you hear, anything, even the slightest whisper, I want to know. Understand?"

"Yer can bank on me, Mr. Balmer," he replied, matching the other's seriousness, tone, "I'll do me best."

Before dropping Georgie off at the corner of Cambridge Street and Picton Road, Balmer gave him two pounds and told him to get down the town that evening to see what he could find out.

The two detectives then drove back to *The Coach and Horses* and spoke to the manager's wife. She confirmed that Jimmy had been in the pub the previous evening and had been very drunk at closing time. And although she didn't know Georgie personally, she remembered the man who was with him and said he'd left Jimmy at about nine-o'clock The full description she gave left Balmer and Morris in no doubt that it was indeed Georgie. They didn't feel it necessary to obtain a signed statement from her or even visit Taffy Roberts.

Despite his promise of co-operation and the two pounds and the fabulous offer of a further fifty pounds, Georgie had no intention , even if he did hear anything, of giving any information to Balmer. The bastard!, he thought. If Jimmy hadn't alibi-ed me he wouldn't have hesitated to drag *me* in for the murders. And with throbbing head and parched throat, he hurried across the road to *The Leigh Arms* for a much-needed pint.

In the *Leigh*' there was only Fred the manager behind the bar. The clock said 12-45 but despite the pubs closing at two on Sundays, the place was still almost empty. Ordering a pint, Georgie invited Fred to have a drink but he declined. He then told him about Balmer's visit that morning, and Doris's house being searched and being taken to the police station and then to Jimmy Skelly's.

"Well that's bloody rubbish", said the manager. "You were in here last night".

"I know that and you know that Fred", he said. "But it still gives you a shock to have your house turned over and be suspected of murdering people." Then gratefully lifting the pint to his lips, he sighed, "God blimey I don't `arf need this. Anyway, good health Fred!."

Gradually, a combination of the hangover and the delayed shock of the morning's events began to wash over Georgie making him feel anxious and unsettled. He decided to sit down - a thing he never did in pubs - and became uncharacteristically introspective, even to the point of mumbling to himself.

He appreciated Balmer was a copper, and he knew the kind of one-track suspicious minds coppers have. But surely even Balmer must know he wouldn't do a stroke like that? His own sense of morality was deeply hurt. He couldn't believe that *anyone* who knew him could suspect him of shooting two men in cold blood like that. It just wasn't him. He wouldn't know how to fire a gun, even if he had one.

Feeling jaded and despondent and far from his usual gregarious self, Georgie had suddenly lost all his enthusiasm for his mother's, his brothers and Charlie's and the Toss School and all that. Content to just sit quietly drinking alone, he couldn't be bothered doing anything - not even tapping Fred for a few bob.

Later, at two o-clock when the towel went on, he said "ta-ra" to Fred and ambled across Picton Road down to Doris's for his Sunday dinner.

Thirty minutes after Georgie had entered *The Leigh Arms* for his much-needed "curer", Jimmy's Skelly's dad, Johnnie, called into "*Charlie Mathews*" for a pint on his way to his elderly mother's. She lived in the tenements in Gill Street which ran between Brownlow Hill and Pembroke Place, near to the Bullring

He visited her every Sunday, and as part of his weekly ritual he would buy her half-an-ounce of Fine Irish snuff from Rabinowitzs' shop in Brownlow Hill before having a pint in *Charlie's* or *Strickland's*, or *Legg's* on the corner of Gill Street.

Johnnie, a well read and well - known convivial character, would strike up a conversation with anyone in a pub, especially if he thought they were a Pay-off.

After calling for a pint of mild, he engaged in small talk with Charlie for a while, asking how he was and if his son Jimmy been in but Charlie said he hadn't seen him. He then noticed, standing further down the bar, a small group of two young men and a scruffy dyed blonde talking loudly and animately.

Hearing one of the men, who looked worried, saying he wished to god he could get a ship, Johnnie, who had been a seaman himself in the Twenties, quickly saw the opportunity of a possible drink. So approaching them, he said to the worried man, "Pardon me friend, I hope you don't mind but I couldn't help overhearing. Lookin' for a ship are yer?" The worried man and the blonde looked at him warily without speaking until their companion dismissively answered "No, it's okay, we're okay. He hasn't got a book. Forget it"

In other circumstances, Johnnie would have conned them into believing that the lack of a seaman's book was a mere inconvenience, but there was something about these three that smelled funny. For a start he'd never seen them before. Their reticence was off-putting; they seemed like out-of towners. And the blonde, he thought, was definitely a whore - and he hated whores. But most importantly to him, who could smell a pay-off a mile away, they were not only drinking glasses of mild, the cheapest drink in the pub, but they also looked most un-wealthy. Deciding to leave matters as they were, he drank up, said cheerio to Charlie and headed across Brownlow Hill to his mother's.

Earlier before leaving his home a short distance away in Myrtle Street, Johnnie had read about the Cameo murders in *the Empire News*. He'd concluded that they must have been committed by some desperate American soldier on the run, because English fellas didn't normally use guns. But now, making his way along Gill Street, he thought of the three strangers in Charlie's and their surreptitious manner. "I wonder..", he thought for a moment. But before he reached his mother's the thought had quite left him.

Chapter Eight

Monday 21st March 1949. 1.30pm.

"Investigations are continuing"
(Liverpool City Police)

Leaving the *Midland*, on the corner of Ranelagh Street, on his way to the *Globe* a few yards away down Cases Street, Georgie had another terrible hangover. He'd been drinking last night in the *Midland* and the *Central* with Doris, his brother Joey and his wife, Aggie.

Entering the *Globe*, he spotted Balmer coming up Cases street. "Hello Mr. Balmer", he greeted cheerily. "Had any luck with the murder case?"

"Nah", he replied shaking his head. "What about you George? Heard anything yet?"

"Not a thing."

"Not to worry", said Balmer, "We'll definitely catch him in the end."

"Hope so anyway", he said.

He'd told Joey in the pub last night about Balmer's visit earlier that day and his brother had reminded him that he'd given a brown overcoat to their eldest brother, Peter, a few years ago. Now, seeing Balmer, he was in two minds whether to mention it. If he didn't, and Balmer later found out it would look very suspicious. On the other hand he wanted to avoid the hassle of being under suspicion. In the event however, it was the Inspector who mentioned it.

"I've been thinking you know George", he said quite innocently, "I seem to remember you used to wear a brown overcoat a few years ago. Whatever happened to it?"

"Oh that one", he exclaimed with feigned surprise, "I gave it to our Peter for work ages ago. It went a bit out of style." Nonetheless Balmer said he still might have to see it for elimination purposes. "Has he still got it do you know?"

"Yeah, I think so", he replied warily. "We'll go down and see him if yer like."

When they arrived at the Pier Head , Peter, who worked as a baggage porter on Princes Landing Stage, was actually wearing the overcoat. He verified that Georgie had given it to him about two years ago. Frayed at the cuffs and shiny with dirt, he only wore it when the weather was bad. After a cursory inspection Balmer was satisfied it didn't fit the description of the killer's coat. "Okay Peter", he said, "Sorry for bothering you."

Before boarding the tramcar back to Cases Street, a relieved Georgie asked Balmer if he was now satisfied. "Yeah", replied the Inspector, "But", he said with a smirk, "I was right about you having a brown overcoat, wasn't I?"

What a prick, thought Georgie, as he jumped aboard the slowly moving tram, leaving Balmer at the tram stop talking to a uniformed sergeant.

He was glad the overcoat business had been settled because you never knew what Balmer might get up to if he thought you were trying to pull the wool over his eye.

Four days later, on the evening of Friday the 25th March, fifteen year-old Harold Jones was taken to Derby Lane police station in Old Swan.

Harold, who had only recently left school, worked at A. V. Milton & Co., a small electrical engineering firm located in Bevington Bush off Scotland Road. On the previous Friday, the day before the murders, he was finishing work and looking forward to the weekend when his foreman, knowing he lived in the Wavertree area, asked him to deliver some nuts and bolts to the Cameo cinema on his way home They were apparently needed in order to bed down the motor fan in the projection room. Harold readily agreed. But before delivering the small package, he decided to go home first and have his tea.

He lived in Gresham Street off Edge Lane, near the *Littlewoods'* building, but he always hung around the Lodge Lane area with his cousin Jimmy Povall, who lived about a quarter of a mile away in Spekeland Road, a few hundred yards from the Cameo.

Sixteen year-old Jimmy was, like Harold, a big lad for his age and quite strong through working as a porter for one of the numerous coal dealers that abounded around the Tunnel Road - Spekeland Road area by Edge Hill railway sidings.

The two lads were members of the *Windsor Snooker Hall* at the top of Lodge Lane, opposite *The Boundary* pub.

After his evening meal Harold got a quick wash and, taking the package, made his way across Botanic park to his cousin's home. Jimmy was already washed and dressed when he called, and since the Cameo was only a short distance away they were there in no time.

The manager, Mr. Thomas, was standing in the foyer by the confectionery kiosk. "Oh! Good Lads!", he gratefully exclaimed as Harold handed him the package. "We're desperate for these". Feeling like acclaimed heroes who had just carried out a brave rescue, they felt even better when their "reward" turned out to be an invitation from Mr. Thomas to see the show for free.

They had intended, after delivering the package, to go to the Windsor for a game of billiards but this was an offer they eagerly accepted. They felt truly important as Mr. Thomas personally took them inside and showed them to the one-and-sixes - the best seats in the house.

During the film Harold remarked what a kind man Mr. Thomas was. He'd done similar favours for other customers, he told Jimmy, but had never been shown such appreciation.

On the following Monday evening of March 21st, the *Liverpool Echo* had carried a police appeal for the "two men" who had visited the Cameo on the previous Friday evening to come forward.

Although the murders were the main topic of conversation in the neighbourhood, neither Harold or his cousin ever read the newspapers so they were unaware of the appeal. Several nights later however, on Friday the 25th March, when they and some of their former school pals were larking about outside the Windsor, four detectives were knocking at Harold's front door in Gresham Street enquiring as to his whereabouts.

The Windsor was often visited by the civilian and military police, looking for young villains or army deserters. The cousins names had been obtained from the members list.

Harold's mother told them he was out with his mates but she didn't know where. So without giving her any explanation they told her to tell him when he arrived home to go to Derby Lane police station.

On his way home at ten past ten, Harold noticed a suspicious looking black car parked at the corner of his street. Sitting inside were four men wearing trilbies. The scene reminded him of the Humphrey Bogart and Jimmy Cagney films they often saw at the Cameo and the Tunnel Picture House. And although unsure whether these sinister-looking guys were gangsters or detectives, he was very soon to find out.

Upon reaching his front door he was suddenly surrounded by the men, who told him they were C.I.D. He was then hustled into the car and taken to Derby Lane police station in Old Swan, where he was surprised to see his cousin already there.

For the next two hours the teenagers were interrogated about their visit to the Cameo on the night before the murders. The detectives were very interested in the fact that Harold, in addition to frequenting the area close to the Cameo, also lived across Botanic park. That was where they thought the killer might have disposed of the murder weapon.

They particularly wanted to know if the lads had been in the manager's office. When they said they hadn't, both their fingerprints were taken and they were finally allowed to leave at 12-30 am the following morning.

At 9.00pm on that same evening of Friday 25th March in the Lancashire cotton town of Bolton, about thirty miles from Liverpool, a fourteen-year-old boy was listening to the wireless and simultaneously trying to read a comic.

Brian Aspinall's mother and father had earlier left their tidy respectable semi-detached council house at number two Ash Grove to go downtown to the pictures. They'd left him in charge of his five-year-old brother John, who was upstairs in bed. His eldest brother Jim, a nineteen year-old Ordinary Seaman, had sailed the previous Tuesday from Birkenhead docks for Japan - via Sardinia - on the cargo ship *Vancouver City* .

Jim had officially joined the ship on Monday March 21st, but that afternoon, after having his smallpox and yellow fever injections, he'd returned, unknown to his parents, to Bolton to spend the last few hours with his girl friend. While he was away the police, who had been checking all the ships in port for any missing crew members, were told by the ship's captain that Jim and three others were unaccounted for. But that evening around midnight, Jim had returned to the ship which had sailed on the following morning's tide.

Brian's tranquillity was shattered by a very loud banging coming from the hallway. On opening the front door several burly men wearing overcoats and trilbies stormed into the house, brushing him against the wall in the hallway. Confused and terrified, he thought the house was being raided by burglars.

Grabbing him by the throat, one of the men shouted, "Okay, where is he?. We know he's in the house!" Still dazed by the suddenness of it all, Brian blurted out, "What's going on?" In reply, the man, wearing brown leather gloves, began slapping him violently across the face.

Meanwhile the other men raced into the living room and upstairs into the bedrooms. Brian again asked what was going on and the big man angrily hissed, "You know fuckin' well what's going on. We're looking for Jim Aspinall. We want him for murder." Brian tried to explain that his brother had gone away to sea. But, still forcing him up against the wall, the man again slapped him again across the face and shouted, "Don't tell fuckin' lies. He's here somewhere isn't he? Now where's he fuckin' hiding?"

Brian could hear his little brother upstairs, now roused from his sleep, screaming as the other men continued their search. "Honest to god," pleaded Brian, "he's gone away to sea. He went last Monday."

When the search was completed the man who had been slapping him asked where his parents were and he hesitantly explained that they were at the pictures in town. "Well, when they come in, " he ordered, "you tell them to get down to Howell Croft police station right away, do you hear, you lying little bastard."

"Who shall I say wants them?" asked a trembling Brian. "You just tell them to get down there", came the harsh reply.

As soon as the men left Brian dashed up the stairs, brought his little brother down and did his best to comfort him until their mum and dad arrived home two hours later.

When he told his parents what had happened they were distraught with worry and fear. It was bad enough having your son wanted by the police for murder but he was now apparently missing as well. What on earth could have happened to their Jim?, they wondered.

There were no more buses or trams at this late hour and because they could not afford a taxi, Mr. and Mrs. Aspinall had to walk in a bitterly cold wind, the three miles to the police station in the town centre. Once there, they were informed that their son was suspected of being involved in the Liverpool Cameo cinema murders, and were then repeatedly questioned until dawn as to his whereabouts.

In the face of the interminable interrogation they could only repeat, again and again that, as far as they knew their son had left last Monday to join his ship. But the detectives repeatedly insisted he had not joined the ship and had been reported missing by the captain. Finally, at 8.00am, still completely perplexed and by now exhausted, the weary parents were allowed to leave the station.

In the following weeks the Aspinall's visibly aged with worry. They had no telephone, and even if they'd had one they didn't know the name of their son's ship or that of the shipping company. But mercifully, towards the end of April, they received a most welcome letter from Jim, post marked Sardinia, where the ship had called at Cagliari to take on a cargo of salt.

Elated at the news that he was safe and well, Mrs. Aspinall immediately caught a bus to Howell Croft to let the police know. But at the police station when she finally saw a detective and attempted to show him the letter, he dismissed her with the casual remark, "Oh, we know all about that. The Liverpool bobbies have already arrested someone." They hadn't in fact arrested anyone.

No apology was ever offered for the traumatic ordeal the two children had undergone at the hands of the police on the night of the raid. Nor was any apology given to their parents for the weeks of anguish they had been caused. Indeed, when he came home from work that evening, Mr. Aspinall remarked to his wife that if she had not gone down to Howell Croft with the good news about Jim, they could have been left worrying forever for all the police cared.

On Saturday, March the 26th Charlie Connolly called at his wife's workplace, the *Maison Lyons* cafe in busy Church Street, with some bad news. Her grandmother was dying. Mary asked for the rest of the day off and she and Charlie went straight to her grandmother's house. But when they arrived it was too late. She had already passed away.

Ten days after the raid on the Aspinall home, on Monday April 4th, an anonymous letter was received at Dale Street police headquarters. The plain white envelope, which carried the franked slogan, "Mind How You Go On The Road", was post-marked Liverpool. And in obviously disguised printed characters were written the words, "Inspector C.I.D., Dale Street, Police Hedquaters (sic), Liverpool".

Since the murder hunt had begun, the police had received numerous such letters, mainly from people trying to settle old scores by denouncing real or imagined enemies as the killer. Similar letters also came from amateur sleuths and from religious fanatics cursing the so-called crime wave and offering names of suspects.

But this letter appeared to be different. To Balmer, who opened it as the Inspector in charge of the case, it seemed to offer the first real breakthrough. It had the smell of authenticity. In a mixture of small and large characters the letter read :

> *"Dear sir, this is not a cranks letter or suchlike, nor am I turning informer for gain. You have been searching Wavertree and district for the persons responsible for the death of the two men killed in the cinema when the persons responsible live nowhere near where the crime was committed. It says in the papers you are looking for one man. I know three men and a girl, not including myself, who heard about his plan for the robbery. I would have nothing to do with it myself and I don't think the girl had. When I met her on Sunday she had not been with them, and another man dropped out on account he wanted to unload the revolver before they went. So only two men went. The man he took with him*

lost his nerve and would not go in with him and said he would wait outside but did not. He has not been seen since nor has the girl he lives with been seen about town, five days ago I seen the man who done the job and we got talking. I said I wanted nothing to do with him and he said I am in it with him. What I want to know is how I stand. I knew they was going to do the job but I did not go with them. I have proof I was in a pub not far from Dale Street till 10.00pm and was talking until 11.00pm in Brownlow Hill with two people. I want to know if I turn King's Evidence or something like that will I be charged. I have a record you see and he might say something to frame me with him. To prove I speak the truth the gun he used he threw it in the pond in the park, the park is in Edge Lane next to Littlewoods'. He cut through the park to a 6A car. I am scared of him, he wants me to go away with him and I can't go down the town. I am afraid of him finding where I stay. I don't know how you can get in touch with me. If I give my address you might charge me with being an accesory (sic) to the killing. If you put in the Personal Columm (sic) of the Ecko (sic) and give me your word that I won't be charged I will give you both there (sic) names also some of the bullets he left with me about 6 weeks ago. I can also tell you where he got the gun from. He wants arresting for selling them. I can also tell you who ran that stolen motor lorry through the pub and killed a person some time back if you give me your word that I won't be charged."

Given that they had absolutely nothing else to go on, Smith quickly authorised Balmer to comply with the anonymous request. And that very evening, a short notice appeared in the *Liverpool Echo's* personal column: *"Letter received. Promise definitely given"*. There was no response. The same message was inserted several days later but still nothing. The police were back to square one.

It was generally agreed among the murder squad that the letter was written by a woman. Balmer made the rather obvious suggestion that she was also probably a prostitute involved with the criminal fraternity. It was therefore decided to check the handwriting of all the known prostitutes in Liverpool. And if that didn't identify the author, then the net would be widened to include all females who had been convicted of *any* petty crime in the last five years.

Chapter Nine

May 2nd 1949. 9.30 am.

"A Dangerous Game"

Twenty two year-old Donald Thomas John Johnson, was in the cells at Wallasey police station. He was due to appear on remand in the Magistrates Court with his twenty three year-old married brother, Francis George Johnson - nicknamed "Judder" - on a charge of robbing thirty shillings from a man on his way home on the night of 22nd April.

Wallasey was a small borough next to Birkenhead, on the Cheshire side of the River Mersey. Its main claim to fame in the 1940s was the thriving resort of New Brighton. And villains such as the Johnson's were regarded as uncouth ruffians and thieving pests who came across the river in search of richer pickings. Bernard Watson however, the man they had robbed after following him off the Seacombe ferry boat, was a mere labourer. And the thirty shillings was all that remained of his week's wages

As "foreigners" from the wrong side of the Mersey, the two brothers from Toxteth knew they had no chance of getting bail - no more than when they'd appeared a week ago. But Donald Johnson had an idea. What if his bail was up to a high-up Liverpool detective instead of these woollyback coppers?

He remembered the night of the Cameo murders about six weeks ago when he'd been pulled by that copper outside *The Boundary* pub and asked for his Identity Card. Close shave, that was. The copper probably didn't know about the murders at the time otherwise he'd certainly have been pulled in on Suss. The job had only happened thirty minutes before. And only half a mile away. The Sunday papers had been full of it the next day.

He decided to ring the bell on the wall. After some minutes a policeman came and lowered the square hatch in the cell door. "What the fuck do you want?" he shouted contemptuously.

If there was one thing Liverpool villains, or any villains for that matter, knew, it was that you never admitted anything to the police.

And you certainly never made a signed statement. But Johnson, with fifteen previous convictions for housebreaking and shopbreaking, was desperate to get bail for himself and his brother. And in order to get it he was about to play a very dangerous game with very dangerous people - the Liverpool C.I.D.

"Listen sir", he asked ingratiatingly, "could you please get in touch with the Liverpool police. I want to talk to them about the Cameo cinema murder."

Enough said! The policeman disappeared in a flash without saying another word.

When the call was received at Dale Street Detective Chief Inspector Morris immediately ordered an unmarked car and, together with Detective Sergeant Farragher, raced through the Mersey Tunnel to Wallasey.

Sitting in the passenger seat, Morris remarked, "This is it! The bloody breakthrough at last". But the more sceptical Farragher asked, "D'you think he really knows anything Jim?"

"He'd better had", Morris replied. "Better not be wasting our bloody time".

As the detectives entered the small interview room, Johnson was already sitting at a bare table, with a uniformed constable standing just inside the door. Morris nodded to the constable who immediately left the room. Then, in measured tones, he coolly said, "Hello Donald, I'm Inspector Morris and this is Sergeant Farragher. I believe you've got something to tell us about the Cameo?" Johnson, looking worried, nodded assent as Morris sat down opposite him across the table. Farragher then left the room without any explanation. "Where's he gone?" asked Johnson. "Oh, no need to worry. He's just gone to have a word with your brother," said Morris. "But me brother doesn't know anything about this", he protested. "Nothing to worry about Donald", said Morris reassuringly. "It's just routine that's all. Now", he went on, "what can you tell me about the Cameo?"

Johnson thought it would be a little too obvious to ask what was in it for him at such an early stage. Morris might think that he really didn't know anything about the murder and was only seeking bail. He might just get up and leave. Thing to do was to play hard to get. If he played his cards right he wouldn't even have to ask for bail, they'd offer him it!

"Well I know quite a lot actually", he muttered. "but I can't tell yer everything I know. I mean I'm not sure where I'll stand meself in all this".

"Listen Don", said Morris, leaning closer across the table, "I can tell you right now. I personally don't think you're the sort of fella who could do something terrible like this. But I think maybe you know the fella who did it." Johnson stared down at the table to avoid Morris's familiarity and to maintain his own air of reluctance. It was a good bargaining posture to adopt.

There was silence for a few moments. The Inspector didn't want to push it; didn't want to spoil this golden opportunity by being hasty. But he was the first to break the silence. "Look Don", he began sympathetically, "I can see you're worried but you've no need to be. You won't be brought into anything. This charge here, we'll have quashed".

Without betraying any sign of elation Johnson thought, Fuckin'ell! This is great! Bail would have been enough. But getting the charge dropped! Fuckin'ell!

Carefully nursing him, Morris gently asked if he had already been interviewed about the murder and Johnson mumbled, "Yeah. Inspector Gardner came to our house and spoke to me mother when I was at work."

"And he seemed quite happy, did he Don?"

" Well, yeah, I suppose so. He never came back, anyway".

If it was true, thought Morris, what a stupid bugger Gardner was! He'd heard rumours that Gardner was going to be taken off the case. Something about him going funny in the head. Meanwhile he wondered if Farragher had found out anything from the brother.

Johnson was dying for a smoke. Asking for a ciggy, he thought, wasn't the same as asking for bail. It was the accepted thing for cons to ask jacks for ciggies - especially when you were being questioned like this. They couldn't read anything into that. "I'll tell you what Mr. Morris,", he said, "I couldn't half do with a ciggy."

This was Morris's opportunity to make his exit to see if Farragher had found out anything. "Look Don," he said in a kindly tone, "I'll go out now and get you some cigarettes. While I'm gone I want you to think it over. Okay?" Johnson nodded his agreement and as soon as the door closed behind him, his mind began racing to work out the rest of his story.

After sending the constable for the cigarettes Morris called Farragher out of the other interview room. "Well"? he asked, "what does *he* know?" Farragher said the brother was actually known as George or Judder, but he felt sure he knew nothing. "He said he was drinking in a pub in the Dingle on the murder night, with his missus".

"Well", said Morris, "Donald definitely does. And, by hook or by crook, I'm bloody-well going to get it out of him. Look," he went on, "I don't want this fella sitting in front of me smoking his bloody head off and taking it easy. Now he has no fags or matches so I've sent out for some fags to loosen him up. Now when he has the first, I'll call you in to give him a match, then you leave. That way, when he comes under pressure he won't be able to call on another fag to give himself a breathing space. Okay?"

"Yeah."

When the constable returned with the cigarettes Morris said to Farragher, "Right, come with me and wait outside till I call you".

Johnson was still sitting, almost slumped over the table feigning despondency. Morris threw the packet of cigarettes on the table. "There you are Don", he said. "Come on now things aren't that bad. Have a fag".

Appearances were deceptive. For just as Morris's friendliness was as phoney as hell, so was Johnson's demeanour, cloaking as it did, an alert and creative brain that had been working overtime for the past fifteen minutes.

He now had what Morris wanted - a story. But first he asked, "Have you got a light Mr. Morris?"

"I don't use them myself Don", he replied, but then called out for Farragher, who entered after a few seconds pause. "Give Donald a light will you Jack", he said. Farragher lit the cigarette then began to leave. "Hey sergeant", asked Johnson, taking a long draw on the cigarette, "how's our kid doing?" Then without waiting for a reply he added, "I've told yer, he doesn't know anything about this business, yer know".

"We know that Donald", said Morris reassuringly. "We know".

Once Farragher had left, Morris pulled his chair up closer. "Now Donald", he asked expectantly, "have you thought things over?"

"Yeah".

"Well what have you got to say?"

"I think I know who done the Cameo murder and I think I know where the gun was".

Morris was finding it difficult to suppress his excitement. Until now he'd been put in the shade by Bert Balmer on the Murder team. Really high profile, was Bert. The Chief's blue-eyed boy, as well. But now it would be his turn. Everyone would now know it was quiet Jimmy Morris and not flashy Balmer who had cracked the Cameo case.

"Good lad!", he exclaimed. "We'll get this charge quashed against you. It's only toffee. You won't be brought into the Cameo case. You won't even have to give evidence". He felt genuinely thankful to Johnson, and for a moment actually liked him. It didn't seem to matter that he was misleading him. That was part of the game. The end justified the means.

As Johnson began his story Morris innocently asked, "D'you mind if I take a few notes while we're talking Don?" The request didn't unduly bother Johnson. He knew the difference between notes and a signed statement. "No, not really," he replied. "Good", said Morris.

"Well", he continued, "I remember reading about the Cameo murder in the Sunday papers, but I can't remember what I was doing or where I was on the Saturday night. I do go to the Cameo cinema occasionally and since January I've been there on an average of once a week. I don't think I was there on the night of the murder, but I had been there that week, either on the Friday night or the Monday, and saw two pictures - one crime and one love. I don't remember anything else about them though."

"Why I came to go on that night was that I was having a drink in *The Boundary* pub at the top of Smithdown Road and Lodge Lane when I met a fella named Charlie Dugan from St. Helens who I met in

Walton prison in 1945. Anyway, he gave me a few rums and asked me to go the Cameo with him and I said, `alright'. Anyway", he went on , "I didn't think much of the film , and left about twenty past nine to go for a drink. He stayed in the cinema. I arranged to meet him outside *The Boundary* the next night at half seven but he didn't turn up."

Morris was listening intently and jotting down notes. "Go on Donald", he coaxed. "Well, about four days after the murder - no it was definitely the Friday after - I was on a tramcar in Church street down the town when I saw Dugan so I got off the car and shouted to him. He turned round and saw me but then he ran into Woolworth's. I wondered why he should do that because we hadn't quarrelled in any way, so I followed him into the store but I couldn't find him".

Pausing to pull out another cigarette, Johnson asked Morris if he could get him a light. But Morris was fearful of an extended pause. For apart from giving him time to think, it might spoil the narrative, which was flowing so well. Secondly, Johnson might suddenly realise the incriminating implication of what he was saying and clam up.

"Let's just carry on for a bit Donald", he said, maintaining his kindly tone," "I'll get you a light in a minute. Don't want to spoil your concentration, you know Don."

Since Johnson did not wish to spoil his own concentration he couldn't really argue with that. And he really did need to concentrate now because from here on in he had to make it plausible if he was going to get bail.

Although only twenty-two Donald Johnson had learned all of the tricks when under police interrogation. Suddenly, clasping his head in both hands in mock anguish, he cried. "Oh it's no use telling lies!" Then in a quieter tone, he went on, "Dugan isn't his real name but if I tell you the truth I'll put a rope around his neck. The real truth is that he spoke to me and showed me a gun, and I know he did the murder. He asked me to go with him but I wouldn't. It's kept me awake night after night worrying about it. I've even been to Confession but the Priest won't give me Absolution until I tell the police all about it. But I promised Charlie on the Holy Eucharist that I wouldn't tell anyone. It will put a rope around his neck", he went on, "and maybe mine as well. What shall I do?"

"Easy, now son", said Morris comfortingly. "Just take it easy and tell me what kind of gun it was". Johnson, not wishing to appear knowledgeable about guns, whimpered, "I don't know anything about them, Mr. Morris". But Morris, offering his notebook and pencil, said, "Okay, Don, just do us a drawing of what it was like then". He then drew a crude sketch of what looked like an automatic pistol.

Unable to believe his luck, Morris didn't press him any further. He couldn't wait to contact his boss. "Look Don", he said, "I'm going to phone Mr. Smith now. Do you want to have a word with *him*?" Johnson made no reply. He knew Smith was the Head of the C.I.D. And for all he knew he might be cleverer than Morris, so he didn't relish the idea of being questioned by him. On the other hand he didn't want Morris to know he knew who Mr. Smith was. In such circumstances it was better to remain noncommittal.

Morris quickly left the room, telling the zombie-like constable to resume his position inside. Now in more generous mood, he shouted back, "Oh by the way, give him a light for his fag will you constable"

Johnson was glad of the cigarette and the respite. He needed more time to think over his story and what he was going to say next.

When Smith received the telephone call, he said he would be over right away and would be bringing Bert Balmer with him.

Johnson had been sitting in the interview room for a further thirty minutes before Morris finally re-entered - this time with Smith and Balmer. Morris had already briefed them on the situation and they had been deliberating about the right tactical approach to use in order to get him to sign a statement.

As the constable again disappeared, Morris handed Smith the notes he had taken and said to Johnson, "Donald, this is Detective Chief Superintendent Smith". Johnson and Smith nodded to each other and Morris felt proud to be in such a pivotal position - especially in front of Balmer. "He's a good lad Chief", he said, "but he's a bit worried about this thirty bob charge he's up on this morning. But I've told him we'll get it squashed for him".

"Yes, of course", confirmed Smith, who then told him to leave them alone for a moment.

Morris couldn't believe his ears! Was the boss really dismissing him after the excellent work he'd done? What is the bugger bloody-well up to, he thought. It wouldn't be so bad but Balmer had been allowed to stay.

Balmer had been in operational charge of the case for the past six weeks and hadn't come up with a thing so far. He had dozens of informers but what good had they been? And the anonymous letter sent to him in April? Much use that was. Nothing had come of that either. In fact, most of the detectives in the Murder team were saying, behind his back of course, that he'd probably written it himself to get himself a higher profile on the case. You couldn't put anything past Balmer. As well as being a publicity-seeker he was ruthless. He wasn't known in the force as "The Exterminator" for nothing. Jimmy Morris, by common consent in the C.I.D., was a much better detective.

After Morris had left the room Smith had second thoughts about Balmer too, whom he knew to be a bull in a china shop. And this situation called for delicacy if nothing else. Also the enticing thought fleetingly occurred to him that Johnson just might cough his guts up to him. If that happened then he alone would take the credit for breaking the case.

Dismissing Balmer, Smith sat quietly down at the table facing Johnson, and asked him first if he was working. "No", he replied, I fell off the ladder." Looking suitably sympathetic, Smith said, "Oh, no", then asked what kind of work he did. "I'm a window-cleaner", he replied.

Smith asked if he was courting. And when he nodded, he said, "Look son, I suppose she's a nice girl and I know you're not a bad lad. You just tell me the truth and I'll help you and your girl to build up a nice home together." But Johnson repeated that he had made a promise on the Holy Eucharist. "I understand that son", he murmured sympathetically, "but if you're ever in trouble you can always come and see me and I'll do my best for you. Now", he said, "all I want to know is who did the murder. You don't have to worry about a thing. I'll keep you well out of it".

"Well", said Johnson, "I think I know who done it".

"And you also know where the gun is, don't you son?" Careful not to commit himself or make any hard and fast promises, he replied, "Well,

I know where it *was*."

Morris suddenly reappeared and told them Johnson was wanted in court. But Smith told him to ask the police prosecutor to hold it back for a little while longer.

This little scene was part of the strategy which had been agreed earlier. They had all agreed that if Johnson was going to be of any use to them he would have to be let out on bail but they didn't want him to think he could be bailed without first signing a statement.

Resuming the interview, Smith told Johnson that if he signed the statement he would get in touch with the Chief Constable and try to arrange bail for him, adding, "It's only toffee, this charge you're up on."

Smith was handling the situation smoothly, and so far had made no demands on Johnson. "Look son", he continued in his fatherly tone, "I hear you've told Mr. Morris quite a lot already. Well, you don't have to tell *me* anything. All you have to do is sign this statement that Mr. Morris wrote down. Is that okay with you?"

Johnson replied that what he'd told Morris was the truth, and that he hadn't been able to work or sleep with worry, but he wasn't going to sign anything. "Well, okay", Smith said patiently, "you don't have to sign anything. Just tell me Charlie Dugan's real name. You won't even be mentioned I promise you".

Unsure whether they'd decided to get him bail, Johnson now made his move. "I'll tell you what", he began innocently, "if I was on the outside I could see him and give him a chance to give himself up. Then I wouldn't be breaking the promise I made. Otherwise, it's more than I dare do to break a promise made on the Holy Eucharist".

It was now a game of pure bluff. But although Smith had much more to lose by keeping Johnson in custody, he wasn't going to throw his hand in just yet. "Okay son", he said with feigned regret, "if that's your position there's not much more we can do about it is there?" Johnson didn't reply.

If we *have* to give this bastard bail without a statement from him, thought Smith, I'm not going to be the one to tell him. "Well, It's up to you Donald", he sighed, as he got up to leave. But, unknown to Johnson, Smith had already requested the Wallasey police to put the Johnson brothers case back until the afternoon, or the next morning if necessary, and for no objection to be made to bail.

Before leaving the room Smith had decided to give it one more try when Johnson suddenly said, " I could find the man tomorrow, and when I've seen him I'll be free from my promise, and I'll tell you who he is and where the gun is. I know where it it's planted."

This was altogether too attractive a proposition to be ignored. Smith had to agree to get him bail as quickly as possible. And if Johnson's family couldn't get across from Liverpool, Farragher would be instructed to stand surety for him.

The following morning when Johnson and his brother appeared in court, Wallasey's Chief Constable, Mr. Ormerod, told the magistrates, "I am not in a position to go on with this case today. These men have been in custody for *some time now* and I feel that any application they might make for bail might be considered by the Bench". (My italics) They were then remanded on bail until May 6th.

Despite the Chief Constable's, "some time now", they had actually been in custody for ten days.

Farragher had duly stood surety in the sum of twenty pounds and twenty pounds. But before the brothers left the court he called Donald into the C.I.D. Office and confidentially asked where the gun was.

Johnson simply repeated his story about the Holy Eucharist. "If I told you where it is", he said, "I'd be breaking a promise." Undeterred, Farragher coaxed, "You won't be breaking a promise. We don't even want you to break a promise. If you take us to where you've got the gun, we'll wipe the fingerprints off." But Johnson resolutely refused, repeating that he had to see the man himself first.

Smith, who had been in court earlier, then entered the office carrying a sheet of writing paper and an envelope. "Look son", he said, "I understand how you feel. But I've thought of a good way to help you and me. All you have to do is write down the name of the man who done the murder, and where he is, and send it in the post to me. It can be sort of anonymous. You don't even have to sign it. Now that's fair enough isn't it?" But Johnson again said his swearing on the Holy Eucharist prevented this.

Concealing his frustration, Smith left the envelope and paper on the table in the vain hope that Johnson would oblige. Then, before finally leaving the room he gave him twenty cigarettes, and two pounds to enable him to visit pubs to try and find "Dugan". "And don't forget", he warned, "stay off the rum!".

Chapter Ten

"When first we practice to deceive..."

Part of Johnson's deal with the Head of the C.I.D was that - regardless of him making contact with the gunman - he was to report to Smith regularly by telephone. An extra precaution taken by Smith, but unknown to Johnson, was that a continual watch would also be kept on him.

On May 4th, in accordance with the deal, he telephoned Smith, who arranged to see him in Fontenoy Street, near the Mersey Tunnel, about a hundred yards from the Central C.I.D. Office. When they met Smith made it plain he was expecting progress but Johnson simply said he hoped to see "Dugan" later on. "I will ring you this afternoon", he said. But at 3.00pm. he again rang Smith and said, "I've not seen him yet. I'll phone you as soon as I do".

On May 5th, at 11.00am., Johnson again telephoned Smith, telling him, "I've not seen him yet but I'm still trying." By now, it was beginning to dawn on Smith that Johnson was giving him the runaround so he demanded to see him immediately in Park Road near his home . When they met half an hour later, Smith warned him that if he didn't come up with something very soon, he was going back to gaol. "I know it seems funny", pleaded Johnson, "and it's worrying me but I can't do anything about it until I see him. The promise is binding on me."

At 11.30 pm that night, Smith received yet another call from Johnson, asking if he could meet him at 1.30am outside the Gaumont cinema at the Dingle end of Park Road. Hoping this might be the breakthrough he needed, Smith drove to the rendezvous alone, telling Morris and Farragher to follow him in another car. They were to park further down on the opposite side of Park Road. And he would flash his headlights if he required their assistance.

When they met, Johnson climbed into the front seat and said, "Mr. Smith, I planted the gun although I wasn't on the job, but I can't tell you where the fella is, as I am bound by my promise. I will tell you all about it though." Having had enough of Johnson's procrastination, Smith immediately flashed his lights and Morris and Farragher appeared. "Mr. Morris", said Smith in an official tone, "this man wishes to make a statement to us." Johnson then said, "Yes, I'll tell you the whole truth of what happened but I still won't tell you the man's name." He was then put into the back of the second car and all three, followed by Smith, drove through the deserted streets to the Central C.I.D office.

Once Johnson had been deposited in one of the interview rooms, Smith decided that the best rapport with him had been developed by the amiable Jimmy Morris. He was therefore assigned, as the "good cop", to try and get as good a statement as possible from him. The role of "bad cop", should he be required, was assigned, appropriately, to Balmer.

Sitting across the small table with numerous sheets of lined paper and several pencils in front of him, Morris told Johnson to speak slowly and clearly. Johnson, nodded and then immediately revealed that he was with the killer on the night of the murders - but only afterwards. "One thing is certain", he said, "and that is I could tell you where the fella who did the killing is and where the gun is now, but I made a promise, and it was a promise on the Holy Eucharist that I would give the chap a chance to give himself up before I said anything about the murder. I had nothing to do with it myself, although he did want me to go with him, but I wouldn't have anything to do with the gun."

In another substantial departure from his account of May 2nd at Wallasey, Johnson went on, "He told me he was going to do a job at the Cameo, and I went with him on the Friday or the Monday before the murder. He asked me to look around the place and weigh up the women who worked there while we were supposed to be looking at the pictures, but I was scared and told him I was going out. He said, `Oh well, I'll see you later`, and he gave me a few bob. I saw him afterwards and he asked me to go with him on the Saturday but I told him I would not He then told me he would see me on the Saturday night at a quarter to eleven outside *The Boundary*. I got there about half past ten."

Johnson then described the incident outside *The Boundary* pub on the night of the murder when the policeman had asked him for his identity card. "After the policeman had gone", he continued, "the man came up to me and said, `Catch hold of this and get rid of it. It's too hot for me.` He then gave me a gun, and I said, `Nitto, but what have you done?` He said, ` Oh, I've just shot a couple of lights out.` I said, `I think you've done more than that`, and he walked away down Parliament Street, saying, `I'll see you tomorrow at the Pier Head.`"

"I then walked down Smithdown Road towards the Cameo, but when I got near, I saw a lot of cars outside and a lot of policemen, and I knew then that he had done more than shoot a couple of lights. I got scared because I had the gun on me, and I didn't want to be stopped with it, so I walked further along Smithdown Road and climbed over the cemetery wall near the hospital. Then I got onto the cemetery wall (between the cemetery and hospital) and walked back a bit and then climbed back into the cemetery. I don't know why I did that, but I was frightened. Then I walked back across the cemetery in line with Smithdown Road and climbed onto another wall, which I found was the backyard wall of some houses. I Then walked along the dividing wall and dropped into the road and saw some blitzed land and realised I was walking back to Smithdown Road, so I turned back and went the other way and found myself in Croxteth Road."

Morris was writing furiously, as Johnson continued, "Next day I saw him again after I had seen the papers and told him that he should go and give himself up but he asked me to give him a week to think it over and I promised him on the Holy Eucharist that I would do so."

For the first time since Johnson had begun his story, Morris spoke. Holding his pencil aloft, he asked, "What happened then Don?"
"I was pulled up, after I had left Croxteth Road the night before, by a policeman, but I'd planted the gun by then. I had wrapped it in my handkerchief as I didn't want any fingerprints on it, but I've been back since and taken my handkerchief away." Then, referring to the gun, he went on cryptically, "Nobody will find it and the only things that might go near it are the birds."   This remark puzzled Morris but he resisted the temptation to interrupt his flow and continued taking down the statement.

" I've seen the fella two or three times since", Johnson continued, "and each time I've given him a promise on the Holy Eucharist that I would not give him away without giving him another chance to give himself up. I saw him when you were searching the lake in Botanic park. We were watching and he said, `You haven't thrown it in there have you?` I said, `No`, and he laughed. I knew something had happened on the Saturday night before I saw him because the police were pulling everybody up."

In anticipation of the avalanche of questions which were bound to follow, Johnson then emphasised, " I *cannot* tell you the fella is because of my promise, but *I* had nothing to do with the job. The only way I've helped him was to get rid of the gun. And I can't tell you where the gun is because you would find his fingerprints, and that would be as good as telling you who he was."

In a further attempt to stave off the inevitable pressure, he went on, "If it wasn't for my promise, I *would* tell you. He's been no good to me. I saw him yesterday and he asked me for the gun back. He said he'd pay me for it, but I told him he could not get it and I couldn't."

Morris, still writing furiously, maintained his silence as Johnson continued his story. "If I could see him again", he said, "and give him a chance to give himself up I would be free from my promise and tell you who he is and where the gun is, but I have made my promise and I can't break it. It has worried me for weeks and I haven't been able to sleep. I haven't been able to work properly, and nobody ever complained about my work."

By now Morris was becoming increasingly sceptical but let Johnson continue on the off-chance that he may just slip up and reveal something which would link him irrefutably to the murders. But Johnson, in a pathetic attempt to gain the officer's sympathy simply said, " At work I fell off the ladder too and that was because I was so frightened. He told me the gun he gave me was the gun he used. He had another gun as well."

Then, in order to make himself so knowledgeable about the killer as to be indispensable to the police and thus remain at liberty, he continued on a different track. "He lives with one girl, but she is no good. He's going about with another girl and she's decent, and I wouldn't like to see her get into trouble. Each time I've seen him since the job", he added, "he's given me a few bob and a few rums."

Morris sat staring at Johnson for a few moments, then said, "If what you've told me is the truth Don, you've got nothing to worry about. So why the bloody `ell won't you tell me his name?"

"I've told you. I *can't*!"

"Okay then, I'm going to read over the statement you've just made. Then all you've got to do is sign it."

"No", said Johnson shaking his head, "I told you, I'm not going to sign anything. But I've been talking to you for a long time and every word I've said is true."

Morris reminded him that he had made a promise to Mr. Smith that he would make a statement, and that Mr. Smith was entitled to expect a *signed* statement. But Johnson, his gaze fixed firmly on the floor, remained silent.

After several more minutes of silence Morris concluded that he alone couldn't take matters any further. It was now the "bad cop's" turn.

In the Chief's office a conference was quickly convened between Smith, Morris, Balmer and Farragher. After Morris had recounted the interview with Johnson, he added, "I think he's bloody well making it up. I think he was only after bail on the other charge." Balmer disagreed. "No, he's not making it up. He knows too much. Nobody could make up that much detail." Then turning to Smith, he said, "He's got loads of form for shopbreaking and housebreaking, fifteen previous convictions. He's a mad bastard as well. Tried to top himself one time in his cell."

Farragher, who had been perusing Johnson's criminal record, said, "None of his convictions were for violence though." But Balmer told him to look on the next page, from which Farragher then began to read aloud, " On one occasion in 1945 he broke into a house in Sheil Road in the early hours of the morning. The occupier, a lady doctor was in bed with the curtains drawn. On hearing the intruder she switched on the light. Johnson, who was in the room holding a spade, switched off the light and brandishing the spade threatened her with the words, `If you value your life you won't switch that light on`".

Suspecting Balmer had himself inserted this, Smith looked at him and quietly said, "Only one thing wrong with that Bert. If he switched the light off first how could she see him brandishing the spade?." Before he could reply Smith cynically drawled, "Never mind Bert, you don't have to answer that."

Urging Smith to let him have a go at Johnson, Balmer declared, "I'll *make* him sign the statement." Then, in a dig at Morris, he added. "After all I *am* in charge of this investigation."

"Hang on a minute Bert", cautioned Smith. "I've got an idea. Wasn't he complaining that the priest wouldn't give him Absolution? Well what if we provide a "priest" who *will* give him Absolution...?"

Johnson was kept in custody and when the interview resumed some hours later Smith told him he had managed to procure a friendly priest who would listen sympathetically to what he had to say with no strings attached. It was an offer he could hardly refuse. The ball was now firmly in his court.

The tall, slim, catholic "priest", complete with dog collar and cassock, sympathised with Johnson and assured him that the conflict raging within him could be resolved. He understood, he said, his great need to unburden himself. And he didn't think it fair his own Parish priest stipulating that he had to tell the police the killer's name before he would give him Absolution. After all, he said, "Confession is a sacred thing between the sinner and his priest. What happens in the Confessional is nobody else's business." He was prepared, he said, to hear his Confession and to give him Absolution.

Johnson almost fell for the daring deception. But, kneeling at the feet of the "priest", listening to his prior blessing, he suddenly noticed beneath the cassock, the navy blue serge police trouser bottoms and the pair of highly polished size nine police boots! It also occurred to him that, so far this "priest" hadn't spoken one word of Latin!

After complaining to Smith about the trickery, Johnson steadfastly refused to say anything more so Balmer was finally given his own way. The "bad cop" would attempt to frighten him into a confession.

Entering the interview room in abrupt fashion, Balmer sternly commanded, "Stand up! Donald Thomas John Johnson, I charge you with the murder of Leonard Thomas at the Cameo cinema on March 19th 1949. Have you anything to say?" Johnson made no immediate reply. He was too shocked. God!, he thought, things have really got out of hand now. He hadn't intended it to get *this* far!

In the event Balmer's ploy did not work, for when Johnson recovered he indignantly replied "You can't charge me with murder. It was him not me". Balmer retorted, "Well sign the bloody statement then!" But Johnson still refused.

Fully aware there was no evidence to support a murder charge, Smith then decided that Morris should charge him with being 'an accessory after the fact'. His precise wording of the charge was: "That well knowing that a man known to you had murdered Leonard Thomas on March 19th, you did, on the same day and other days afterwards, receive, comfort, harbour, assist and maintain the said man."

Moments earlier Johnson, in a final attempt to avoid being charged, had told Morris, "If you don't charge me I'll get the gun for you tonight", but by now the police had had enough of his filibustering. Their patience had ran out. Later that morning he appeared in the tiny No 3 Court at Dale Street and, with the police objecting strongly to bail, he was remanded for a week in custody,

Immediately before his third remand appearance on May 27th, Johnson, with his solicitor, Mr. Leslie Black, in the presence of Smith, Balmer and Morris, made a brief statement - the only one he ever signed. It simply said, "I do not know anything about the Cameo murder. I do not know who did it."

When shortly afterwards Johnson and his solicitor left the C.I.D. Office, a furious Smith told the others, "I want everything you can get on that little bastard. Block his bail again, and block it at every remand. And every screw who escorts him is to pump him for any information and report to us. Any cons he talks to in Walton, I want to know what he says. I want him three-ed up in a cell. Then he's bound to open his mouth to somebody. Because you know what he's going to do don't you? He's going to say he told us a load of lies just to get bail And he's going to say we offered him a deal."

After being remanded in custody, Johnson and his brother were taken by police car to Wallasey Magistrates court on the thirty shillings robbery charge and were remanded to the Chester Assizes, due to start in a few days time. Additional charges against both of wilfully damaging fittings in the police cells at Wallasey were dropped, and

"Judder" was granted bail.

On the Cameo charge, Johnson appeared at the Liverpool Committal Court on 30th May and was sent in custody to the Summer Assizes beginning in two weeks at St. George's Hall.

Chapter Eleven

"In the merry month of may...."

May 1949 proved to be most eventful. For apart from Johnson's entrance into the Cameo case, George Kelly and James Skelly had been picked up for the March assault on the police at the bottom of Brownlow Hill.

When they appeared before the Stipendiary Magistrate, Arthur McFarland, on May 12th, Skelly was charged with "Assaulting Constable George Taylor when in the execution of his duty", and Kelly with the more serious offence of, "Unlawfully and Maliciously Wounding Constable Allen George Beresford with Intent to cause Grievous Bodily Harm". They were both also charged with stealing a pair of rubber boots valued at five shillings, the property of person or persons unknown.

The charges had arisen out of the incident on the afternoon of March 8th when they had been on their way to Boots chemist at the corner of Renshaw Street and Mount Pleasant to get a tin of Elastoplast dressings for Kelly's mother who had accidentally cut herself.

Crossing from *Lewis'* they'd seen Johnny-One-Cunningham, wrestling with two policemen on the pavement outside the *Adelphi* hotel. Whilst one officer held him by the throat the other was striking him with his truncheon. Apparently he'd been resisting arrest after being accused of stealing a pair of Wellington boots from *Lewis'*.

Recognising their friend, Kelly and Skelly, who, like Cunningham, had also been drinking, had remonstrated with the officers but had been ordered to "fuck off". Whereupon Skelly, wrenching the truncheon from one officer, had punched him on the chin, and Kelly, dragging Cunningham away, had kicked the other officer on the ground, causing a slight cut on his eyebrow. All three had then made good their escape up the side streets off Brownlow Hill to the Bullring.

The two men had pleaded not guilty and were remanded on bail until May 26th.

Apart from them being innocent of the theft of the rubber boots, they had learned through experience that pleading not guilty was the only way to discover what evidence the police had. You would then know whether you stood any chance of successfully contesting the case. It was also a convenient way to avoid being sent for sentence in custody to a higher court - which was the usual practice.

The following day, Friday the 13th, Jacqueline Dickson was arrested at 11.30am in a Church Street store where she was spotted stealing a woman shopper's handbag containing, purse, cash, clothing coupons, savings book and various items of jewellery. Northam, who had been waiting outside the store, had run away when he saw her struggling with shop staff.

This was the second time she'd been arrested for this type of offence. She'd been lucky in January, when caught in Chester Market robbing a woman shopper. On that occasion she'd simply been sent up to Carlisle, where she was wanted, and had had the Chester charge taken into consideration. But it was still on her record, and it was only four months ago. She was aware she was facing another prison sentence if she didn't think of some way of getting out of it.

When she was taken to the Bridewell in Cheapside, Donald Johnson, who had earlier that morning appeared on remand, was in a large holding cell which was quickly filling up with those who, like him, had been remanded in custody. She was put in a nearby communal cell for women.

At 6.00pm when Johnson and the other prisoners were escorted in handcuffs outside to the Black Maria and taken to Walton, Dickson remained at Cheapside for her court appearance the following morning.

Becoming increasingly apprehensive about her perilous situation, she finally, at 11.00pm, asked the turnkey to fetch Sergeant Farragher. She had, she said, some important information for him.

Dickson had known Farragher for some time. It was he who had been in charge of the case when McManus had got the five years for assaulting her. And she always gave him information about any jobs she'd heard about around the town. He owed her a favour.

When he arrived she asked if he could get her bail in the morning.

"What's in it for me Jackie?" came the cynical response. "I have an idea who might have done the Cameo job", she replied. Sensing something bigger than he could handle, Farragher told her she would have to speak to Inspector Balmer. She was then taken out of the cell through the corridors to the C.I.D. Office and given a cup of tea and a cigarette whilst Balmer was sent for.

Dickson didn't like Balmer. Even though it was him who had put Woolerton away for pimping on her last year, he was still scary. His name was notorious among the girls around Lime Street. Scotch Esther said he used to send American servicemen to her for free sex under the threat of harassment and arrest if she refused. And some of the other girls said he was always threatening to put them away unless they gave him information.

She was surprised to discover that instead of asking her what she knew, Balmer immediately asked for a sample of her handwriting, and in particular for her to write words like *Echo* and *accessory* and *column*. This puzzled her but these words, misspelt, had of course been contained in the anonymous letter. Yet apart from proving to be almost illiterate, he was satisfied her handwriting did not match.

Balmer then asked what she knew about the Cameo and, desperate to get bail, she told him she knew a man whom she thought was involved in the murder. "I don't know his first name", she muttered hesitantly, "but I think his second name is Connolly. He's always hanging around Lime Street, and he always wears a trilby like it said in the papers."

Balmer knew Lime Street and its inhabitants very well but he had never heard of Connolly. Asking Farragher to check the criminal records for anything on him, he continued to question Dickson more closely.

Showing her the anonymous letter, he asked if she knew who might have sent it. She replied that she'd heard it was a man who had written it pretending to be a woman. But when Balmer pressed her on the source of her information, she became even more vague and said it was simply something she'd heard - she didn't know who from. "What makes you think this Connolly fella had anything to do with it?" he asked. Because, she replied, she'd seen him in *Littlewoods'* cafe shortly after the murder and he looked very worried and suspicious, and she thought he fitted the description of the murderer that was in the papers.

Sensing that this was no more than whores gossip Balmer nonetheless decided to have Connolly brought in for questioning.

With Dickson kept in the police cells overnight, Farragher complied with her request to contact Jimmy Northam so he could bring her some cigarettes. And when he arrived at midnight Balmer asked him if he knew anything about the Cameo. But Northam said he knew nothing and that he had only come down to give her the cigarettes.

The following morning, Saturday May 14th, Dickson appeared in court and was remanded until Monday. And on the promise of keeping her ears to the ground for any further information, the police did not oppose bail.

Later that morning, emerging from the *Marionette* Billiards Hall in Lime Street, Connolly was approached by two detectives and told Balmer wanted to see him down at Dale Street. When he asked why they told him it was just part of routine enquiries about the Cameo murders. There was no need to worry, they said, everyone in town was being questioned. He was then asked if he wished them to accompany him but he declined, saying he would go down on his own -which he immediately did.

At C.I.D Central, he was welcomed with assumed friendliness by Balmer and told that they were simply making routine enquiries. Chief Superintendent Smith was present but took no active part in the interview.

Connolly was first asked for a sample of his handwriting, again with particular emphasis on the words "Echo" and "accessory". He was then shown several police mugshots of women and asked if he recognised anyone. After glancing through them for a while he said, , "I know her", indicating Dickson, " "She knocks around Lime Street. In fact I saw her only the other week in *Littlewoods'* cafe." Well, thought Balmer, at least Jackie was right about one thing.

"Do you know where she is now Charlie?" he asked. Then added, "Or do you know where she lives?" Connolly said he only knew her by sight and didn't know her whereabouts or where she lived. He didn't even know her name. But trying to be helpful, he added "She knocks around with a fella named Woolerton. He always hangs around in *Lewis's* and the Milk Bar in Lime Street. If I see him I'll tell him to get in touch with yiz."

Since Dickson had been charged and bailed until Monday Balmer knew her whereabouts. The purpose of his questions to Connolly, since he had nothing else to go on, was to try and establish a closer link between her and a man she had named as being involved in the murders.

Connolly was asked if he would answer a few more questions. "Sure", he replied. Where was he on March 19th?, Balmer wanted to know. He replied that he was working at Bibby's Flour Mills in Great Howard Street on the Dock Road.

"What time did you knock off?"

"Must've been ten o'clock because I mostly worked the 2 to 10 shift." How could he so readily remember, asked Balmer, what shift he was working two months ago. "Because", he replied, " I gave my notice in around the middle of March and I'd been doing the same shift for weeks before I left."

"Okay Charlie", said Balmer, apparently satisfied, "you can go now. Thanks for all your help."

Connolly, who hardly drank, frequented the Billiard halls and cafes of Lime Street. He was around the area so often because he had to travel into town each day in order to catch a bus from Lime Street to his work. And his wife, a waitress, had worked in various city centre cafes, including *Lewis's* restaurant and the *St. George's* next to the *Marionette* club. Sometimes, when on the two to ten shift, he would get downtown early and consequently had time on his hands. On these occasions he would go into *Lewis's* to see his wife and sometimes get a free meal. Or go for a game of Billiards in the *Marionette* opposite the Punch and Judy Stall. Similarly, when he'd finish work on the early shift, he'd hang around waiting for his wife to leave work.

Now since packing in the Bibby's job and having more time on his hands, he was even more frequently around the town, hanging about waiting for his wife who now worked in *Maison Lyons* in Church Street.

When Connolly had left the C.I.D. Office, Smith, Balmer and Farragher were agreed that he could not have written the anonymous letter. His handwriting was totally different. But glancing through his criminal record sheet, Balmer said, "Seems too smooth to me." Then, spotting the conviction and fine for assault on the police when he was sixteen, he added, "A bloody bobby-baiter as well, eh. Must fancy himself."

"Should do," said Farragher, "he was an amateur boxer in the Navy. Good war record as well by the looks of it." Ignoring this, Balmer continued, "And his name's Charlie, the same as Johnson's friend Charlie Dugan!" Farragher reminded him that Johnson had later said that Dugan wasn't his real name. "Anyway Jack", said Balmer, "check his story out with Bibby's just to make sure. He just could be our man. And", he added , "he admitted he knew Jackie Dickson, and that he was in *Littlewoods'* cafe when she said he was."

Walking back along Lime Street to the *Big House* for a game of billiards, Connolly approached Woolerton who was coming out of the National Milk Bar next door to the *Futurist* cinema.

The short, stockily-built, twenty-six year-old pimp George Woolerton was known around town as "Bobby." He had found it more expedient to adopt the name of his happily married, hard working brother in order to confuse the police and prostitutes and also to cover up a trail of bad debts he left behind wherever he went.

Connolly told him that he had been questioned about the Cameo murder and that the police were looking for the girl he knocked around with and suggested he should go down and speak to them. But he replied that he had no intention of going anywhere near Dale Street and that if the police wanted him then they'd have to come and get him. "Well, that's up to you", said Connolly, and with a shrug walked off.

On Monday 16th May, Jacqueline Dickson was remanded for one day, then another day, then for six days, until 24th May, when she failed to make an appearance. Desperately afraid of being remanded in custody if she didn't get information for Balmer, and terrified of receiving a gaol sentence, she'd decided to jump bail and go to Manchester with Northam.

Meanwhile, after the enquiries at Bibby's, the police discovered that Connolly had not, as he had said, been at work on the night of March 19th. And although they accepted he had probably made a simple mistake, Balmer decided to keep this knowledge up his sleeve for possible future use. He did not tell Connolly what he had discovered. That wasn't his style.

When Kelly and Skelly appeared before the Stipendiary On May 26th the serious charge of Grievous Bodily Harm against Kelly had been reduced to Assault on the Police. They were both convicted of assault on the police and the theft of the rubber boots and each given three months consecutively on both charges, making a total of six months in all. The two men immediately gave notice of appeal and were released on bail. Their appeals would be heard later in the year at the Quarter Sessions, by the Recorder of Liverpool, William Gorman K.C.

Chapter Twelve

On 14th June Donald Thomas John Johnson appeared before Mr. Justice Lynskey at the Liverpool Assizes. He was represented by 35 year-old Miss Rose Heilbron K.C., whose first major criminal case this was since becoming a Kings Counsel. Leading for the Crown was Mr. A.D. Gerrard K.C. with Mr. Melville Kennan.

The indictment was read out to Johnson by Ian Macaulay, the Clerk of the Court: "... the charge against you is being an accessory after the fact of *murder*, in that you , well knowing that a man known to you on March 19th 1949, at Liverpool, had murdered Leonard Thomas, did on the same day and other days afterwards receive, comfort, harbour, assist and maintain the said man"

After the jury had been sent out in order for the judge to hear legal submissions Miss Heilbron immediately applied for the indictment to be quashed. Johnson, she asserted, could not be charged with being an accessory. A man can be charged with the alleged murderer or after conviction of the murderer. But he cannot, she maintained, be charged alone with being an accessory before an alleged murderer is even charged, much less convicted. And in this case nobody had been charged with murder.

Quoting various legal authorities, she submitted that the charge was unsustainable because of the anomalous situation which could arise if the alleged murderer himself was subsequently apprehended and acquitted or convicted of the lesser charge of manslaughter. In both eventualities, she maintained, the situation would not only be anomalous but grossly unjust, because the punishment for being an accessory after the fact of murder was twenty years or penal servitude for life but for felonies such as manslaughter the penalty was only two years.

Despite the charge being that of, "accessory after the fact of murder", the judge said that as Johnson's trial proceeded the jury might find it was manslaughter. Therefore, according to him, there would be no problem. "Whether or not another jury might take some other view of it", he added, "I am not concerned." Then dismissing Miss Heilbron's submission, he ruled that the accused could be tried as an accessory either with the principal felon (i.e. the alleged murderer), or after the felon, or before the felon. Thus, he concluded, the indictment would stand.

This seemed a most peculiar decision. For the learned judge seemed to be saying that, irrespective of the specific indictment, it was up to the jury to decide whether or not Johnson had been an accessory to a murder or an act of manslaughter - before the actual killer had been convicted of either! He was also apparently unconcerned about the possibility of a legal farce whereby the killer may be subsequently found guilty merely of manslaughter whilst the accessory had already been found guilty of being an accessory to murder - or vice versa!

When the jury were recalled prosecuting counsel Mr. Gerrard proceeded to relate the circumstances of the murder on March 19th and called Constable John Thompson, who testified to seeing Johnson at 10.15pm that evening acting suspiciously by a bus stop in Lodge Lane outside *The Boundary* public house. Thinking he might be trying to pick pockets, he asked him to produce his identity card, which he did. "That satisfied me", said Thompson, "that he was not there for picking pockets and I had no legal authority to question him further." The constable went on to state that if Johnson had not had an identity card he would have charged him with a felony. But precisely what felony, he never said. Neither did he make a note of the name on the identity card Johnson showed him because, he said, no offence had been committed.

In reply to Miss Heilbron, Thompson said he first recognised Johnson on May 13th, in the magistrates court when he was standing on the steps leading to the dock. Miss Heilbron suggested that he never saw Johnson standing on the steps. "That is not correct", he replied. She then said she would produce the warder who had brought Johnson directly from the cells straight to the dock.

Concluding her cross-examination of P.C. Thompson, Miss Heilbron said, "Eight weeks elapsed before you saw this man at the police court, and during that time you have seen hundreds of people, and I suggest to you that you cannot possibly identify this man as being the man you stopped in Lodge Lane."

"He was definitely the man", insisted Thompson, "and I have no doubt about it whatever."

Later, when Detective Chief Inspector Morris was giving evidence about seeing Johnson at Wallasey on May 2nd, he was about to refer to the first statement made by the accused when Miss Heilbron objected to it's admissibility. The judge then ordered the jury to retire again whilst he heard her submissions.

She contended that the evidence of Morris and the other senior police officers about unsigned statements made by Johnson was inadmissible because the statements had been obtained through threats and inducements held out to him. These included, she said, the police offering to have other charges against Johnson and his brother dropped; Detective Sergeant Farragher standing bail surety of £20 for Johnson; the police offering to keep him out of the Cameo case in exchange for information; the Head of the C.I.D. giving him cigarettes and sums of money; Detective Chief Inspector Balmer originally charging Johnson with the murder of the cinema manager.

Before ruling on the admissibility of the statements, the judge allowed the C.I.D. Officers to be questioned. And with the jury still absent, one after the other they went into the witness box. All denied the allegations, with the exception of Farragher, who admitted standing surety for Johnson. And when Miss Heilbron questioned Detective Chief Superintendent Smith about the probity of this he said he had felt Johnson would be of more use to the police at liberty than in custody.

During a further exchange between Smith and Miss Heilbron she said, "It is a lie that you did not give Johnson a sheet of foolscap paper and an envelope to make a statement on the Cameo murder." Looking hurt, the C.I.D. Chief indignantly replied, "I am surprised at you Miss Heilbron, suggesting to me it is a lie. It is not a lie."

Balmer followed Smith into the witness box and when challenged that he had charged Johnson with the murder of Leonard Thomas in order to frighten him into signing a statement, he defiantly replied, "That is definitely not true. He was never charged."

The following morning, before the hearing resumed, the jury were called into court in order to have their presence officially recorded. The judge then took his seat and told them that the discussions that needed to take place in their absence had still not been concluded and that they would therefore have to be sent out again.

When they had filed out of court, Miss Heilbron called Johnson to the witness box and asked him to tell what happened on May 2nd at Wallasey.

Dressed in a brown striped suit and white shirt with a pen collar, Johnson entered the witness box and admitted telling the police various stories in order to get bail. Before May 2nd, he said, bail had been strongly opposed by the Wallasey police. But on May the 2nd Mr. Morris told him that he'd come over to see him about the Cameo murder. He had told him that the only interest he had in the Cameo case was like any other member of the public and that he knew nothing about it. Morris then said he would go out and get him some cigarettes while he thought it over. "Did you obey his instructions to think it over?", asked Miss Heilbron.

"I thought up a story", he replied.

Johnson admitted telling the police officers that he knew where the gun was and all about "this supposed" Charlie Dugan and the promise on the Holy Eucharist. But, he maintained, he had never dictated a statement and had never been cautioned for a statement.

"Did you believe Inspector Morris when he said he would get the case quashed? asked Miss Heilbron"

"Yeah, certainly",

"When was bail mentioned?"

"Just before I went into court."

"After you were released on bail what happened?"

"Superintendent Smith gave me an envelope and paper and told me to write out who was the murderer and where he was. He gave me two pound notes and twenty ciggies and told me to stay off the rum." At this remark laughter broke out in the public gallery but was quickly stifled by the judge.

When Miss Heilbron asked Johnson if he understood that he was given bail in order to see the man and pass the information on to the police, he replied,. "I wouldn't have got bail otherwise. That's why I told them the story. None of those statements are true."

Johnson said Smith had earlier told him he would get in touch with the Wallasey Chief Constable and try to arrange bail for him. He agreed he told Smith he thought he knew who done the murder and where the gun was. But everything he told the police was simply in order to get bail for himself and his brother. He agreed with Miss Heilbron that he subsequently signed a statement, in the presence of his solicitor, denying any knowledge of the Cameo murder or the person who may have committed it.

After Johnson left the witness box Miss Heilbron made a final submission to have the case thrown out. "My Lord," she said, " I contend these statements are inadmissible in that they were obtained by inducement. Pressure was exercised by the police, quite proper pressure. But if they apply pressure the penalty they suffer is that they cannot use it in any evidence."

When the jury were recalled, the judge told them, "In your absence we have listened to a good deal of evidence as to whether certain statements, which the prisoner is alleged to have made, were admissible in evidence as having been made freely and voluntarily and not because of some hope of favour."

Finding that there had been inducement by the police, the judge said, "I have to rule, having heard the evidence, that only one of the statements made by the prisoner is admissible and that the others were induced by him being offered the opportunity of bail, and a police officer going surety for him. The result of that ruling is that, although there is ample evidence before you that a murder has been committed here, there is no evidence...that this man, in the words of the old law, did 'receive, harbour, assist or maintain' the man who is *alleged* to have done the murder." (My italics) The prosecution", he went on, "have come to the conclusion that the one statement (the first) which I have said is admissible...does not give sufficient evidence on which...to convict this man. It is therefore my duty to direct you to return a formal verdict of Not Guilty."

The use of the word "alleged" in Mr. Justice Lynskey's ruling was rather odd. There was no man who was "alleged" to have been the murderer because no man had been charged. Indeed, his ruling seemed to be begrudgingly given. He had stated for example that, "On Superintendent Smith's own evidence", he was satisfied that the police had not been "too strenuous in their opposition to bail". Given that a detective on Smith's instructions, had actually stood bail because, as Smith had testified, Johnson was of more use at liberty than in custody, this was a massive understatement - presumably made in order to minimise the police's irregular conduct.

After their not guilty verdict, the jury must have been somewhat puzzled to see Johnson being escorted down to the cells instead of walking out of court. But they were not to know that he was already serving a sentence of four years Corrective Training, passed on him earlier in the month at Chester Assizes for the Aggravated Robbery charge at Wallasey.

The jury were not the only ones to be puzzled. Inspector Balmer was puzzled and most curious. But it had nothing to do with Johnson. It had more to do with Charles Connolly. For Balmer had not only spotted him during the trial standing in the crowded public gallery, he had also seen him outside in the passageway commiserating with Johnson's mother.

The now unemployed Connolly, like many others with little money and plenty of time on their hands, often passed a few hours watching cases at St. George's Hall. And, although he did not know Mrs. Johnson or her son, when he'd seen her crying he thought she could have been his own mother so he had quite spontaneously tapped the distressed woman's shoulder and told her not to worry, that everything would probably turn out right.

Superintendent Smith's instruction about prisoners and prison officers reporting on Johnson quickly began to bear fruit. And had Johnson's trial been allowed to continue the police had stockpiled an array of incriminating evidence to be used against him, including a statement from his brother.

As early as the 6th of May, "Judder" had made a statement which went as follows:-

"My name is Francis George Johnson. I am twenty three years of age...when I was in the cells at Wallasey my brother went away from his cell and when I heard him come back I shouted to him, `Where have you been?" He said, 'Upstairs.' I said, 'What for?' He said, 'The jacks have been giving me a grill.' I said, 'What about?' and he said, 'The Cameo murder. I asked what he knew about it, and he said, 'You'd be surprised what I know. I could tell you something about it.' I asked what he could tell me and he said, 'Never mind.' This talk I had with him was on Monday night this week. He went out on bail on Tuesday morning. One day in the week following the murder, I called at my mother's house. My mother said the police have been here asking where Donald was on the night of the murder. I said, 'What did you tell them?' She said, 'I said he was at home.' I said, 'What time did he come in that night?' She said, 'I don't know.' I said, ' Blimey, I hope he's had nothing to do with that.' She said, `if he had I'd turn him over to the police, but he couldn't have had.` I don't know where Donald was on the night of the Cameo murder because he wasn't with me. I was at the Dingle public house in Park Road from about seven o'clock till ten o'clock. My wife might have been with me but I can't remember exactly. While we've been in prison Donald has been very worried."

Despite this prejudicial statement casting suspicion on his brother, a prisoner named Bernard Joseph McBride was on stand-by to testify that Donald Johnson had told him that he, Judder, had committed the murder. McBride's statement, made on 7th of June at Walton prison to Detective Chief Inspector Morris, in the company of Balmer, read as follows:-

"I am at present serving a sentence at HM. Prison in Walton For the past eight months I have been engaged as a hospital cleaner. At 2-30 pm on Sunday 29th of May while I was in the hospital Donald Johnson - I had known him three years ago when he was a patient on remand in the hospital - said, 'Are you the same fellow I met in Wandsworth in 1946?' I said, 'Yes, you seem to be in a load of trouble' He said, 'Well it wasn't me who did the job it was my brother. I was in a woman's house that night when my brother came in and told me he had shot two men. He showed me a gun and asked me if I would take it. I told him I had taken the can back for him before but he would have to get himself out this time. I went outside to have a wash and while I was out he must have put the gun in my pocket but I didn't find it till I got home to my mother's house. The next day he came around and asked me for the gun but I told him he couldn't have it because I had hid it where no one could find it. I hid it with a handkerchief and if the police ever got hold of it they would only find one set of fingerprints and they would be my brother's.' "On the Tuesday or Wednesday", the statement continued, "Johnson spoke to me. He'd had a visit from his solicitor after he'd been to court on the Monday. He said to me, 'My solicitor has told me that my girlfriend, Clara Gallimore, is in the family way and if I don't tell the police all I know in three or four days, she will'. He didn't tell me that Clara Gallimore knew anything about the gun but from the trend of his story I got the impression she knows something."

The police had also obtained damning statements against Johnson from various prison officers. One from Prison Hospital Officer, J.L.E. Poidivon, dated 30th May 1949, confirmed McBride's story. Officer Poidivon stated that McBride told him that one of the murdered men was a relative of his, and that Johnson had told him (McBride) that his brother had committed the murders. The murder gun was in Johnson's house up till a couple of days before his arrest on the Wallasey charge. Johnson told McBride, 'I've carried the can for my brother because he is a married man with two children.' Apparently his wife knows all about it. The other Johnson (Judder) had also shot a man in the *Ocean* club and injured his eye. Donald Johnson was put up for identification but nothing had been proved. He had taken the blame for several crimes of his brothers due to him being a family man. This is what he told McBride, according to Officer Poidivon.

Earlier, on May 13th, a statement had arrived at Dale Street from Prison Officer, H.M. Sharp. It said:-

"Whilst waiting at the foot of the stairs to No.3 court Johnson quite voluntarily started talking, saying, 'The old lady has let me down telling the police that I was playing cards at our house that night. I've never handled cards before.' He went on to say that he was at the Pavilion theatre that night where a fight ensued through a girl asking to change seats. He named the person he was fighting with as Nobby Clark. There was also talk of his girlfriend and his brother George and receiving three pounds from a detective in Wallasey. Later I asked Johnson if the police were in possession of the gun He replied 'Christ, No'. I would add that Auxiliary Officer Parkinson was present and heard all that was said".

On the 13th June another letter signed by Prison Officer F. Corke was sent to the police. It said:-

"I Respectfully state for your information on Friday 10th June, I accompanied Johnson to Chester Assizes. In consequence of my conversation about the Cameo murders, he gave me to understand that the gun in the case had been thrown into the River Mersey. I questioned him as to whether there were any fingerprints on it. He said, 'I never leave fingerprints.' He then corrected himself and said, 'The bloke wouldn't be stupid enough to leave fingerprints.' During the course of the trial at Chester I was again in conversation with him after he had been sentenced to four years corrective training. I informed him that his brother... had been bound over for two years. He replied, 'This is the third time I've allowed myself to take the rap for our kid.' During further conversation he said, 'How do you think I'll get on on Tuesday at Liverpool Assizes?' I reminded him of the grave charge and told him the sentence would be very heavy if he was found guilty. He said, 'If they find me guilty I shall own up to it.' I said, 'Own up to what?' He said, 'The Cameo job.' I asked him why should he own up if he had not committed it. He replied, 'He (his brother) has more to lose than I have.' He then started talking of how bad the living conditions were in his brother's home and how often he had done robberies solely for the purpose of helping his brother's wife and two children. I said, 'You must have got on well with your brother's wife and kids.' He replied, 'I idolised them.' I said, 'To the extent of taking the rap again for him?' And he said, 'Let's see how things go on Tuesday. If I'm found guilty I'll talk.'...''

At this juncture in his statement Prison Officer Corke appeared to assume the combined role of investigating officer and prosecuting counsel. For it went on, "I respectfully suggest that should the prisoner be found guilty, it may be possible to defer sentence until later in the day during such time he may make a statement. I am convinced he will make a statement and break down the silence."

In addition to these incriminating statements, the Governor of Walton prison had sent to Liverpool's Chief Constable, a copy of a letter written by Johnson to his brother's wife, Florence, in which he said,

"Judder will get off. I assure you on that. I made a sacrifice as you know." It is however unclear as to whether these comments refer to the Wallasey or the Cameo charge.

After Johnson's trial a letter of a different sort, which Detective Chief Superintendent Smith did *not* expect, was sent by the Director of Public Prosecutions to the Chief Constable. This letter resulted in a severe dressing down for Smith and the Cameo murder team. In it the D.P.P. complained about the police conduct of the Johnson case and the subsequent acquittal, and went on to say, " I cannot find in the papers that were submitted to me on the 18th May, any reference to these actions of the police officers. Mr. Bishop (the prosecuting solicitor) was not informed." The caustic letter ended," I should therefore be obliged if you would let me have the benefit of your observations as there are apparent omissions."

The "actions" referred to were of course the inducements and other violations of proper police practice, as laid down in the Judges Rules, which were used unsuccessfully to threaten, cajole and coerce Johnson.

As a result of this letter the Chief Constable of Liverpool, Mr. C.C. Martin, called Smith, Balmer and company before him and severely berated them. But if the Chief Constable's reprimands had a salutary effect on Superintendent Smith - who was due for retirement anyway - subsequent events would prove that they had not deterred the determined and ambitious Chief Inspector Balmer.

Chapter Thirteen

June - September 1949

> *"Fools are made the dupes of rogues,*
> *And rogues each other cheat.*
> *He is very wise indeed,*
> *Who never meets defeat."*
> *(Anon.).*

Kelly and Skelly were advised by their lawyer, Harry Livermore, that if they were to have the slightest chance of winning their appeal, or even pleading mitigation, when they appeared at the Sessions, it would help if they could show they were honestly and gainfully employed. To this end Kelly obtained work as a labourer in early June with Liverpool building firm, William Thornton & Sons at the Stanlow Oil Terminal across the river at Ellesmere Port. The job however, didn't last long.

On a hot July day he was late returning from the local pub, having consumed several lunchtime pints. After being censured by the foreman he was ordered to fill up a wheelbarrow with wet concrete and push it some 200 yards up a narrow wooden ramp to the concrete layers. "Yer what?", he laughed. "Yer fuckin' jokin' aren't yer? I wouldn't push that full of cotton wool." Whereupon he was instantly dismissed.

Also in June, Connolly, still hoping to emigrate to a new life in Australia, managed to obtain employment as a porter at Lime Street Station. This was a much better job than Bibby's: he could usually slip out in his lunch-hour for a game of billiards in the *Big House* or *Marionette* Club. He could also see his wife more often - who was still waitressing at *Maison Lyons*.

In mid- August, Skelly met Paddy McGrath, his old adversary with whom he had fought in the *Midland* some months earlier. There was no animosity between them. It had been a fair fight and they had shaken hands afterwards.

Skelly told him about the court case and his need of a job until his appeal in October. A few days later much to his surprise, McGrath, a Seamen's Union delegate, offered to get him a trip away to sea, despite his lack of a seaman's book or union card. Never having sailed before he gratefully accepted the offer.

The ship was bound for North Africa and he would be away for six weeks. So before it sailed he informed the police, promising to be back in time for the appeal hearing. To his surprise they raised no objection.

Whether or not this arrangement - which allowed a convicted criminal on bail to leave the country for six weeks - was sanctioned by Balmer or not it would in the coming weeks prove to be extremely helpful to his "enquiries"..

In the first week of September the Inspector received a telephone call from Doris O'Malley whom he was still discreetly seeing. She was distraught, complaining that Kelly had beaten her up and given her a black eye. So what's new, he cynically thought. He was well used to their stormy relationship. Indeed, he himself often had to patch things up between them when he'd call at the house in the middle of a row. And he knew Doris could give as good as she got. He didn't feel in the slightest protective towards her. Why should he? As far as he was concerned *their* perfunctory relationship was based on nothing more than lust.

After going through the motions of commiseration he was about to hang up when she suddenly cried, "Yer know he done the fuckin' Cameo murder, don't yer?" At this his ears pricked, but remaining calm, he told her to compose herself. "What do you mean Doris?", he asked gently. "Has he told you anything?"

"He's been a bag of fuckin' nerves ever since the Cameo", she cried hysterically. Then she went on between sobs, "And that Sunday after the murder, when you came and searched the house and took him to Skelly's, well, when he came back home from the *Leigh* he said, 'I wish I'd still had the fuckin' gun on me, that bastard Balmer wouldn't have stood there so cocksure of himself.'"

"Did he now?", said Balmer. Then, feigning disinterest lest she alerted Kelly when they'd made up, as they always did, he quietly told her to take no notice; that it was probably all bravado to impress her. "Look Doris", he went on, apparently dismissing the importance of the message, "you take no bloody notice of him. Just tell him when you see him that if he lays another finger on you I'll have him pulled in, okay?" Suitably reassured, she thanked him and hung up.

Even if Doris was telling the truth, which he doubted, knowing Kelly as he did Balmer guessed his remark would have been made out of a combination of temper and vanity. One thing was certain: as evidence it wasn't worth a bean. What she had said however, did give him food for thought. Kelly's alibi, he recalled wasn't airtight. He remembered also what his taxi-driver friend, Jimmy Corrie, had told him about Kelly coming into *The Leigh Arms* on the night of the murder all flustered. He just *could* have done the murders. And even if he didn't maybe he could be made to fit the bill.

As with the knowledge of Connolly not being at work when he said he was, and his sympathetic attendance at Johnson's trial, Balmer would keep this little piece of incriminating information up his sleeve. He wouldn't even mention it if he met Kelly. Never show your hand until you're ready to move. That was his style.

A week after this incident, on September the 15th, a further development of much greater importance occurred. A Preston man, forty-one year-old Robert Graham, who was nearing the end of a twelve month sentence for false pretences, contacted the Preston police telling them he had some very important information for the Liverpool police about the Cameo murders. Balmer was soon on his way to Walton Prison to interview him.

Graham said he had been in the prison hospital with Johnson in June. "Just before his trial began", he went on, "Johnson's counsel, that Rose Heilbron one, visited him and after she'd left Johnson was very upset. He told me, 'my case all depends on legal arguments. If it fails I'm gonna tell the truth and end up on I wing', you know, the condemned cell. 'I couldn't do twenty years in here', he said, and he kept saying that."

"But he was acquitted", said Balmer warily. "Oh I know, and he was in great spirits when he got chucked But he said to me, 'I can tell you now because they're finished unless they find the gun, and they'll never find that."

"Did he tell you how he done it?"

Graham hesitated then coyly replied," Well, he told me one or two little things."

"Never mind", said Balmer, "we'll go through it together and refresh your memory and get the story right."

"I'll do me best", said Graham, adding, "I like to help the police if I can. Yer never know when yer need the police. Know what I mean."

Balmer could hardly contain his excitement as he drove back to Dale Street. He had great news for his boss. His excitement however proved to be short-lived.

"There's Graham's signed statement", he proudly told Smith. After reading it the Chief said sarcastically, "Very neat Bert. Do you believe him?"

"I'm satisfied he's telling the truth", said an unconvincing Balmer. "Yes, but we got another statement at the time, from another cleaner named McBride, saying Johnson told him his brother done it."

"It's a matter of who you believe", said Balmer defensively. "Well, we believed McBride at the time didn't we? said Smith with growing irritation. He was even going to be a witness wasn't he?"

"Yeah but Graham's statement is a lot more detailed."

"Look Bert", said Smith, "we had our chance with Johnson, we can't touch him again. Anything else now would just look like vindictiveness. In any case", he went on, "where's the corroboration?" There was no reply from Balmer.

"Leave it Bert", said Smith wearily. "What we need is a *genuine* informer. There must be one among all your whores and thieves and taxi drivers. Get me one Bert. One who knows something we can get our teeth into."

Smarting at his boss's dismissiveness, Balmer nonetheless replied with determination, " Okay, I will. Leave it to me".

As early as April 20th the police had completely drained Botanic Park lake in search of the murder weapon. Teams of detectives wearing gum boots, had then systematically dredged the mud with garden rakes and an electromagnetic detector. Whoever had written the anonymous letter was wrong about the gun being dumped there. Now, five months later, Smith told his men he was scaling down the murder enquiry. They had visited 9,000 homes, interviewed 64,000 people, fingerprinted 1,800, and taken handwriting samples from 1,840 females. And they were still no nearer to making an arrest.

Then suddenly the breakthrough came. Norwegian Margie - who had gone home to Stockport during the handwriting blitz on the city's prostitutes - arrived back in Liverpool. She was soon roped in and asked to write down the misspelt words, *Echo, accessory* and *column*, contained in the anonymous letter. But being a Grammar school girl, she spelt them correctly. A deflated Balmer was about to let her go when he decided to have one last shot.

He had noticed that, despite the misspelt words and the disguised handwriting, the small "g", of which there were many, had been written identically throughout the letter. Acting on this hunch, he told Margie to copy a whole section of the text. When he saw the result he was ecstatic: all of her 'g's were identical to those in the letter. After almost seven months he had finally found the author of the anonymous letter.

An overjoyed Balmer quickly decided to detain her for further questioning. Margie however persistently refused to sign any statement. She would not even utter a word until he promised not to charge her with anything to do with the murders. And when he readily did so the story she began to tell had him on the edge of his seat.

The only people she could name, she said hesitantly, were Jacqueline Dickson and Stutty Northam. And although she gave descriptions of the other two men in *The Boundary* pub that night, she said she did not know their names or who they were. About a week later however, in the *Beehive* pub in Mount Pleasant, she said she had bumped into the man who had left *The Boundary* with Dickson and Northam. He had recognised her and bought her a drink, and then began fishing to see how much she knew. Foolishly she told him she had heard everything that night and that after reading the newspapers the following morning she had put two and two together.

"I told him I didn't want anything to do with him" she went on, "but he threatened me with a gang. And when I told him I wasn't frightened of him or his gang, he said I should be because I'd been in Jackie Dickson's company the night of the murders and heard everything so I could be charged as an accessory, and that I was in it with him and Jackie and Northam"

Now that Margie had opened up, an eager Balmer had a salvo of questions to fire at her. First: how did she know, as she'd stated in her letter, where the man got the gun from, if she didn't know him? And how did she know, as she'd also said in the letter, that he was selling guns? How could he have given her bullets, as she stated in the letter, six weeks before she wrote the letter if she didn't know him? Also how did she know, again as stated in her letter, that he lived nowhere near where the murder was committed? Who was the person, she had mentioned in the letter, who'd ran a stolen lorry through a pub and killed someone.?

Margie explained that she had seen Northam passing the gun to the unknown man in the. *Boundary's* passageway. The man she had mentioned in the letter who deserved to be arrested for selling guns was a different man, a Birkenhead chap named Gouldson. She'd seen him once in the *Spanish House* selling a gun to another man. He was a friend of Northam's so she had assumed that he had given the gun to him, which Northam had passed to the man in *The Boundary*. It was also Gouldson who had given her bullets to mind for him some weeks before the murder. "He sometimes drinks in The *Caledonian* in Lime Street and *Yates' Wine Lodge*", she volunteered.

"When I said they lived nowhere near where the crime was committed", she went on, "I meant Northam and Dickson because he lives in Birkenhead, and I thought Jackie Dickson lived with him."

She explained that Dickson had told her ages ago it was Northam who had driven the lorry through *O'Connor's* pub in Lime Street and killed a woman. "But", she continued, "Jackie told me the lorry wasn't really stolen. Gouldson had loaned it to Stutty to do a job. And Gouldson had told him that if anything went wrong he was to dump it and he would report it stolen".

According to Dickson, said Margie, Gouldson used to put young fellows on to jobs, " I believe he'd lend his lorry and he'd also give them a gun if one was needed, and then he'd get a cut from the jobs they did." Dickson had also told her that he had put Stutty onto a stick-up job upstairs at the *Ocean* Club in town, and even offered him a gun to do the job, but Stutty had refused.

The mention of the *Ocean* club rang a bell with Balmer. Although what Margie was now saying was only hearsay, hadn't there been something in the Johnson case about his brother shooting someone in there? Was there a connection between Johnson's brother and Northam? Or Johnson's brother and Gouldson. It was certainly something to be checked out.

Meanwhile, Balmer wanted to know who was the man in the letter, who wanted her to go away with him; the man she was so frightened of. "That was the fellow with the gun", she replied, " the fellow who went out of *The Boundary* with Jackie and Stutty. The one who threatened me in the *Beehive* after the murder".

"Why", he enquired, "would he ask you to go away with him if you didn't know him?"

"Because he said he fancied me. But I thought he only wanted to get me away to kill me or something. That's why I left town for a few months. I'm dead scared of him."

Again referring to the anonymous letter, Balmer wanted to know how she knew the gunman threw the gun in Botanic Park and got a 6A tram? "Jackie Dickson told me that when I saw her the next night", she explained. "She also told me that Stutty was supposed to wait outside the picture house but he lost his nerve and ran away. That's why I put that in the letter as well."

"Now let's get this straight", said Balmer, "are you telling me this Gouldson fella set the Cameo job up?".

"No, I didn't say that", she replied. "He wasn't there that night in *The Boundary*. Like I told you, I know Gouldson but I don't know the fellow who went with Stutty and Jackie. I'd never seen him before...or the younger fellow who was with him; the one who stayed in the pub. But it was probably Gouldson who supplied the gun and the bullets because, like I said, I've seen him selling them and he did give me some bullets to mind for him but I threw them away."

"But this fella who Northam gave the gun to in *The Boundary* wanted you to go away with him didn't he?", asked a sceptical Balmer. "Yes, but I didn't know him", insisted Margie. "He'd remembered me from the night in *The Boundary*."

Balmer then asked, if Dickson left the pub with the two men why did Margie say in the letter that she didn't think she went with them. "Well", she replied, "that's what she told me when I saw her the next day in the *Caledonian*. She said Stutty and the other fella had jumped on the tram just as it was leaving the stop outside *The Boundary*, but that she wasn't quick enough to catch it so she never bothered, she just went home."

"What do you mean by "home"? he asked. " Well, I suppose she could've meant Birkenhead or Upper Parliament Street", she replied. "She used to have a room there, I believe, but I don't know the number."

When the Inspector suggested Margie could not have been in *The Boundary* until about 9.30pm if, as stated in the letter, she'd been drinking in Dale Street till 10.00pm., she explained how she had left *The Boundary* and got a taxi down to the *Spanish House* at the bottom of St. Johns' Lane and Whitechapel. She purposely hadn't mentioned *The Boundary* in the letter in case it put the police on her trail. But, she maintained, the bit about talking to two men in Brownlow Hill at about 11.00pm on her way home was true. Adding that she had even gone with one of them for a short time down a back street.

Reminding her of her promise in the letter, Balmer again asked for the names of the two men in *The Boundary* but she insisted she didn't know them. When she'd said in the letter she would give "both their names", she had meant Northam and Dickson. "That's why I said the people who done it lived nowhere near Wavertree."

"But you've just told me that Jackie Dickson had a room not far away in Upper Parliament Street.", he retorted.

"Yes but Stutty Northam comes from Birkenhead and she lives with him doesn't she? "And with not knowing the other two fellas I thought they must be from Birkenhead as well. And, she added, "Jackie said she never went with them anyway."

Balmer now realised why Dickson had skipped bail in May. And although not really expecting a positive outcome he nonetheless ordered her and Northam to be brought in. Predictably however, the detectives were told at 227 Upper Parliament that Dickson hadn't been seen since May. And at 122 Wood Street Birkenhead, Northam's parents said they hadn't seen him for months.

When the officers returned with the bad news, Balmer immediately ordered photographs and details of the couple to be circulated to all police forces, and to be published in the *Police Gazette*.

Faced with Margie's insistence that she did not know the two men in the *Boundary* with Northam and Dickson, Balmer began showing her dozens of mugshots, including those of Kelly, Skelly and Connolly. Then with the *Ocean* club connection in mind, he singled out "Judder Johnson's" photograph and said, "He's the man who had the gun in *The Boundary*, isn't he Marg?" Looking pale, she hesitated for a moment then, shaking her head vigorously, she said, "No, I've never seen him in my life before." Undeterred Balmer then pointed to the mugshots of Donald Johnson and said, "And that's the other fella who was with him, isn't it? But again Margie shook her head.

When she eventually gave a sign of recognition it was merely to remark, "I know those two. That's Georgie Kelly and Jimmy Skelly. I know them". Balmer was unimpressed: he already knew they were known to her, and, more importantly, that they were in the clear.

Next Balmer wanted to know why, after being given the assurance she had requested, in the personal column of the *Echo*, she did not respond. She said she had panicked and decided to go to her sister's in Stockport.

After several hours a frustrated Balmer threatened Margie that if she didn't sign the statement and name Northam's male companions she would be charged as an accessory to murder. But protesting that he had broken his promise of immunity, she told him she still had the cutting from the *Echo's* Personal Column in which the police had made the promise, and that if he charged her with anything she would produce it in court. Unsure as to whether, like himself, she was bluffing her words nonetheless had a sobering effect on him -particularly in view of the roasting he and his colleagues had received from the Chief Constable after the Johnson case. At present she was his only witness. And to that extent he was only too aware that she held all the cards.

After receiving the anonymous letter Balmer had sent it and the envelope to the Forensic laboratory for examination. It had been returned with the information that what he'd taken to be a red franking mark was in fact a smear of lipstick. So he now asked Margie if she had deliberately smeared it. "Not really", she replied, "but I've had my handbag robbed so many times I always carry my money and my make-up in my coat pocket these days. So maybe some of the lippy in my pocket smudged it."

Before finally releasing her on police bail, he asked where she had posted the anonymous letter. At the fork junction of Crown Street and Grove Street, she told him. Opposite Mrs. Kravitz's where she had a first floor room.

Three weeks later, on Saturday September 24th, Balmer got an even bigger break: Dickson and Northam were located in Manchester living in a bedsit. Balmer went personally with Detective Sergeant Farragher and brought them back to Liverpool.

When Margie's story about plotting the crime in *The Boundary* was put to them, they completely denied it. And later, when confronted with Margie at the Central C.I.D. Office they denied even knowing her.

In the face of their denials the Inspector was only too aware of his predicament. For, apart from Margie's uncorroborated story, there was not a shred of evidence to connect them with the Cameo murders. Certainly not enough to charge them. Nonetheless, he ordered Dickson's former bedsit in Upper Parliament Street and Northam's parents home to be thoroughly searched for anything incriminating. But nothing was found.

Gouldson was interviewed at length but denied everything Margie had said. He said he was a legitimate businessman, a firewood dealer and light haulage contractor, and claimed he did not know Norwegian Margie or Dickson or anyone named Judder Johnson. He did however admit knowing Northam on a casual basis, simply because he was, "a Birkenhead lad, like meself." But he denied all knowledge of any shooting at the *Ocean* club. He also admitted his lorry had been stolen a few times but that the police had been satisfied on each occasion that the theft was genuine. Having taken the precaution of checking the files however, Balmer told Gouldson he was a liar. Hadn't he been convicted at Chester Assizes last year of conspiracy to steal from Birkenhead docks?. And hadn't the case involved four young men who had used his lorry, which he had reported stolen? Gouldson had to admit that this was true but maintained he'd been wrongly convicted.

Although Gouldson had been caught out in a blatant lie, there was nothing, apart from Margie's word, to link him with the Cameo murders so Balmer reluctantly had to let him go.

Persisting in his vain attempt to get Dickson and Northam to name the gunman, he explained to each of them separately that if they co-operated they could turn King's Evidence and would not be charged with anything to do with the murders. But to the wary pair this sounded too good to be true.

Northam, with a long criminal record, and suspicious, from hard experience, of police promises, insisted he knew nothing about the murders . And Dickson, knowing only too well how unscrupulous Balmer was, remained tight-lipped .

They both felt that if they didn't admit any involvement they would be safe from prosecution. Margie didn't worry them unduly. It was their word against hers. And, given that six months had gone by without Johnny's friend, or Johnny himself, being arrested, they were unlikely to suddenly give themselves up now.

Balmer decided to try another ploy. Showing Northam numerous mugshots, he told him he need not say anything or make a statement. All he had to do was simply point to the gunman.

The photographs were the same as those shown to Norwegian Margie. But in response to each one an expressionless Northam simply shook his head. When he came to "Judder" Johnson's mugshot Balmer said, "You know him don't you Stutty? He's the fella you went with to the Cameo?"

"I ddon't knnow what you're ttalking about", he stammered.

"And he's the fella you went with on the other job at the *Ocean* Club? Isn't he, you lying bastard?" But resisting the Inspector's belligerence, Northam quietly said, "No, I've nnever seen him in mmy llife before."

Later, Dickson was shown the same photographs. But this time they included some of Kelly's brother, Joey. Passing over the shots of Kelly, Skelly and the Johnson brothers without any sign of recognition, she pointed to Connolly and said, "I recognise him. I told yer about him last May. Remember?"

"Yeah, I remember", said a sneering Balmer, "And you told me then that he was involved in the murders."

"Well I thought he was", she replied defensively.

"But he wasn't the fella in *The Boundary* Jackie, was he?"

"I've told yer", she replied, " I don't know anything about *The Boundary* or any murder."

"And you don't know these two neither, do you?", he said sarcastically, pointing to mugshots of the Johnson brothers. "No I don't," she replied defiantly.

There had only been the hearsay of Margie's and the third hand statement of prison officer Poidivon to make any connection between Northam, "Judder" Johnson, Gouldson and the *Ocean* club. So, realising he had gone as far as he could with this particular bluff, Balmer said to Dickson, "No matter Jackie Keep looking."

Coming to the full face and side shots of Joey Kelly, Dickson said, " I know him, That's George Kelly. I used to knock around with him. The last time I seen him he took me for a drink in the *Caledonian*. Bought me whiskies as well. He was loaded"

"Was he now", said Balmer curiously. "And when was that Jackie?"

"Oh, a few months ago, before I went to Manchester. About March or April I think"

Intrigued, Balmer asked, "What makes you think his name's George Kelly?"

"Cos he told me that's why", she replied. "I told yer, I used to knock around with him for a little while. That day he took me in the *Cally* I'd told him Bobby Woolerton was gunning for me and that he was always hitting me all the time so afterwards he went to the Milk Bar in Lime Street and sorted him out".

Balmer was puzzled. She obviously believed Joey Kelly was Georgie. But why was Joey using his brother's name?

There seemed to be quite a lot of name swapping going on in the town. Woolerton was another one. He too went around calling himself by his brother's name. Balmer had discovered that last year when he'd charged him with living off Dickson's immoral earnings.

To make certain she wasn't mistaken Balmer again showed Dickson the mugshots of George Kelly and asked, "Are you sure you don't know him?" After studying them for a few seconds, she shook her head. "No I've never seen him before", she replied. "But he looks a bit like George Kelly doesn't he?"

"He should do Jackie", said Balmer. "That's his brother. That's the real

Georgie!"

In the early stages of the murder investigation Joey Kelly had been interviewed and ruled out as a suspect. He had stated that from about 9.20pm on March the 19th he and his wife were drinking in "Back Bent's" pub behind Trowbridge Street tenements. And his wife had confirmed this. But, thought Balmer, Georgie was a different proposition. From 9.15pm, when he'd left *The Leigh Arms*, to 9.45pm, when he was next seen in there, there was nobody who could alibi him. He'd been alone for half an hour in the area very close to the Cameo. In fact he'd admitted that he'd been for a short period in *The Spofforth* pub, which was even nearer the cinema. And hadn't Jimmy Corrie seen him coming into the *Leigh* all flustered?

Was there, he pondered, some sort of collusion or cover-up arrangement between the two brothers? Was that why Joey was calling himself Georgie?

Since ascertaining that Connolly had not been at work on March 19th Balmer had been looking more deeply into his past and was very interested to discover that both he and George Kelly had been at the Royal Navy training school, HMS. *Raleigh*, at the same time in 1941. Connolly had no alibi either. Hadn't his story about working at Bibby's on March 19th proved false? And why had he been so interested in Johnson's trial in June? Hadn't Johnson said the gunman's name was Charlie? And what about Kelly's remark to Doris, "If I'd had the gun on me that bastard Balmer..."

Things were beginning to look more hopeful . If he could make the pieces fit he might be able to make out a case after all. And if Margie or Dickson or Northam wouldn't name the *real* gunman then he might have to provide them with a name. And if their "evidence" was to accord with the contents of the anonymous letter - the only real evidence he had - then he might have to provide them with *two* names.

Balmer knew that Northam and Dickson were never going to admit anything, about the real killer - mainly because they didn't trust him not to charge them as accomplices. He also knew there was insufficient evidence to charge them even with being accessories. But he may nonetheless be able to frighten them into becoming witnesses...if he could procure two others to fit the role of the killer and accomplice.

That would be the ideal solution, he thought. For whoever they were, those two others by virtue of their own non-involvement, would obviously deny it and therefore couldn't possibly incriminate Northam and Dickson. That would be their guarantee. They wouldn't have to rely on his promise of immunity - although that would still be given. And that would consolidate the guarantee!

Chapter Fourteen

25th September 1949

The Conspiracy begins...

Having detained Northam and Dickson, Balmer bluffed them that they were in deep trouble. He threatened that Dickson would be charged with attempting to pervert the course of justice in the Cameo case; with the original Church Street theft charge and with absconding from bail. All in all, he told her that with her record she was looking at a minimum of seven years imprisonment.

As for Northam: Balmer lied that he had evidence he had stolen the lorry which had killed a woman in Lime Street. He was therefore now considering whether to charge him with murder or manslaughter. He would also be charged, like Dickson, with perverting the course of justice in the Cameo case, and with aiding and abetting Dickson to abscond from bail. At best, said Balmer, he could expect ten years. At worst he could be hanged.

There *was* a way out for both of them however. He told them he had two suspects of his own for the Cameo murders. If they would co-operate with him in providing evidence against these two men he was willing to drop all other charges, and ensure that Dickson got a conditional discharge for the Church Street theft and skipping bail. Neither would have to go to prison.

Northam and Dickson wanted to know who his two suspects were. When he replied, " George Kelly and Charles Connolly", Northam protested that he didn't even know them. "Don't worry about that", said Balmer, "you soon will do."

Dickson complained that although she only knew Connolly by sight she'd heard he was a hard case. She was frightened of what he might do to her. She also wanted to know for certain whether Kelly was the *real* George or his brother Joey because she didn't know the real George. "But you do know a man who you *believe* to be George Kelly", coaxed Balmer, "so technically you will be telling the truth when you testify that you know him, won't you?"

Reassuring them there was nothing to be frightened of, he said that once they had made their written statements they would be placed in a safe house under police protection. Dickson would not have to confront Joey Kelly. The suspect wasn't her erstwhile boyfriend, it was the real George Kelly.

What guarantee was there, they wanted to know, that having got their signed statements Balmer wouldn't go back on his word and charge them? Producing a file which contained the cutting from the *Echo's* Personal Column, Balmer replied, "Because your statements will say that you both wrote the anonymous letter. And as you can see we gave a promise in the *Echo* last April that we wouldn't charge you with anything if you came forward and gave us the names. How long do you think the case would last if we charged you two after publicly giving that promise? The case would be thrown out of court. So you see, I couldn't possibly go back on my word even if I wanted to. Not only that", he went on, "if I did welsh on the deal, you two would probably retract your statements and refuse to testify, and I wouldn't blame you, and how would we look then? We'd have no bloody case would we?"

Closely scrutinising the cutting, the frightened pair were somewhat assured by Balmer's logic. After some hesitation Dickson, terrified at the prospect of years in prison, caved in and agreed. Northam, suddenly feeling leader-less and very nervous, quickly followed.

Over the next five days they were shown police mugshots of Connolly and Kelly, and other photographs of both men taken around Lime Street by various street photographers. They were both given copies of the anonymous letter to study and were assiduously questioned on its contents. They were also provided with potted histories of the two men and told to memorise these along with their physical descriptions.

Balmer, aware that Kelly never drank in *The Boundary*, realised that the "venue" for the plotting of the crime would have to be changed; somewhere more plausible; a pub which Kelly could not deny regularly frequenting.

After giving the matter considerable thought he decided on the *Beehive* at the bottom of Mount Pleasant. It was a pub where Kelly regularly drank, and which he himself had often used for his black market deals with people like the manager of the *Hope Hall* cinema and the cafe owner, "Uncle" Bill Beresford.

It was perfect. Dimly lit, with a long ornate glass-fronted passageway leading into a seedy back parlour, the *Beehive* relied mainly on a passing trade of prostitutes and their clients. In that respect alone it would be ideal should it become necessary to pressurise some of these prostitutes into giving evidence. It was also nicely situated opposite a billiards hall, a factor which would make Connolly's presence there quite believable. And to cap it all the Number 8 tram, which ran up to Smithdown Road past the Cameo, stopped directly across the road. Altogether, he concluded, it would be much more believable than the larger, suburban, more brightly-lit, family-oriented *Boundary.*

After four days and nights of constant tuition Northam and Dickson, although still very apprehensive, had nonetheless been sufficiently rehearsed in order to make authentic sounding statements. Now it was time to get it all down in writing.

On September 29th both their statements were signed. Dickson's began, "I am the wife of Richard James Dickson. I live at 163 Upper Brook Street Manchester..."

Dickson said she'd known both Kelly and Connolly for several years. On the afternoon of March 19th 1949 she and Northam had gone to Birkenhead to his parents. After tea, they came over to Liverpool and arrived at the *Beehive* at about 7.30pm. They went in the passage and there saw Charles Connolly whom she knew. She introduced him to Northam. Shortly afterwards Kelly arrived and ordered drinks all around. A discussion then ensued between the foursome about likely "jobs" to be done. A warehouse in Islington was mentioned but somebody said it was alarmed. Kelly suggested breaking into a stall at the funfair in New Brighton where he said there would be lots of cash and cigarettes. Then Connolly said there was a taxi-driver at the Copperas Hill rank a few hundred yards away at the side of the *Adelphi.* His name was Harry. Connolly said he was a stoolie and he was loaded.

Connolly asked Dickson to go down and lure him up a back street and they would roll him for his money. She refused. Connolly then said he knew a smashing job at a picture house up in Webster Road but that a gun or a dummy would be needed. At that, Kelly said, "I've just the thing" and pulled out a gun. He then began to load it in the passageway.

Her statement went on, "He took some shells from his pocket and pulled out the butt end of the gun and whilst he was placing the shells inside I said, 'You want to be careful in case somebody sees you'. But he said, 'I don't care, I'm Kelly'. He then pulled out a handkerchief and put it around his face as a mask but it was too small. A dark, heavily made up girl then came over and gave him a small brown apron which he put in his pocket."

Kelly then asked if Northam was coming with them but he refused. Dickson went out of the pub and across the road to the No. 8 tram stop with the two men. But when the tram arrived she changed her mind and went back to the *Beehive*. She and Northam then returned to Birkenhead.

"The following day", the statement continued, "the witness Northam and I stayed in Birkenhead.". About two weeks later Northam wrote a letter and sent it to the police. "He felt better after that". She posted it on the corner of Crown Street and Upper Parliament Street at about half past four on the Sunday. "It got lipstick on it from my pocket", she added .

Her statement ended, "When I saw the accused Kelly in the *Beehive* public house on the 19th March he was wearing a dark raincoat or overcoat with a belt around it".

Northam's statement was largely a carbon copy of Dickson's, even to using the same police phraseology when referring to her as, "the witness Dickson" and, "the accused Kelly."

"When I first saw the accused Kelly in the passageway", it went on, " his Mac or coat was open and I could see a pair of pliers sticking out." The statement continued, "Kelly said the gun was a 38. I saw the magazine was empty. Kelly put one shell into the breech of the gun and six in the magazine. He then put the gun into his back pocket. Then he put a small dark brown apron into his pocket."

Northam's statement went on to say that he next saw Kelly on the

21st March, in Lime Street, when he confessed to committing the murder and told him, " I ran across the park and got a 6A car back home."

Regarding the anonymous letter, Northam stated, " I started to write it to the Superintendent but couldn't spell it so I wrote 'Inspector'. I gave it to Jackie to post and it got lipstick on it."

Nowhere in either of these original statements of September 29th was there any mention of Kelly borrowing an overcoat from Northam before leaving the *Beehive*. Nor of any meeting the following afternoon with Kelly and Connolly in the *White Star Vaults* public house in Brownlow Hill (*Charlie Mathews '*). Nor of Connolly having tea with Dickson a few days after the murder and giving her a handkerchief full of bullets Or of her being taken by Kelly to a Lime Street pub, given whisky and being threatened by him.

As far as Balmer was concerned however, the statements could always be embellished later if necessary. For now, they were solid enough to warrant the arrest of Kelly and Connolly. Moreover, by their reference to the dark, heavily made-up girl, aiding and abetting Kelly by providing him with a mask, he hoped to pressurise Norwegian Margie into providing corroborative evidence.

Having been twice remanded into police custody on the 26th and the 27th of September - in order to keep the pressure on her - Dickson finally signed her statement on the 29th. Minutes later Northam signed his.

Later the same day Dickson again appeared in court on the Church Street theft and absconding from bail charges. She was given a conditional discharge, the lowest penalty - other than an Absolute Discharge - which a court can impose. It meant her immediate release.

Gathering his team together Balmer broke the good news: Dickson and Northam had coughed. It was they who had written the anonymous letter. And they had named the killers: George Kelly and Charles Connolly were their men!

Chapter Fifteen

Friday September 30th 1949. 2.30 am

"The Spider and the Fly".

Three unmarked squad cars, with headlights blazing, raced along deserted Liverpool Road, lighting up the blacked-out art deco *Eagle & Child* pub as they sped towards Woolfall Heath Avenue. Screeching haphazardly to a halt outside number 110, several detectives, led by Detective Chief Inspector Balmer, poured out and began rapping on the front door: "Open up! Police! Open up!"

Charles Connolly and his wife, both naked, were just about to make love upstairs in the front bedroom. But startled by the commotion, and the full headlights reflected on the bedroom ceiling, Connolly quickly drew on his trousers and moved to the window. His wife, frightened at the sudden din cried, "Oh Jesus! What's up Charlie? What's going on?"

"It's alright love", he said gently, trying to reassure her, "It's the coppers. I'll see what they want."

Meanwhile, his mother-in-law, alarmed at the noise, had gone downstairs and opened the door. As she undid the bolt the detectives hustled past her and raced up the stairs.

"What's this all about?" asked a shocked Connolly. "Never mind" said Balmer dismissively, "Get dressed".

"What for? What's it all about?", he again demanded.

Some of the detectives carrying torches, were busily searching the bedroom: in the chest of drawers, the wardrobe and under the bed. Mary Connolly, still shocked and unable to speak, was sitting upright in bed with the bedclothes pulled up to her chin to cover her nakedness. As he hurriedly finished dressing Connolly was still demanding to know why they were raiding his home like this. Balmer said, "I'm arresting you for the murders at the Cameo cinema"

"I don't know what you're talking about", replied a bemused Connolly.

One of the officers, becoming suspicious of Mary, suddenly snatched the bedclothes out of her grasp and forced open her clenched fist. Screeching in alarm, she quickly recovered the bedclothes to cover herself and her embarrassment. The detective's "find" was an unused condom. "There was no need for that!" protested Connolly. "Haven't you'se got *any* respect.?" Looking very sheepish, the detective apologised to Mary.

With Connolly squeezed between Balmer and Detective Sergeant Farragher on the back seat of the police car, they were first driven to the nearest police station in Stockbridge Lane, then into the city to Lawrence Road station, a few hundred yards from the Cameo.

They hadn't told him anything more than the charge. And when he demanded to know the details he was met with a wall of blank, stony faces. Fifteen minutes later, after some conversation between Balmer and the uniformed desk sergeant, he was given a cup of tea and then driven down town to the city's police headquarters in Dale Street.

With Connolly taken away, the remaining detectives systematically set about searching his mother-in-law's home. Scant regard was paid to his distraught wife, their three year-old daughter or his in-laws, as they turfed out almost every item of furniture into the front and rear gardens and ripped up the floorboards in every room. They never said what they were looking for. Nor did they subsequently find anything to implicate him in any crime.

In the interview room at C.I.D. Central, Connolly, sitting in an upright wooden chair, was surrounded by the three detective inspectors, Balmer, James Morris and Hector Taylor. "Look", he pleaded, "I have a right to know who's implicated me in this. Tell me the full strength". Balmer after a long pause quietly said, "Charlie, all I can tell you for now is that you're under arrest for the murders at the Cameo cinema last March." Recovered now from the initial shock of his arrest, an angry Connolly blurted out, "Yer what! Murders? What murders? What Cameo? I don't bleedin' well know what you're talkin' about. I've never been in any Cameo cinema. I don't know the place."

Balmer, ignoring his pleas and maintaining his quiet, almost casual, tone, said, "Look Charlie, we know you didn't fire the gun. All we want to know is who was the actual person who went inside, and who was it who stayed outside?" Connolly, still dazed replied, "I don't friggin' well know what you're talkin' about. I don't know anything about any murder or any Cameo. Look", he pleaded, "tell me the strength will yer. I have a right to know who's implicated me. I have a right to know all the details."

"Okay", said Balmer resignedly, "if that's the way you want it. We'll leave you to think it over." And without another word being said the three detectives left the room.

Half an hour had elapsed before a uniformed constable entered and, without speaking, removed the three empty chairs.

The interview room, with its glazed windows and a single bright bulb shining down, was now bare save for Connolly sitting in the middle of the floor on the remaining chair. It was very uncomfortable and he was very tired. But each time he began to drop off a different policeman would enter the room, sometimes to offer him a cigarette, then a few minutes later to give him a match. And all the time they would be advising him to, "Make a clean breast of it to Mr. Balmer and make it easy on yourself."

After several hours of this, an exhausted Connolly decided to defy them by curling up on the bare cold floor and going to sleep. But still they kept at him, ostensibly killing him with kindness, offering him cups of tea and cigarettes and then matches; anything to keep him awake and wear him down.

Later that morning at 5.45am Balmer sent two plain-clothes officers to deliver a note to Kelly's mother's house in the Trowbridge Street tenements. Walking quietly up to number 39D on the top landing, they pushed the handwritten note under the door and stole away.

At 10.15am Kelly, who had stayed the night in Doris O'Malley's, called into his mother's, who gave him the note, then went across Brownlow Hill to the rented rooms in Pleasant Street where his brother Joey lived. When he gave his customary whistle up to the first floor window, Joey's wife shouted down, "What d'yer want?"

"Is our kid there? Tell him I want him." He was still asleep said his wife.

"Well when he wakes up tell him Balmer's left a note in me mam's asking me to go down to Cheapside. He's got me a ship. Tell our kid

I'll see him later in *Tracey's*."

"Yeah, okay," she yawned.

In the Central C.I.D. Office, Balmer sat with his feet on his desk, musing upon a familiar quotation :-

"Will you walk into my parlour, said the Spider to the Fly,
'Tis the prettiest little parlour that you ever did spy.
The way into my parlour is up a winding stair.
And I have many curious things to show you when you are there..."

The passage from Mary Howitt's charming little poem was most appropriate, epitomising as it did, Balmer's preferred method of apprehending villains.

Kelly in buoyant mood, swept into the office and asked the uniformed duty officer, "Mr. Balmer in? Believe he wants to see me."

"What's the name?" asked the officer dryly.

"George Kelly."

Just then Balmer, appeared. "Georgie!", he greeted, "Just the fella I want to see. "Come through George."

Kelly was surprised to see Morris and Farragher standing there looking very grim. "What's all this then Mr. Balmer?", he asked apprehensively. "Thought this was a private matter?"

"Well it was", replied Balmer, "but sometimes things change very quickly -especially around here. Know what I mean George?"

"No, I don't," said a puzzled Kelly.

"Well", said Balmer, "I'm afraid you're under arrest George."

"Under arrest!" he shouted. "Under arrest? What the bleedin'ell for?" With all trace of familiarity now gone, Balmer, staring gravely at him, replied, "The murder of the manager and assistant manager of the Cameo cinema".

"Murder?!" he cried in disbelief. Then recovering his composure somewhat, he slumped down onto a seat, running his fingers through his hair." Honest t'god Mr. Balmer I don't know the first thing about any murder. How could I murder anyone? You've gotta be jokin' about this Mr. Balmer." Resuming his seat behind the desk, and with the other two staring at Kelly, Balmer coolly said, "Oh no George this is no joke. I'm deadly serious".

It had been so easy. The Fly had walked straight into his parlour!

During the next four hours the only information Kelly was given was that he had committed the murders at the Cameo in company with Charles Connolly, and that it had been planned with a Jacqueline Dickson and James Phillip Northam. " I don't know any Charles Connolly. I've never seen him in my life", he vehemently protested. "And I've never seen the other people in my life". Ignoring his pleas, Balmer told him it was believed it was he who had actually shot the men. "That's fuckin' crazy", he cried. "I've never had a gun in me life. I don't even know how to fire one".

At 3.30pm Kelly was put on an identification parade and picked out by Jacqueline Dickson. Connolly was not at that time nor subsequently ever put on an identification parade for Dickson - presumably because he had volunteered in May that he knew her by sight.

At 5 o'clock in the afternoon, Connolly was escorted through several rooms and connecting corridors, until he arrived in the charge-room at the Main Bridewell. Facing the uniformed sergeant at the charge desk, the cuffs of his jacket gripped by two detectives, he heard a commotion behind him. Looking briefly over his right shoulder, he saw a dark-haired man with unkempt hair, tie-less and a five-o'clock shadow, tentatively approaching him. The man was escorted by Balmer and Farragher. As he got nearer, the man inclined his head searchingly, trying to see his face. Connolly wondered who he was. Perhaps it was a so-called witness. Well if that's the case, he thought, I've got nothing to hide. He can have a bloody good look! So he turned fully and looked the man straight in the eye. As he did so the man, his head still inclined to get a better look at him, asked quietly with a quizzical expression, "You don't know me do you?" Equally perplexed, Connolly replied, "No, I don't." That was the first time in their lives that Charles Connolly and George Kelly had met .

At 5.10pm both men, in accordance with legal procedure, were charged only with the murder of Leonard Thomas. Connolly had been in custody for fifteen hours, Kelly for six, yet neither man had been interrogated about the murders for which they had been charged. Nor were they ever to be so.

Later that evening Balmer accompanied by Farragher, went to

Superintendent Smith's office, gave him the good news about the arrests and proudly handed him the statements of Dickson and Northam, After Smith read them, far from the congratulations Balmer expected, he was faced with a barrage of criticism. "You haven't got a case Bert", said the Chief dismissively. Balmer, somewhat taken aback, retorted, "I've got two bloody major witnesses".

"Witnesses to what Bert?. For a start they're two accomplices involved in it up to their necks and..."

"Its more than we had before", interrupted Balmer.

"I've told you, you haven't got a case", repeated Smith. "Where's the evidence Kelly and Connolly ever got to the Cameo, much less went inside?

"Dickson saw them getting on the tram outside the *Beehive*."

"So what? They could've bloody well got off at the next stop for all she knows. How could she testify to anything else? According to her statement she went back to the *Beehive* after they got on the tram"

Balmer tried to retrieve the situation by pointing out that Dickson and Northam had actually been party to the plan in the *Beehive* and had seen Kelly with the gun and mask. But an increasingly exasperated Smith said, "Look Bert, given the time you spent in the prosecutions department I shouldn't have to tell you this, but at best all you've got is conspiracy to rob. And your two witnesses are self-confessed accomplices who've been promised immunity! Where's the corroborative evidence? Where's the gun, where's the eyewitnesses, where's the bloody overcoat for God's sake!?"

"I'll find something", protested Balmer. "Now that we've broken the silence other stuff is bound to start coming in".

Brushing this weak assurance aside, Smith wanted to know where the names of Kelly and Connolly had come from. "She named them", answered Balmer"

"I believe you Bert", said a cynical Smith, "thousands wouldn't."

Unabashed, Balmer went on to insist Kelly could have committed the murders. "He has form for violence and he fits the cinema witnesses description of the gunman. He even admitted to me the day after the murder that he'd been in *The Spofforth* pub the night before - only five minutes from the Cameo. He definitely fits the bill."

"Why Connolly?", Smith wanted to know.

"She's named him", replied Balmer. "and she named him back in May"

"So what? She was wrong then. Why should we believe her now?"

When Balmer pointed out that Connolly's alibi proved to be untrue; that he'd been in the same naval barracks as Kelly in 1941; that he admitted knowing Dickson and that he'd been a very interested spectator at Johnson's trial, Smith gradually became less cynical. "Okay Bert", he said. "I'll leave it to you. If you can make a case good luck. But", he added ominously, "I'm warning you, if this turns out to be another fiasco like the Johnson business I'll make sure it's you who takes the can back this time."

"It won't", said Balmer. "I promise you, I'll make a case. And I'll make it stick"

As Balmer and Farragher were leaving the office, Smith called after them, "Since the two villains are denying even knowing each other, perhaps you'd better start by finding some people who will testify that they do."

"Don't worry about that", Balmer called back, "I will".

With the two men locked away in Cheapside to await their appearance in court the next day, the police turned their attention to Kelly's mother's home in Trowbridge Street. At 9.30pm on Balmer's orders, they raided the top floor tenement flat and set about taking the interior apart. Nothing was left untouched as they ransacked the rooms, throwing beds, furniture and clothing onto the landing. They even dismantled the living room's cast iron combined fireplace and cooking range, which was the family's only source of heating. During the raid, Kelly's father, a deeply religious man who was suffering from shingles, knelt on the floor amid the chaos and prayed, whilst his horrified wife and daughter Sally, simply stared in shocked silence.

When the police finally departed the scene of domestic destruction and chaos, they were loudly jeered and booed by the neighbours who, alerted by the unholy din, had congregated on the landings and in the square below.

Having been kept in separate cells overnight, the two accused men, unshaven, tired and dishevelled, appeared the following morning before Arthur McFarland the Stipendiary Magistrate. The court, which was the largest in the Dale Street building, was crowded with members of the public and police officers, including twenty detectives who surrounded the dock. The Chief Constable of Liverpool and Detective Chief Superintendent Smith were also present

After being charged, Kelly had asked Balmer if he could contact solicitor Harry Livermore and ask him to attend court on his behalf, which he did.

Kelly was on first name terms with Livermore through regularly introducing him to prospective compensation claim clients. And Livermore and Balmer knew each other very well through their adverserial roles in the magistrates courts during the war years when Balmer had been a police prosecutor. Indeed, it would seem that the intricate construction of the case against Kelly and Connolly was due in no small measure to Balmer's knowledge of the rules of evidence, court procedure and *Moriarty's Police Law*.

Mr. J.R. Bishop, the prosecution solicitor, said he didn't propose to go into the evidence at this stage but reminded the court of how the city had been shocked by the murders of the Cameo manager and his assistant the previous March. He then went on state, "Within *the last few hours* very important additional evidence has come into the possession of the police that has resulted in the arrest of these two men." (My italics).

Firstly the term "additional evidence" gave the false and unfair impression that there had been prior evidence against the men. Secondly, the evidence in question, which would prove to be the false statements of Dickson and Northam, had been obtained, not over 'the last few hours', but over the past five days.

This was the beginning of the prejudice and official lies which were to bedevil the accused men throughout the Committal proceedings and their three trials.

Despite his initial declaration that he would not go into the evidence, Mr. Bishop then proceeded to tell the court that there was evidence that the two accused men had met and discussed the robbery, and that one of them was seen loading a gun and that both then set off for the Cameo. There was also evidence, he said, that they were seen together after the crime and that both made statements to people afterwards.

After Balmer had described the arrest and charging of the two men, Connolly, who was not represented, was asked if he wanted to say anything. Rising to his feet and leaning against the dock rail out of sheer exhaustion, he said "I wish to apply for bail and legal aid. I have a right to know who is supposed to have given evidence against me in this." Told by the clerk of the court that that could not be gone into at this stage, he then sat down despairingly with his head between his hands.

Sitting alongside him, Kelly nervously bit his lip and glanced around the court as Livermore declared, "I am instructed that there has been a very tragic mistake made by the police as far as my client is concerned."

The Stipendiary told both men they would be granted legal aid but refused bail. They were then remanded in custody for ten days.

At 11.05am Kelly was taken from his cell at Cheapside and put on an identification parade for Northam. To ensure he didn't make any mistake, Balmer told him, "Don't forget, if you get a bit confused, Kelly will be the one with a ridge on the end of his nose". After twenty minutes hesitation Northam finally picked him out. Fifteen minutes later he also identified Connolly.

At 4.00pm on that Saturday afternoon the two men were handcuffed and taken with several other prisoners in a Black Maria to Walton prison. One of the prisoners in the van was a well known Liverpool hard man named Dennis Barker. What Barker had to say that day was to subsequently cause even more problems for Connolly.

Whilst they were on their way to Walton, James Skelly was being taken off his ship at the Mersey Estuary. Four detectives had travelled out to the Mersey Bar by pilot boat and escorted him ashore in handcuffs to the Main Bridewell. His appeal against the six-month sentence he'd received in May was to be heard in two days time before the Recorder, William Gorman, at the city's Quarter Sessions.

It seemed that Balmer could trust a convicted man to leave the *country* for six weeks whilst on bail, but not to leave Liverpool once he had returned! It also happened to be most convenient for Balmer to have Skelly, Kelly's main alibi witness, out of circulation where he could be of no further help to his friend.

Chapter Sixteen

Sunday October 2nd 1949

"The vilest deeds like poison weeds,
Bloom well in prison air..."
Oscar Wilde

As was customary for persons accused of murder and other serious offences, Kelly and Connolly were lodged in separate cells in the hospital wing at Walton. Ordered to be kept under observation, their cells, instead of having the normal solid heavy wooden doors with a tiny spyhole, were fronted by vertical bars much like those in an American prison. Although causing intense cold at night, this openness had its advantages, the main one being that - combined with the echo effect of the stone corridor - it facilitated rather than prevented conversation between the two men. For although Connolly's cell was on the corner of the main corridor and Kelly's a short distance further down the side corridor, thus preventing them from seeing each other, both cells were only four yards apart. In addition, although not allowed to exercise together, they sat next to each other every Sunday in the prison's Roman Catholic chapel.

During the first few days in Walton, the muted nightly conversation between the two men consisted merely of accusations and counter accusations. Connolly was convinced that Kelly knew all about the murders and continually demanded to know who his accomplice was. Similarly, Kelly was sure that Connolly was involved.

Matters finally came to a head on the morning of October the 3rd whilst they were waiting in the queue outside the Medical Officer's room. Connolly, at the end of his tether, suddenly attacked Kelly. Grabbing him around the throat and pushing him up against the wall, he roared, "Okay you little bastard! Now fuckin' tell me who it was with yer or I'll knock the fuckin' shite outta yer!"

Struggling to get his breath whilst trying to prise the strong boxer's hands from his neck, Kelly pleaded, "Honest to God Charlie, on me mother's life, I don't know anything about it. I'm just like you I don't know anything about it either." Just then Gerry Mahoney, a cleaner, whispered to them to break it up because a screw was approaching. Connolly let go but, composing himself, warned Kelly that he'd get the truth out of him sooner or later.

Unknown to Kelly, his friend Skelly had that day appeared before the Recorder at the Quarter Sessions and had his appeal dismissed. He was now in H Wing in the main block starting his six-month sentence.

Back in his cell, Connolly, desperate at his plight, decided to write to Balmer asking him to visit him so that he could tell him of what he'd heard from Dennis Barker in the prison van. Receiving his letter the following day, Balmer immediately drove to Walton to interview him. Connolly had by this time been appointed a solicitor, Mr. Maxwell Brown but Balmer didn't feel it necessary to consult him before visiting his client.

He began the interview by asking if Connolly wished to make a signed statement but he said he didn't want to sign anything. "I just want to tell you what happened."

"Okay then", said Balmer, "I'm listening. Fire away."

"Well, he began, "I want you to find who Nobby Clarke of Bootle is, and where he is. Also to tell yer that a man named Skelly is a mate of Kelly's. He is the same build as me but a little bit heavier. I know Kelly told this to Dennis Barker when we were in the Black Maria on Saturday. I heard him, and I heard him say that Skelly and him were together all night".

Balmer was writing this down when Connolly said, "No, don't write that, I don't mean all night. Kelly was with Skelly up till eight o'clock and then Kelly left him. I heard Kelly say that quite plainly. I want yer to see Dennis Barker. He'll tell yer Skelly looks like me. He'll back up what I say. Dennis also told me that Nobby Clark knows something about the murders. No, I don't mean the murders. Just put that he knows something. What I mean is this. It may be Skelly who was with Kelly that night and they only said they split up at eight o'clock. It seems funny they should leave each other like that so early. Yer see what I mean? I'm told by me mate, I won't tell yer who he is, but he says that Skelly's away at sea and won't be home for six months. No, cross that out, I mean six weeks. It seems funny that he should suddenly go away just after the murder. It was his first trip too because I believe he was in the army and that. I don't mean that exactly. I mean, I'm surmising it was his first trip. I don't know Kelly at all. Never seen him before in me life. Fitzsimmons of Huyton knows him well. You'll know Fitzsimmons, you had him down once. He'll tell yer that Skelly is very like me. Now don't go to Skelly and show him what I've said. Don't forget this is not a statement, this is something I'm telling yer I want you to do."

"I know that", said Balmer, "I'm just taking notes of what you're saying."
"Well don't forget", said Connolly, "as long as it's only notes."

Continuing, he said, "Can't yer see though, Kelly had his alibi fixed up right away. I've got to find one now. But I feel a lot better now because me missus and me family have been casting their minds back and they're pretty sure they'll remember where I was. That's all I need, someone to jog me memory."

Balmer again asked him if he would sign the notes but Connolly replied, "No, if yer don't mind, I've been told by my mouthpiece not to sign anything."

What Connolly did not know, and what Balmer did not tell him, was that he knew all about Kelly and Skelly; that Skelly was right now only a few yards away across the yard in the main prison doing six months, and that he had discounted him from having any involvement in the murders from as early as March 20th. And although it might have seemed strange to a bona-fide seaman like Connolly that a man who was on bail after being convicted of assaulting the police; who had never been away to sea before; who didn't even have a seaman's book, was allowed to leave the country for six weeks, he wasn't to know that it could indeed happen... especially if the police wanted it to happen.

Putting down his pencil, Balmer asked why Connolly had said he was at work when he wasn't. "I genuinely thought I was", he replied. "Look", he continued, "I'd been working for Bibby's for over six months. I was working nights. Why would I be involved in a murder on me night off?. I'd only been paid the night before, and I also had about fifteen quid holiday pay coming to me. Why would I want to rob anyone?"

Ignoring this plea, Balmer wanted to know what the situation was between him and his wife. Unsure of why he wanted to know but expecting a little sympathy, Connolly told him that the domestic situation was pretty strained due to the overcrowding, and the fact that his mother-in-law didn't like him anyway. Otherwise there were no problems between him and his wife. "Well, why are you knocking around with this Moore woman then?", asked Balmer. Connolly protested that he wasn't knocking around with any other women; that he didn't even know anyone named Moore. Where had that lie come from, he wanted to know? He had witnesses, said Balmer, who had seen him with her several times around the town.

That particular piece of misinformation had come from two prostitutes after Balmer had shown them photographs of Connolly wearing his trilby and asked if they'd ever seen him with Jacqueline Dickson. They hadn't but said they had often seen him with a woman named Moore from Brownlow Hill. They were however, mistaken. The man often seen with Moore, a perfectly respectable woman, was her husband Charlie Reid, also from around Brownlow Hill. Reid, who had nothing to do with the case, looked like Connolly and was the same build and height. Like Connolly, he too always wore a trilby, and for the same innocuous reason - his rapidly thinning hair.

After emphasising to Connolly the dire situation he was in, Balmer said in a kindly tone, "Look Charlie, why don't you do yourself a favour. Sign a statement to the fact that you called me up here to confess your part in it. I know you only waited outside. I'll arrange for you to turn King's Evidence and the charge against you will be dropped." He then added ominously, "You don't want to bloody-well hang do yer?" Momentarily taken aback, Connolly was nonetheless disgusted at the suggestion. "I don't tell lies", he said. "Why should I confess to something I haven't done?"

"Okay Charlie", said Balmer with a shrug as he rose to leave, "it's your funeral. Don't say I didn't offer to help you."

From the moment Kelly and Connolly were remanded in custody Balmer had set about consolidating the case against them. He knew that one of the biggest obstacles to overcome was the fact of Kelly being with Skelly in *The Coach and Horses*, when Dickson's and Northam's statements had put him in the *Beehive* plotting the crime with themselves and Connolly. It was imperative to get a good statement from Elizabeth McDonald, the licensee's wife.

On Sunday, October 2nd at 7.55pm, seven months after Balmer had last spoken to her, a signed statement was obtained from Mrs. McDonald. Her memory of the night of March 19th was not as clear as when she'd been interviewed the day after the murder, when she'd even described the man with Skelly as wearing a brown birds-eye suit.

She was now told that, although the man they'd arrested was insisting he was in her pub from 8.00pm to 9.00pm, the police had evidence that he was in fact downtown in the *Beehive* during that time, plotting the murder with three others. And they were certain they had got the right man.

The result of this was the following inconclusive statement :-

"I am the wife of Randall McDonald. On the night of the Cameo murder, Saturday 19th March, I was in charge of the *Coach & Horses,* 6 Low Hill. My husband was out. He is the Licensee. About half-past eight I was in the Lounge when I saw Skelly. He had had some drink and was very noisy and wanted to sing. Another man in a brown suit, thin dark hair, brushed back, thin build, was with him. They had been there for half-an-hour at least. This would make them come in about eight to a quarter past. I spoke to Skelly twice about his behaviour and told him to be quiet. The other fellow was quite sober and very quiet. About a quarter past nine, somewhere between nine and a quarter past, the man who was with Skelly went out and talked to me about the weather as he went. He was still very quiet and no trouble. Skelly left at ten o-clock and was still very noisy, and was taken home by Taffy Roberts. The reason I knew it was nine to a quarter past, was that it was half-nine on the clock, and the clock is always a quarter of an hour, or a little over, fast. I don't think I would know the man again because I've never seen him before or since".

Signed: Elizabeth McDonald.

It wasn't felt necessary to show the licensee's wife, a photograph of Kelly so that she could make a positive identification. After all, hadn't she said she wouldn't know the man again? That was enough for Balmer. All in all a pretty good statement, he thought.

The following day, October 3rd, he instructed Farragher to take a statement from James Corrie, his taxi-driver, drinking acquaintance. Corrie had already been coached by the Inspector on what to say during their Bass-drinking forays in the *Shakespeare* and *Royal Standard* pubs. It was however, more prudent to have another detective take his actual statement - particularly since many people were aware of the friendship between them.

Balmer had overcome Corrie's initial reluctance to embellish the facts, by first hinting that his Hackney Police taxi licence and his docks baggage pass may be at risk. He'd then inflamed him with the false story that Kelly and Connolly in the *Beehive* had tried to get Dickson to lure him away from the taxi rank to an alleyway off Mount Pleasant, where they'd intended to beat him up and rob him. Luckily said Balmer, she had refused otherwise it could well have been him who ended up murdered that night, particularly since Kelly had a gun on him.

This was enough for the sycophantic Corrie. Full of indignation he agreed to sign a statement saying , not simply that Kelly was in *The Leigh Arms*, but that he came into the buffet bar as late 9.50pm looking the worse for drink and very agitated; that he was obviously trying to draw attention to himself by offering to buy him and Mrs. Butterworth and the staff drinks, and that he'd stood at the bar with his fists clenched telling them he'd just been, "having a go", and that, "nobody takes liberties with Kelly.".

The opening of Corrie's statement bore a striking similarity to that of Edward Ellis, the licensee of *The Spofforth* Hotel.

Here is Corrie's phraseology:- "When I read in the papers the following morning about the murder at the Cameo cinema, *my mind went back* to the previous night and Kelly's behaviour in making himself so conspicuous and drawing attention to himself when he came into the public house..." And here is Ellis's:- "When I read in the papers on the Sunday morning about the murder at the Cameo cinema *my mind went back* to Kelly being in the public house. He was not wearing a hat or an overcoat when he was in the public house..." (My italics)

Whilst Balmer was at Walton interviewing Connolly, two members of the Murder Team, passing the *Primrose Cafe* in Cases Street, exchanged greetings with Paddy Dowling, an ex-sergeant major and member of the Corps of Commissioners. Dowling had, several months earlier, been given Kelly's job as doorman by Jacky the Greek.

Referring to the newspaper reports of October 1st, he remarked, "I see you've arrested Georgie Kelly for the Cameo murder, eh lads?" "Yeah", one answered, "we got the bugger in the end". "Well", he said, "I don't think he could've done it yer know." When they asked him why, he told them he had seen Kelly that Saturday evening coming out of the *Globe* next door at about 7-30. "So how could he have been at the Cameo up Smithdown Road?" "Are you sure", one of them asked. "Yeah",, I think so", he replied. "I see him every Saturday night about that time. He always goes in the *Globe* to change the money, yer know, his mother's takings off the barrow."

"Thanks Paddy", said the detectives as they hurried down to Dale street with this excellent news. Balmer would be over the moon. They had found a witness who could put Kelly within five minutes of the *Beehive* on the murder night. It would however take a further six weeks for Balmer to finally persuade Dowling to sign a definitive statement.

On the same day, October 4th, signed statements were also obtained from Fred Thomella, the licensee of *The Leigh Arms*, and "Irish Paddy", the Lewis's store detective.

"Paddy", whose proper name was James Daniel Sangster, was an old acquaintance of Balmer's. Like Corrie, he'd been previously briefed on what to say. And because they were so friendly, Balmer again ensured that another detective took his statement. In this Sangster made it quite clear that Connolly and Kelly definitely knew each other. He had seen them together numerous times on the blitzed site opposite the store and in various pubs, and had actually spoken to them separately. Strangely, however, although he stated he had seen them together on six occasions during the past year and knew, "both men so well that there is no possibility of me being mistaken", he could not say he had ever spoken to them when they had been together.

With particular reference to Connolly, he stated that on two occasions he had requested him to leave the department store's cafeteria because he'd been sitting there too long. Each time Connolly had showed resentment but left without being physically ejected.

Given Connolly's boxing history and his physical build, compared with that of the diminutive Sangster, this part of his statement was a combination of poetic licence and wishful thinking. Nonetheless Balmer was very pleased with this clear cut unambiguous statement. The store detective would make an impeccable witness.

When he saw Thomella's statement Balmer was not so happy. It was too vague. Thomella had stated, "Although I saw Kelly at about 9.00pm and again just before closing time, *I cannot say whether or not he was in the house between those times...*When Kelly came in the pub he was not wearing a hat or an overcoat." It was a Saturday night, he said, and the pub was *crowded.* (My italics)

This was too inconclusive for Balmer. According to Thomella's statement, Kelly could well have been in the pub when the murders were being committed. Something would have to be done about it before the trial. But how? Thomella, an ex-police officer with twenty three years service behind him, wasn't going to change it so readily. The Inspector realised he was going to have a job on his hands to get him to do so.

Apart from the unsatisfactory statement from Thomella, Balmer's promise to Smith that he would make a case that would stick, was being fulfilled with each passing day. He now had six good witnesses: three who could directly and indirectly implicate Kelly and Connolly; an independent one who could refute their assertions that they didn't know each other, and another, who could deny Kelly his *Coach and Horses* alibi.

What he now needed more than anything else was corroboration of Dickson's and Northam's story about the plot in the *Beehive*. And the best person to provide that was Norwegian Margie.

Over the next three weeks, despite heavy pressure and threats that she would be charged as an accessory if she didn't co-operate, Margie refused to make a false statement against Kelly. She had told Balmer the truth about the planning of the crime in *The Boundary* and she was not going to swear an innocent man's life away.

Although Balmer's case had to go to the Committal court without her, he still had her pencilled in his scenario as the dark, heavily-made-

girl in the *Beehive* who had handed Kelly the brown apron for a ask. And, he warned her, that when the proper trial started at the sizes she would be *forced* to give evidence because she would be ubpoenaed. Meanwhile, he threatened, she would get no peace; his fficers would be watching her day and night for the slightest breach of ie law.

Walton on the morning of Wednesday October 5th, Kelly in esperation wrote the following letter to Doris O'Malley:-

"Dear Doris,

hoping you and Doreen are okay. Well Doris you know in your own heart and soul that I know nothing about this murder. Have you been up to see Fred in the pub, (the Leigh Arms) he is the man who will save me, as for the rest in the pub, there was the Harrisons, all the Poveys and a lot more people who know me. All that night I was with Jimmy Skelly, but this girl said she seen me in the Beehive with a gun, now everyone knows that is all lies. That night I came home it was 10 pm and you was in the house, also little Boe Kelly.

Doris this is a frame-up by the police. Doris, Fred knows that I was in his pub from 8-45pm until 10 pm so how the hell could I kill anybody. Will you please ask Fred to come and see me, they have got me in the Prison Hospital. This is a terrible thing to get the blame for, when you know you haven't done it. Doris the whole trouble is Barmer(sic) and Smith don't know who as (sic) done it so they've blamed poor Kelly for it. I am going mad with the worry of it on my head all the time. I know you will come to see me, bring Fred with you. Did Mr. Livermore see Fred yet. Doris, I must get away with this because I know nothing about it, it is just a frame-up job. Please help.

Still lots of love, George.

xxxxxx

This letter, like those of all prisoners, went through the prison censor's hands. The police typed out a copy. But since they wrote on this copy that they also had the original, it seemed that , even after Kelly's arrest, Doris O'Malley was still on very good terms with Balmer!

The typewritten copy was edited by Morris and the following passages were scored in the margin and underlined on the page:- " Have you been up to see Fred in the pub"; " That night I came home at 10.00pm and you was in the house also little Boe Kelly";. "All that night I was with Jimmy Skelly"; "...from 8.45pm until 10.00pm so how the hell could I kill anybody".

These imprecise passages, clearly a summary written by a distraught Kelly, would subsequently be used as the basis for Balmer's verbals against him, and by the prosecution to infer that he had been attempting to get Doris to nobble Thomella.

Kelly was unaware that the police had already obtained a statement from Thomella the previous day. But when Balmer saw Kelly's letter he knew it was even more imperative to get Thomella's neutral statement changed. For, apart from it needing to be more definite about Kelly not returning to the *Leigh* before 9.50pm, Kelly's solicitor might persuade him to make another one, even more favourable to Kelly.

After writing the letter Kelly was escorted with Connolly to the RC. Chapel where they were seated on the back row. A warder sat between them and another warder sat nearby.

Until today they had become a grotesque spectacle in church, with a black net hanging down in front of them effectively segregating them from the other prisoners. But they had protested at this treatment so vehemently that the governor had ordered the practice to cease.

As the prisoners stood to sing the hymn *Faith of our Fathers*, the pugilistic-looking Dennis Barker and Johnny One Cunningham, dressed in white surplices over their prison brown, paraded before the altar to assist Father Lane in serving Mass. The bizarre spectacle of two of Liverpool's hardest cases dressed as pious altar boys trying to look angelic, prompted Kelly and Connolly to burst into laughter. But they were quickly silenced by the warder.

As the service was ending an incident occurred which caused Kelly to make a statement at 11.30am in the Governor's office. In it he swore:-

" I went to the RC. Church this morning and I was put in the back row. Somebody in church must have pointed me out to this man Johnson. I had never seen him in all my life until this morning. He was two seats in front of me. He said to me, ` You have not got a worry in this world and keep your chin up`. He then said, `I know who done the Cameo murder, I will get you cleared of it all`. I said to him, `Will you swear to that and his reply was, `Yes`. All the men in church heard what he said to me. He said he will tell the Governor also the police and my counsel."

Fifteen minutes later, again in the Governor's office, another prisoner, J.P. O'Neil, made the following statement in the presence of Johnson:-

"This morning in the RC. Chapel the prisoners, Connolly and Kelly, came in behind us. I heard Kelly say to Connolly, `There's Johnson`. Connolly said, `Where? Where?`. Connolly then said to Johnson, `We don't know anything about this`, and Johnson said, `Alright, send your lawyer to me and I'll fix it`. I then spoke to Johnson, who looked white and strange, and asked him if he was all right. And he replied, `Yes but I feel sick`. Later he spoke to Connolly and Connolly said, `I'm worried about this because my wife is in hospital having a baby`. And Johnson said, `You'll be alright, don't worry`."

Asked what he had to say about this, Johnson said, "I have nothing to say except that Connolly hasn't got a wife. And I would like to call Officer Southern who was in chapel standing by Connolly and Kelly at the back".

When Southern arrived Johnson asked O'Neil, "Can you distinguish Connolly from Kelly?. Do you know them apart?" O'Neil answered, "Yes, Kelly is in civilian clothes and Connolly is in prison brown". Johnson then asked Southern the warder," Were you standing near us in church?" "Yes".

"Was I looking any different to what I am now?"

"Not that I know of. Nothing unusual".

"Did we have any conversation with the unconvicted prisoners Connolly and Kelly?"

"None whatsoever." Then O'Neil's statement was a pack of lies?, said Johnson. Southern replied, "I did not receive the prisoners until they were inside the church in the balcony. And I did not hear any conversation there. I was sitting next to Connolly and Kelly." O'Neil then asked Johnson if he would repeat those questions in the presence of Connolly and Kelly. Johnson replied. "I decline to answer". He then refused to sign anything or make any further statement.

It was clear from the opening lines of O'Neil's statement, "Connolly and Kelly came in behind us", that he was referring to an incident which occurred as the prisoners were entering church. Therefore the prison officer Southern, who admitted he only received the men after they had arrived in the church's balcony, would not have heard the conversation described by O'Neil. Moreover, the incident described by Kelly and the conversation he said took place between him and Johnson was probably a totally different one - which nonetheless Southern denied hearing. Connolly however was not called to confirm or deny the truth of what Kelly and O'Neil had said. And, although the incidents were recorded and signed by A.C.W. Richards, the prison governor, nothing further was heard about them.

Chapter Seventeen

October 9th - 19th, 1949

> *"Some do the deed with many tears,*
> *And some without a sigh..."*
> Oscar Wilde

Before Kelly and Connolly appeared at the Committal hearing there were several important developments which would ensure a much firmer case against them when they finally came to trial. These would primarily be, the radically altered statements of Northam and Dickson and the emergence of the alleged murder overcoat.

In addition, a gun was discovered but because this apparently did not help the prosecution's case its discovery would be kept quiet.

It was a Beretta 9 mm automatic pistol found in the River Birkett in Birkenhead on October the 9th. Its discovery was never mentioned by the police or the prosecution. And although it was sent to the Forensic Science Laboratory at Preston on the 11th October for examination, the results were never disclosed.

The new statements to be signed by Northam and Dickson came about after a meeting between Balmer and Smith, when the latter said he wasn't happy with the progress of the case.

"Why?" asked Balmer. "I'll tell you why", said Smith, because you've got no evidence that they actually arrived at the Cameo, that's why."

"But " protested Balmer, "Jackie Dickson went out of the pub with them and saw them boarding the No 8 tram opposite the *Beehive*."

"That doesn't prove that they actually arrived at the Cameo Bert. We've got to have something or someone to show that they were at the cinema, and better still, some sort of evidence that they actually did the job. Remember Bert", he went on, we've got no tangible evidence either. No gun, no overcoat, no hat, no mask, nothing."

Reluctantly nodding his agreement, Balmer left the meeting saying he would see what could be done.

On the 10th of October, a brown overcoat, which would

subsequently be presented as that worn by Kelly on the night of the murders, was allegedly handed to Balmer by Northam, who then, together with Dickson, signed his changed statement.

The substantially amended statements of the two "accomplices" now described how Northam had been carrying this overcoat on his arm when he and Dickson entered the *Beehive* on March 19th. The earlier references to Kelly wearing a mac or dark overcoat when he arrived in the pub, had been deleted, as had Northam's reference to a pair of pliers sticking out of Kelly's waistband.

Later, as Kelly was loading the gun, Northam's revised statement now had Connolly saying it looked like an air pistol and Kelly saying, "This is no air pistol, it's a 38".

When the Cameo job was finally decided on Kelly asked Northam if he was going with them but he said no and told him he didn't like guns or those who used them. Kelly then asked to borrow Northam's overcoat, and donning it he said, "It's a smashing fit." Still wearing the overcoat, Kelly then left with Connolly and Dickson but Dickson came back after a few minutes. Whilst she was away, said Northam, he remained in the passage standing next to the unknown dark-haired girl who had earlier offered the brown apron to Kelly to use as a mask. He never spoke to her because he was self conscious about his stammer. When Dickson came back in the pub they both left immediately for Birkenhead.

Both statements now said that they had not stayed in Birkenhead all the following day. They now stated that before leaving the *Beehive* it had been arranged for all four to meet the following day in the *White Star* pub in Brownlow Hill. And that when Northam and Dickson arrived there at 1.00pm, Connolly was already there talking to a man named Jimmy Skelly. Connolly looked pale and frightened and said he was going to leave the country and Skelly offered to get him a ship. Shortly afterwards Kelly arrived with the dark heavily made-up girl of the night before. Connolly again said he was going to leave the country and Kelly called him a yellow bastard and said he would be foolish to leave the country, and that he (Kelly) was staying put. He then said, "That bastard Balmer was up at our house this morning. *If I'd had the gun with me he wouldn't have stood there so cocksure of himself.*"

(My italics)

Kelly said he had an alibi all fixed up and told Connolly he would have to get one as Balmer was bound to be up to see him. Connolly said he would fix up an alibi with his wife. Kelly then told Connolly that if Balmer saw him, he was to say they didn't know each other. Before the party broke up at about 2.00pm., the statements continued, Kelly warned them all to keep their mouths shut otherwise he or his brothers would shut them. Northam asked for his overcoat back and Kelly said he would fetch it tomorrow.

The following day, Monday March 21st, the couple came over from Birkenhead, and Dickson left Northam by *Lewis's* and was gone for about an hour. During that time, stated Northam, he met Kelly at about 2.00pm on the bombed site next door to the *Palais De Luxe* cinema, opposite the Big House pub in Lime Street, and asked for his overcoat. Kelly went away and came back with it fifteen minutes later, saying, " I would have slung it but it might have been traced back to you. The best thing you can do is burn it" Northam said to him, "You made an awful mess of that job at the Cameo." but Kelly told him to shut his fucking mouth. Northam asked how it came to turn out like that and Kelly said , "Your type of fellows have no guts and Connolly is the same." He said if Connolly had stood by the door properly as he should have done, he would not have been surprised and there would have only been one man shot instead of two. Kelly told him that Connolly only went as far as the side door but would not go in. Kelly said they had first been talking on the opposite side of the street waiting for the lights in the cash desk to go out but when he'd asked Connolly to go in with him he said he would wait outside. Connolly, he said, should have warned him when this man was coming up the stairs.

Northam's statement then recounted what Kelly allegedly told him of the actual murder: He got up to the manager's office and walked in. There was an old fellow sitting down. Kelly said he wanted the takings and pointed to the bag on the table. The man said, "Don't be a fool. Take that thing away. It's only a toy" Kelly said, "This is no toy, I want that bag." The old man then stood up and said, "You can't take that, it belongs to the company. You can have some of my own money if you like." Kelly said the man then stood up and tried to brush the gun aside but, said Kelly, `I couldn't be bothered with him anymore so I shot him"

His statement went on that Kelly told him, "I picked up the bag, put the gun in my pocket and turned to go out. I got two or three paces from the door when the door opened and another man came in. He stood with his back to the door and his hands behind his back. The bag was in my left hand and my right hand was free. The man moved towards me as if to put his arms around me and tried to grab the bag. I then butted him and, taking the gun out of my pocket, shot him in the chest. The man fell on his knees and started to tear at his shirt. He tried to tackle me again so I shot him again and he fell."

Kelly then told Northam the money was scattered all over the floor. Thinking that the second man had locked the door behind him, he shot off the lock. He then had to pull the man away from the door, and dashed down the spiral staircase. He couldn't see Connolly anywhere so he got away through the park by *Littlewoods'* and jumped a 6A tram car home. He then told Northam, "I have a cast iron alibi. The police cannot break it in a thousand years - especially Balmer".

If this new statement of Northam's was more substantial and incriminating against Kelly and Connolly than that of September 29th, Dickson's was even more detailed and pernicious.

She now stated that, she met Connolly on two occasions after the murder and on the second of these had actually had tea with him in *Littlewoods'* cafe. On the first occasion, March 21st, Connolly looked pale and frightened. He told her that Kelly had gone inside the cinema but he had waited outside. When he heard the gunshots he had run away. He then gave her a handkerchief containing heavy objects and said to her, "Give this to Georgie Kelly next time you see him". But she gave the handkerchief to Northam. They discovered that the objects inside were bullets. Northam kept six of these out of curiosity and gave her the remainder back, telling her to return them to Connolly and tell him do his own dirty work.

When she saw Connolly on the second occasion in *Littlewoods'* she gave him the bullets back. He was frightened, said he was going to, "blow town", and asked her to go with him to "The Smoke". Later she was searching in Northam's pockets and found some of the bullets.

She took them and threw them down drains in Hawke Street at the back of the *Adelphi* hotel.

Some days later, her statement continued, she saw Kelly outside the *Palais De Luxe*, and he said, "Good God Jackie what's up with you?" She told him she was frightened of a man called Bobby Woolerton who was going to batter her. Kelly took her to a pub down a side street at the back of Lime Street by the fish market. She thought the pub was called the *Caledonian*. He bought whiskies for both of them and told her, "This is the stuff you need". She told him he seemed to have plenty of money to throw away on the stuff. He said he would have had more if he'd got what he went for at the Cameo. She again told him she was scared of Woolerton finding her so she was going to Birkenhead. Kelly said, `There's no need to be scared while I have this` and tapped something in his pocket. She didn't see what it was but said to him, "Why don't you get rid of that thing?"' He said, "I will. I will take it to bits and throw it down some drains somewhere." Kelly then threatened her that if she said anything to anyone he would knife her, and that if he didn't somebody else would. She started to cry and he took out his handkerchief and said, "Hey nark that or people will think I've done something to you."

When they left the pub she went to Central station underground with him and he bought two tickets. She was terrified. She thought he might follow her down a back street in Birkenhead and shoot her or something. But he said he was going to meet his brother instead.

After reading over his new statement, Northam voiced his concern about the part which referred to him lending his overcoat *after* the Cameo had been decided upon, and *after* he had seen Kelly with a gun. Left like that, he thought, it would allow Balmer to charge him with being an accessory whenever he wished. His fears were soon dissolved however when the Inspector agreed to change the statement to read that, in the *Beehive* Kelly had borrowed the overcoat because he said he was feeling cold, *before* any jobs were discussed. Feeling much happier now, Northam readily signed it.

That morning of October 10th, Kelly and Connolly appeared in court. After they were further remanded in custody Kelly was again put on an identification parade and was picked out, this time by Sangster the Lewis's store detective.

As he was leaving the room Kelly angrily shouted, "I won't forget you for this Balmer!" Harry Livermore, his solicitor told him to be quiet but Balmer said to Detective Sergeant Farragher, "Note that down Jack, `If it's the last thing I do I'll get you for this Balmer`. That's what he said."

Half an hour later, Connolly was also identified by Sangster

When, later that day Balmer reported the latest developments to Smith and showed him Northam's and Dickson's new statements, the C.I.D. Chief was visibly pleased. "That's more like it Bert", he said. "Good work".

During the following weeks in Walton the initial shock of their arrest was beginning to wear off the two men. And with each gradually realising that the other knew nothing about the murders, they became friendly and began to grow more confident. The nightly chats through their cell bars along the short corridor continued. And almost every night Kelly would entertain the whole block with such songs as, *When I Leave the World Behind, Some Enchanted Evening;* his mother's song, *When I Lost You* and the jollier, *Lazy Mary*, a humorous adaptation of an old Italian folk song. He also sang such songs as *Valencia* and *They Didn't Believe Me* by a new singer named Mario Lanza, whose records his seafaring brother Frankie had brought home from New York, but these didn't get such a warm reception because nobody knew them.

Connolly however, began to suffer from blinding headaches and had to be given phenobarbitone each night. At these times he would become so irritated with Kelly's singing that he would shout down the corridor for him to shut up and, "give your fuckin' arse a chance!"

Kelly, having discovered that his friend Skelly was in the main prison serving the six months they'd both received in May, began sending him messages written on toilet paper. They consisted mostly of him asking if he knew Northam, and if he didn't could he find out anything about him. But Skelly did not know Northam and, being a prisoner himself, wasn't able to be of any help.

Meanwhile Kelly had discovered that his brother Joey knew

Dickson quite well. On one of his visits, with their brother-in-law, Tucker Gill, Joey had admitted he had been, "knocking around with her last year." But he didn't tell his brother he had been using his name. Kelly was taken aback at this news about Joey and Dickson but Joey pleaded with him not to mention anything about it. If it got out, he said, it would wreck his marriage.

The following day in the queue outside the Medical Officer's room, Kelly told Connolly of what he'd learned. Connolly said he must tell his solicitor when they next appeared in court. Rather naively however, Kelly didn't seem to think it was all that important. He was more worried about ruining his brother's marital relationship. "As long as *I* know in me own heart and soul that *I* don't know her", he told Connolly, "then that's all that matters. A mean, what good would it do to let anyone know. Our kid and his judy would be the only ones to suffer."

In the event Connolly told his own solicitor, Mr. Maxwell Brown, who then conveyed the news to Harry Livermore.

Chapter Eighteen

"Thou shal not bear false witness..."

On Wednesday October 19th, the Committal proceedings, which were to last for four days, began before the Examining Magistrate Mr. C.G.S. Gordon in No 2 Court in the Dale Street building.

Mr. J.R. Bishop acted on behalf of the Director of Public Prosecutions. Kelly was represented by Harry Livermore. And although he now had a solicitor, Mr. Maxwell Brown, Connolly was represented by barrister, Mr. Gordon Clover.

Each day the courtroom was packed to capacity and the daily proceedings were expansively reported each evening in the two Liverpool newspapers, the *Liverpool Echo* and the *Evening Express.*

On the first day Harry Livermore immediately requested that the proceedings be heard *in camera* on the grounds that the widespread publicity would be prejudicial to a fair trial when the case went to the Assizes. This however was rejected by the examining magistrate who, as the case progressed, was to prove unsympathetic if not overtly obstructive to the defence.

Opening the case for the prosecution, Mr. Bishop gave a resume of the circumstances of the murder, and the arrests of the two men on September 30th.

Dealing with Balmer's visit on the morning after the murders to 67 Cambridge Street, he stated that Kelly, when asked to account for his movements the night before, said, "I can easily do that. I was with Jimmy Skelly in *The Coach and Horses* just after opening time. He was on the booze so I left him and arranged to see him down the town. He did not turn up so I went up at nine o'clock and saw he was drunk I then went to the public house opposite our street and stayed there until ten o'clock."

After explaining that the public house in question was *The Leigh Arms*, Bishop said Kelly continued, "When I got home I found a note from Dolly in the sugar basin saying she was at *Bramleys* and we had a row about it."

This was of course a gross distortion of what Kelly had told Balmer that Sunday morning. But in view of the licensee's wife, that same day, confirming Skelly's and Kelly's presence in the '*Coach* the previous evening, it cleverly conceded that Kelly *had* been in the *Coach* but still allowed time for him to have been in the *Beehive* plotting the crime at the time Dickson and Northam had stated. It furthermore paved the way for the discrediting of the evidence of Skelly, the only witness who could refute Kelly's alleged presence in the *Beehive*.

Despite Balmer's clever construction however, Kelly's alleged unsigned statement was both fanciful and illogical. The court was being asked to accept that he met his friend at opening time in the *Coach & Horses*, saw that he was "on the booze", left him to go downtown for three and a half hours, came back alone at 9.00pm, saw that he was drunk, then left him to go and stay in *The Leigh Arms* until closing time.

The implausibility of this account was matched only by the opportunity it gave the prosecution to claim that Kelly could have been with Connolly, Dickson and Northam in the *Beehive* between 7-30 and 8.00pm.

Bishop went on to state that on May 14th Balmer and Farragher saw Connolly at his home at 1.50am and took him to Dale Street to see Superintendent Smith. When asked his whereabouts on Saturday March 19th, he said, "I was at work on the afternoon shift. I did not get back till ten o'clock".

Not only did the visit to Connolly's home not take place on May 14th, it was an untrue account of what he had actually told them at Dale Street on that date. It was however conveniently worded so that it presented him as a liar who was deliberately trying to account for his movements between 8.00pm and 10.00pm on the murder night. And by falsely stating that the police had specifically called at his house in the early hours of the morning, rather than truthfully stating that he was routinely interviewed after being seen in Lime Street, the clear implication was that Connolly had been a serious suspect from as far back as May. Otherwise, it may have been asked, if Connolly was under suspicion since May then why had he only been routinely questioned? And why had it taken until September to arrest him? It wouldn't do for Balmer to appear incompetent.

These lies and distortions, whilst always containing a germ of truth, were to increasingly become Balmer's personal hallmark - along with the repeated use of the particular words "definite" and "definitely" in witnesses statements and his own evidence. It would become, throughout the prosecution's case, as indelible as the red lettering through a stick of rock. And if these alleged unsigned statements of the two accused were somewhat implausible, they would subsequently appear as mere subtle refinements compared to some of the more crude and fantastic allegations which would later be made against them.

Coming to the initial confrontation between the two men in the charge room at Dale Street on September the 30th, Bishop told the court that Connolly was 'sitting in an office by the main Bridewell' when Kelly was brought in by Inspector Balmer. And that when he was some twelve to fifteen feet away, Kelly shouted across to Connolly, who was facing the other way, "You have never seen me in your life before have you? "You don't know me at all?" Connolly replied, "No, I don't".

True to Balmer's vow that he would, "make a case", Bishop then described a scene between Kelly and Doris O'Malley which he said took place after the two men had been remanded in custody on October the 1st. On that occasion, he said, Kelly was granted a short interview with Doris O'Malley at which Balmer was present. She said to Kelly, "Oh Georgie isn't it terrible." Kelly replied, " You need not worry about me. I am all right. I was at *The Coach and Horses* with Skelly and then I was with you." But O'Malley said, "No Georgie, don't you remember. I left a note for you in the sugar basin where I had gone and you carried on afterwards because you did not find me?" Kelly then said, "Oh yes. I am all right. Don't you worry about me. I have never seen the other fellow before. I asked him, `have you seen me before`, and he said, `No`."

These two incidents were designed by Balmer, firstly to imply that the two men did in fact know each other and that Kelly was trying to warn Connolly. Secondly that Kelly was lying about his movements on the night of the murder and trying in some coded way to get O'Malley to back him up.

The description of the first incident was a distortion of what occurred in the charge room. And the second of course - with the exception of Kelly telling O'Malley about asking Connolly if he knew him - never happened. It was contrived following the interception of Kelly's prison letter to O'Malley, and was based on the passages where Kelly had summarised matters by stating he was with Jimmy Skelly "all night", and that when he came home at 10.00pm she was in the house with little Bowie Kelly. Indeed, when Balmer in the witness box later testified to the veracity of this conversation, Kelly loudly protested.

Recounting the incident at the 10th of October identity parade when Sangster had identified Kelly, Bishop said that as the Chief inspector was walking out of the Bridewell Kelly shouted, "If it's the last thing I do I'll get you for this Balmer!" That dramatic, but untruthful, threat made the headlines that evening and provided another black mark against Kelly.

The next two days saw Northam, Dickson, Smith and Balmer enter the witness box in succession to make a most damning case against the two accused.

During his cross-examination Northam flatly refused to divulge his and Dickson's address, claiming they had been threatened. He would not say by whom nor was he asked. Nonetheless the implied accusation of subornation of witnesses was not lost on the court or the evening papers. It was a little more mud to be thrown at the two men which Balmer hoped would stick!

When Livermore raised the vitally important matter of the anonymous letter, which was the basis of the prosecution's case, the examining magistrate ruled that it could not be entered in evidence or even referred to. And when Northam and Dickson refused to divulge to Livermore where they were living at the time they were brought back to Liverpool, their refusals were upheld by the bench.

During the cross-examination of Superintendent Smith, Livermore asked if he knew where Dickson was living at the time she was brought back. He said he did, adding that she was seen by the police on September 29th. But when asked if she was brought to Liverpool on that date, Smith agreed this had been some days earlier. He would not however specify which date. And when Livermore tried to establish the circumstances in which she was brought back, the examining magistrate, supporting an objection from Bishop, ruled that it was not relevant. At this, Livermore complained, "if we are going to hide this under a veil of secrecy..." But interrupting him, the magistrate testily declared, "There is no veil of secrecy."

An insistent Livermore asked Smith if *he* was prepared to tell where Dickson was living when she was brought to Liverpool. But before he could reply the magistrate again intervened and said. "I rule that out of order."

In a later reply to Livermore Smith, despite agreeing that he was "in charge of the enquiries in this case" admitted that he was not present at any of the interviews with Kelly. This admission would have been astonishing if Kelly, as someone charged with murder, had as he should have, been diligently interviewed. But of course neither he nor Connolly ever were. Was this why the Head of the C.I.D. didn't hesitate in giving such an unabashed reply?

When Northam entered the witness box his replies were almost inaudible. He explained this by stating he had been blown up by a landmine whilst in the army during the war, and that this was also why he stammered. He had, he said, known Kelly for five years, adding that when Dickson introduced him to Connolly in the *Beehive* he laughed because he had already known him for about four years.

Replying to Livermore, Northam said he was certain he had known Kelly for five or six years, including the years 1946 and 1947. Unfortunately he was not pressed on this. Had Livermore done so he could have proved this to be untrue because between November 1943 and September 1945 Kelly was serving two prison sentences in Manchester and Liverpool of nine and twelve months. And from January 1945 he was actually serving a three year sentence in Bristol, imposed at a naval court-martial for desertion and prison-breaking.

Asked if he knew about the case of Donald Johnson, Northam admitted he did. Why then, asked Livermore, if he knew as far back as March who the murderer was did he not come forward at the time of Johnson's trial in June? But before he could reply Bishop objected. Livermore however, persisted: " I only want to ask this. When you read or heard about these proceedings against Johnson did you then come forward to the police?"

"No." Intervening once again, the magistrate said he would not allow the question or the reply to go on the deposition. And when Livermore complained about this, he said the question was not justified, had nothing to do with the current proceedings and that he was ruling it out of order.

Northam later stated that when Kelly produced the gun in the *Beehive*, Connolly said it looked like an air pistol but Kelly replied, "It is not an air pistol. It is a 38". He also claimed that when Kelly returned his overcoat in Lime Street on the 21st March, he asked him if he still had the gun and Kelly replied, "do you think I am fucking mad".

These were two further elaborations on Northam's already amended statement of the 10th October, the second of which begged the question: if Kelly felt it would be mad to still have the gun in his possession two days after the murder, wouldn't he have felt it equally mad to be seen carrying the alleged murder overcoat in the city centre?

Blonde-haired Jacqueline Dickson was the next witness. She had obviously been primed to expect aggressive questioning. For despite Connolly's barrister Gordon Clover treating her most courteously, her insolent attitude towards the defence was apparent from the outset. This first became apparent when a cynical Livermore asked if it was true to say she was very friendly with Northam and she replied, "Does it matter?"

"Yes, it matters to me", retorted Livermore. "Will you answer the question?" But staring at him contemptuously, she refused to answer. He then asked if she and Northam were living at the same address, to which she replied, "I prefer not to answer that question. It has nothing to do with this case."

"The magistrate will stop me if these questions have nothing to do with this case", said Livermore. But the adamant Dickson emphatically declared, "I'm not telling you."

When Livermore later asked where she was living at the time she was picked up by the police and brought back to Liverpool, the magistrate once more interceded, warning him, "You are going to be on rather dangerous ground." The solicitor protested that he was entitled to ask her this but the magistrate said it had been agreed, "to keep a certain place confidential." Bishop then added his objection to the question being asked.

Becoming increasingly exasperated at Dickson's recalcitrance and the frequent interventions of the magistrate, Kelly's solicitor bravely ploughed on. "Let me put it this way", he asked, "where you at the address you are now at when the police first saw you about this matter?" "No".

"Will you tell me where you were when they first saw you about this matter?"

"No."

"Were you living with any relatives when the police saw you?"

"No".

"Why won't you tell me where you were staying?"

"Because I don't want to."

When Livermore said he could insist on her answering the question and that she must do so, Dickson declared that she had been threatened with having her face cut open unless she changed her statement and said it was a case of mistaken identity. He was however more interested in logic than sympathy. Dismissing the story of the threats, he wanted to know why she was refusing to divulge the address if she was no longer living there, and if there were no relatives living at that address. Dickson lamely replied, "Just because I don't want you to know."

This defiant attitude, adopted throughout her evidence, clearly demonstrated that Dickson, having been advised not to willingly co operate with the defence, was overdoing it. She was being obstructive for the sheer hell of it. Undeterred, however, Livermore told her, "I am going to insist upon an answer. I am entitled to know." And brushing aside an objection from Bishop that the question was irrelevant, he declared that he only wished to know the circumstances, time and place where Dickson came to be seen by the police. "I don't understand what the secrecy is about threats", he angrily declared. "It is pure rubbish because the girl is not living now at the address at which she was then."

At this point, Dickson, as if suddenly remembering forgotten lines from her script, irrelevantly interjected that it was the previous Sunday when she was threatened. But Livermore, as dismissive as ever of her purious claims, said, "That has nothing to do with where the police saw you three or four weeks ago". Then addressing the Bench he went on, "I am entitled to know the circumstances under which the police came to see this witness - where, how and when."

When the clerk of the court intervened to suggest that Livermore might be content to simply be told the town she was living in, he pleaded, "Am I not entitled to know the circumstances under which the police came to see this witness? That is all - where they saw her." Bishop, knowing the bench was on his side, smugly remarked, "I very much doubt it." At this point Dickson impertinently interjected, "Even if the police say I must tell you, I will not. So there is no use you asking."

Rather than condemning this blatant contempt, the examining magistrate, to everyone's astonishment, stated that he thought the question had been unduly pressed and that the defence should now regard the question as being answered. But Livermore was not so easily put off. "Surely", he pleaded, "I must have a reason for pressing it otherwise it would not be pressed". He then added that Dickson's refusal to answer because of alleged threats was nonsense. He did not accept there had been threats. And anyway, the so-called threats had nothing to do with where she was living when she was seen by the police in May or September, and were therefore totally irrelevant.

Despite his persistence Livermore never got an answer to his question. Nor did Dickson ever explain who had threatened her. Yet, the examining magistrate allowed these vague, unqualified and unsubstantiated charges to be put on the record and thus plastered all over the pages of the '*Express* and the '*Echo* that evening.

Referring to the bullets which Connolly allegedly gave to Dickson, Livermore asked her if she hadn't thought of handing them over to the police. She hadn't because she and Northam had been threatened and were afraid to go to the police. That was why she had left town and why the police had taken so long to find her. She then added, in reply to a further question, that she supposed Northam had kept six of the bullets for curiosity.

Instead of suggesting to her that she could have come back to Liverpool whenever she wanted, which merely drew the blank reply, "I did not come back", Livermore could have more profitably put a much more illuminating question. Namely, Why, at the time of absconding in May, was she afraid to go to the police if she had already sent them the anonymous letter in April and had been given the required assurances?

Moving on, Livermore asked her if she knew a man named Joseph Kelly. She agreed she did. Did she also know a man named Gill? This was a reference to Thomas "Tucker" Gill, husband of Kelly's sister Sally, who associated with Joseph Kelly. When Dickson denied knowing him, Livermore turned to the public benches in the crowded court and asked him to stand up. She then agreed she knew him.

In a further exchange with Kelly's solicitor, regarding other men she may or may not have known, Dickson's defiance continued unabated. Asked about Woolerton and why she allegedly told Kelly that he was going to batter her, she replied, "My private life doesn't come into this at all". When pressed for an answer, she told Livermore, "If you have all the evidence you ought to know all about it."

"Do you refuse to answer?", he asked.

"Yes I do because it is private."

After questioning her about her alleged conversation with Kelly in the *Caledonian* after the murders, and expressing doubt that Kelly would give her incriminating information and then threaten her, Livermore suddenly asked if she knew a man named Donald Thomas John Johnson. Dickson went pale, hesitated for a moment, then said, "I don't know whether I have seen him or not. I know a lot of people but I don't know their names." Livermore however did not pursue the matter.

On the second day, following the brief evidence of Detective Chief Superintendent Smith, Balmer entered the witness box. His replies would prove to be as sententious as Dickson's were obstructive.

After verifying the prosecution allegations about the interview with Skelly, the conversation between Kelly and Connolly in the Dale Street charge-room, and that between Kelly and O'Malley in the Bridewell, he was asked by Livermore about the hours immediately following the murder. Agreeing that the search of 67 Cambridge Street the morning after the murders revealed neither gun, overcoat or mask, he nevertheless stated that he had no knowledge of any other houses in the vicinity being searched during the night of March 19th and morning of the 20th. He wasn't called in until the Sunday morning. Pressing him, Livermore said, "I am asking if you know that a search was made in the neighbourhood on the night of the nineteenth?" Agreeing that a search was indeed made, he pedantically added, "Now you are getting more definite."

It was clear that Balmer did not intend to be any more helpful to the defence than Dickson and Northam.

Continuing, Livermore asked if the search was extensive, to which Balmer inconclusively replied that it would be, as far as the circumstances permitted. But pressed on this point, he reluctantly agreed that an extensive search of the neighbourhood was indeed made on the Saturday night/ Sunday morning.

When it was put to him that he had offered Kelly fifty pounds for information about the murders, Balmer, shaking his head, vehemently denied it. He then stated that he had paid Kelly on occasions for information but not about the Cameo murders.

Referring to the visit to Skelly's house, Livermore suggested that he first took Kelly to Prescot Street police station to get Skelly's address. "Definitely not", the Inspector replied. At this, Kelly shouted from the dock, "You took me to the police station!" Livermore, already considerably exasperated, turned on his client. "Look Kelly", he admonished, "just let me proceed."

After the furore subsided Balmer was asked about notes he had made regarding the visit with Kelly to Skelly's house on the Sunday morning. How could he remember exactly what Skelly had said but not Kelly? Giving a spontaneous answer which he hoped would explain Kelly's present antagonism towards him, he lied, "He just explained why he didn't like me."

As Balmer continued his evidence Kelly made further protests from the dock When describing the events surrounding Kelly's arrest and stating that he told him it was believed he had planned the crime in the *Beehive* with the others, Kelly's voice again resounded through the courtroom. "You didn't tell me that!", he cried. And later, when Balmer was relating the alleged conversation between Kelly and O'Malley in the Bridewell, he shouted out,

" I didn't say that. It is a confounded lie!"

Earlier, when Police Constable James Nugent had testified that he had seen Connolly and Kelly together on various occasions, Kelly had shouted out, "Its all lies!"

During these exchanges Connolly, unlike the excitable Kelly, although feeling equally indignant, remained calm, as he did throughout the hearing.

Resuming his evidence the following day, Balmer stated that Kelly's arrest followed an interview over an entirely different matter. And in answer to Livermore, he agreed that Kelly had denied throughout any involvement in the murders.

On the latter point, Balmer could hardly disagree. On the former, he did not tell the court that he had tricked Kelly by inviting him to Dale Street on the bogus promise of getting him a ship. And although Livermore was aware of this he never put it to the Inspector.

When Sangster, the store detective was cross-examined by Connolly's counsel, Gordon Clover, about his identification of the two men at the main Bridewell on October 10th, he said that up to four months ago he had seen Connolly about three times a week for about eight months. He agreed he knew a man named James Skelly. But Skelly, he said, was much broader and not quite as big as Connolly. "You could not mistake either of them", he said. Then added that he had seen Connolly in the company of Kelly on several occasions in town.

When the Committal proceedings finally closed on Saturday the 22nd October, Kelly and Connolly were sent in custody for trial at the next Liverpool Assizes. On the advice of their lawyers they reserved their defence and were granted legal counsel under the *Poor Persons Act.*

In addition to the widely-held belief that the police did not charge innocent people, the detailed daily reporting of the case in the local press had ensured widespread prejudice against the two men. Despite this however, and the fact that the jurors would be selected from the local area, it was never contemplated that the trial should be held anywhere else but Liverpool. Any suggestion to the contrary was unthinkable to the Prosecution and would be vigorously challenged.

Chapter Nineteen

Friday October 28th, 1949

"Heads you win, Tails I lose"

The prosecution, wishing the case to be tried locally and as quickly as possible, made application at Liverpool Assizes on October 28th for the trial to commence on Monday November the 7th. The defence, quite understandably, did not agree.

With smartly-dressed Kelly and Connolly sitting quietly in the dock, Miss Rose Heilbron K.C., who had been briefed to represent Kelly, argued before Mr. Justice Morris, that the defence would not have sufficient time to prepare their case if the trial was heard at these assizes. She requested that the trial should be transferred to Manchester, both to allow for more time, and because of the likelihood, following the widespread press coverage of the committal proceedings, of a prejudiced jury.

Appearing for the prosecution, Mr. William Gorman K.C., the Recorder of Liverpool, protested, stating that the trial should start the Monday after next. Stating that the prosecution alone had over forty witnesses, "…almost entirely police officers, professional men and residents of this city", he then rather curiously claimed that the case would only take a week to hear.

Reminding the court that the committal hearing had only finished the previous Saturday, Heilbron said, "The police have had since last March to make their enquiries and the defence have had only since the end of the committal proceedings." The date requested by Gorman was too soon. "There are forty one witnesses for the prosecution", she said, "and although the enquiries for the defence are by no means complete, there may be an equal number for the two prisoners."

She then submitted that the fairest way would be to transfer the trial to Manchester Assizes. This would give adequate time to prepare the men's defence without keeping them too long in custody.

Her application was supported by Connolly's junior barrister,

Gordon Clover, in the absence of his leading counsel, Basil Neild K.C.

Apparently unheeding of Heilbron's objection, and her clearly stated reasons for the objection, Mr. Justice Morris asked if she would be ready to proceed on November 7th as Gorman wished. "I hardly think so", she patiently replied, explaining that there were tremendous ramifications in the case and that defence witnesses were still being interviewed. This argument however didn't appear to elicit much sympathy from the judge, who then asked, "When was the defence instructed? Adding, "You have had some time already."

"A very short time", she immediately responded.

Heilbron explained that the men were arrested on September the 30th. The committal hearing took three and a half days but only the prosecution case was heard. "And", she said, "it was difficult to start dealing with the defence case until the prosecution's case was made known."

Asked by the judge if the defence would be ready sometime later during the week suggested by the prosecution, Heilbron, her patience now wearing thin, abruptly replied, "No it would not." She had, she said, been informed by her instructing solicitor that unless he was given adequate time he would not be able to do justice to the defence. "It is a difficult matter to rush", she went on. "Evidence may be overlooked if it is rushed - and vital evidence."

Arguing that it would be wrong to send the case to Manchester (a mere thirty miles away), Gorman, attempted to justify his objection by stating, "The whole circumstances are Liverpool circumstances. The whole of the witnesses are Liverpool witnesses." Apart from the irrelevance of this statement, it seemed the Recorder of Liverpool had either forgotten or conveniently overlooked the fact that his star witness, Jacqueline Dickson, was in fact a native of Manchester?

Continuing his rather spurious argument, Gorman told the court that the list for the next Manchester Assizes was extremely long, and that it would be wrong to transfer, "...*a case of this length* from the place where it is proper for it to be heard..." (My italics) Had he forgotten, or had he conveniently overlooked, telling the court earlier that the case would only take a week? And was Liverpool, after all the prejudicial press coverage, really the "proper place" for the men to

The Globe, Cases Street, today; unchanged since 1949.

3.

finding WHERE I STAY, I DONT KNOW HOW
you can get in touch with me i7 i
give my address you might charge me
with being an accesory, to the killing
i7 you put in the personal column o7
the Eiko And give me your word that
I wont be charged I will give you
both there names also some o7 the bullets
He le7t with me about 6 weeks ago
I can also tell you where he got
the gun 7rom He wants arresting for
selling then I can also tell you
who ran that stolen motor lorry
through the pub and killed a person
some time back i7 you give me your
word that I wont be charged

Section of the anonymous letter. Note the same 'g's.

MIND ————
HOW YOU GO ?
ON THE ROAD

Inspector — C.I.D.
Dale Street
Police Hedquaters
Liverpool

The envelope which contained the letter.

ENVELOPE ADDRESSED TO: MRS.DORIS O'MALLEY, 67 Cambridge Street,
Picton Road, Liverpool 15.

In replying to this letter, please write on the envelope:-

Number 7915.   Name: KELLY G.
                                         Liverpool Prison.

Dear Doris,

Hoping you and Doreen are okay. Well Doris you know in
your own heart and soul that I know nothing about this murder. Have you
been up to see Fred in the pub, he is the man who will save me, as for the
rest in the pub, there was the Harrison's, all the Poveys and a lot more
people who know me, all that night I was with Jimmy Skelly, but this girl
said she seen me in the Bee Hive with a gun, now every one knows that is
all lies, that night I came home it was 10p.m. and you was in the house
also little Boe Kelly. Doris this is a frame up by the police. Doris,
Fred knows that I was in his pub from 8.45p.m. until 10p.m. so how the hell
could I kill any-body. Will you please ask Fred to come and see me they
have got me in the Prison Hospital. This is a terrible thing to get the
blame for, when you know you haven't done it. Doris the whole trouble is,
Edt.Barmer and Smith don't know who as done it so the've blame poor Kelly
for it. I am going mad with the worry of it on my head all the time. I
know you will come to see me bring Fred with you. Did Mr.Livermore see
Fred yet, Doris, I must get away with this because I know nothing about it,
it is just a frame up job. Please help.

                         Still lots of love,

                         (SIGNED)   GEORGE.   XXXXXXXXX

Edited copy of Kelly's intercepted letter, bearing police markings

Harry Livermore, later knighted as Lord Mayor of Liverpool.

Liverpool's Pier Head circa 1949. The recently completed *Ark Royal* is in the river.

Johnnie Skelly in *Charlie Mathews'* 1958.

Miss Rose Heilbron. K.C.

Mr.. William Gorman. K.C.

Mr. Basil Nield. KC.

Mr. Justice Oliver.

Mr. Justice Cassels.

Lord Goddard.

St. George's Hall Liverpool; Scene of the 'Cameo' trials.

In replying to this letter, please write on the envelope:—

27. 2. 50

Number. 7.9.1.5... Name.... G. KELLY

....................................Prison

Dear, Harry

Doris as been up to see me and she as give me some very good news, But its no good if these people dont take action about it, Harry I cant believe I am sentenced to Death, I dont know the first thing about this Murder, why these people as blamed me

God only knows

No. 243   (21442—3-11-42)

Letter from George Kelly in the condemned cell to his friend Harry Harrison.

The Cameo Conspiracy

Well there his a lot of
people who knows I am
innocent of this crime, But
what Can we do about it,
Tell all The Boys I was
asking about them, Please
do me a favour, if I get
Hung for this Hurry please
try some day to prove
me innocent, I know it
will be to Late then, But
it will Clear my familys
Name, also it will get
those people in trouble
who Blamed me for it.

P3

There his one thing I can
do I can face God with
a Cleaur ~~Conscience~~ Conscience
so why should I werrey,
Herry Nobody knows what
it his like to be sentenced
to Death, when I know
in my own Mind That
I am a innocent man,
People can only do there
best fer me, That Latday
Night I left The Lee. Arms
pub, and went down to
the (spoford) fer a pint
Just to see if Dores

4

was there, I went in
there about 9.15 and
stayed there till 9.20.
I could not see Doris
so I went back to
the Lee Arms pub and
stayed till 10.PM. So Here
I am Convicted of Murder
The people who Blamed me
for this I have never seen
them in all my life, also
the Men who was charged
with me, I cant understand
it please. write me a letter
                  from George. Kelly.
             Good. Luck.

George Kelly

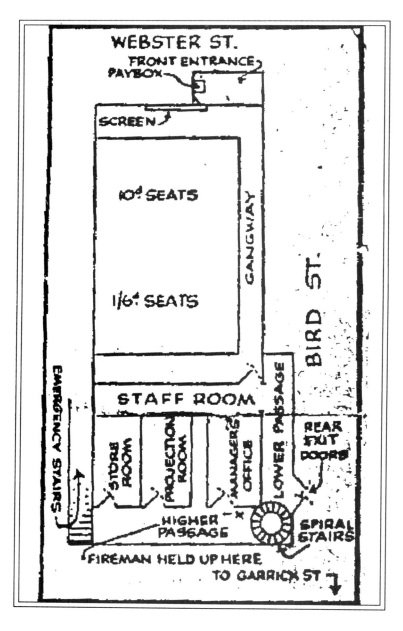

Layout of the Cameo Cinema, March 1949.

be tried?

Deriding the defence plea for more time, Gorman told the court that Kelly had been represented by a solicitor in the committal court and Connolly by a barrister, and that Kelly's solicitor had protested there should not be any delay in bringing to trial these men who he (Kelly's solicitor) said, "have a perfect answer to the charge."

But Heilbron pointed out that that remark had been made very early in the magistrates court in order to bring forward the committal hearing so that the accused would know the details of the case against them. "That evidence, voluminous evidence, has now been given", she said. And with regard to the alleged lengthy list at Manchester, she told the judge, "Whether there is a big list at Manchester is a matter your Lordship should consider as against justice in this case."

Addressing Gorman, the judge said that if the defence said they couldn't possibly be ready by the date he had requested, then must not he (the judge) accede to their request? Retreating somewhat in the face of this inescapable logic, Gorman replied, "I should be the last person on earth to take advantage of the defence." But then added, "I suggest that a few days elapse to see what progress has been made."

There was however to be no outright victory for the defence. The judge intimated that if he did postpone the trial it would not be to Manchester but to the next Liverpool Assizes starting in January. If that were the case, protested Heilbron, the two accused would be in custody for a long time, "...with this dreadful charge hanging over their heads." She then again submitted that the two men should be tried at the first available assizes, subject to their defence being ready - the implication being that this would be Manchester. The judge however, suddenly decided to adjourn the hearing until the following Tuesday, saying the defence should renew their application at that time.

When the hearing resumed on November the 1st Mr. Justice Morris ruled that Kelly and Connolly would be tried at the Liverpool Assizes starting in January next year.

It appeared the judge had thrown both the prosecution and the defence a bone. But although the trial might take a little longer to come on than Gorman would have liked, there was little doubt he had won the argument... and the first round.

Chapter Twenty

November, 1949

"In suspicious circumstances."

With Kelly and Connolly, and Kelly's alibi witness Skelly, safely locked up and out of circulation, Balmer diligently set about consolidating his case against the two men. Chief Superintendent Smith, however, continued to stress the fundamental weakness of their case - the lack of corroborative evidence. In order to redress this Balmer was most anxious to get a firm statement from Patrick Dowling, the Primrose cafe doorman, who had in October merely told the detectives that he *thought* he saw Kelly coming out of the *Globe* at about 7.30pm on March 19th.

He was also determined to obtain a statement from Norwegian Margie, that she had handed Kelly a dark apron in the *Beehive* to use as a mask on the murder night, and, more importantly, that she was present the following day in the *White Star* public house, when Kelly, in the company of Connolly, had admitted carrying out the murders. To this end his threats intensified.

Warning her that Northam and Dickson had made statements to the effect that she was the heavily made-up woman who had handed Kelly the apron, and was with him the next day in the *White Star*, he threatened that unless she co-operated she would be charged with being an accessory to the murder. Margie however, still refused to be intimidated. And although fearful of Balmer, she was adamant she was not going to swear an innocent man's life away - especially Kelly's, of whom she was quite fond.

Her attitude was most worrying to Balmer. If her determined resistance continued he was only too aware of how dangerous a loose cannon she could be. What if she came forward at the trial and told the truth about what really happened on March 19th? His case against Kelly and Connolly would be blown sky-high. His career would be in ruins. He might even end up in prison himself!

The pressure on Margie to sign a statement had to be kept up at all costs. And it was…until the early hours of November 11th. For just after midnight she was found dead in her rented bedsit at 44 Grove Street.

The previous evening she had arrived home at 9.10pm and, as was her usual practice, had gone into the front sitting room to have a chat with the landlady's married daughter, Evelyn Townsend, who was about the same age as herself. When Evelyn retired to bed at 11.30pm Margie went into the back parlour to have a chat with her mother, Mrs. Miriam Kravitz. But after about 15 minutes she suddenly left the house. When she returned shortly afterwards she went straight upstairs to her room. Moments later Miriam heard her daughter shouting down the stairs, "Quick, get the keys to Margie's room!"

Mother and daughter found it difficult gaining access to the room because of coats and a roll of newspaper packed behind the door. But when they eventually succeeded they were met with the sickening smell of coal gas and the horrifying sight of Margie lying fully-clothed on her bed, with a tube, leading from a wall gas bracket, stuck in her mouth. The latch was on the window and Margie's cat, Tiddles, was locked outside, crying on the window-ledge crying to get in.

Less than a quarter of a mile away at Olive Street police station, P.C. Granville was on desk duty when Evelyn arrived at 12.55am to report what had happened.

On arrival at the house, the constable noted that the window was open but the gas tube was still lodged in Margie's mouth. Tiddles was now on the bed mewing around her lifeless body.

At the inquest a few days later, the verdict was that Margie had "committed suicide whilst the balance of her mind was disturbed". She had apparently left a suicide note. But her sister, Mrs. Frances Penfold, who had been contacted in the small village of Brinnington near Stockport, doubted that Margie had written it. In a sworn affidavit, she stated, "I have seen the (suicide)note and the writing does not look like my sister's. But *I have been informed that she was under the influence of alcohol* before the occurrence and this may account for me not knowing the writing." (My italics).

This was very strange because although Frances had been "informed" that her sister had been under the influence, the pathologist's report, whilst sufficiently detailed to record blood levels and stomach contents etc., made no mention whatever of any alcohol in the body Also, the original statement made by Mrs. Kravitz, appeared to have been altered to indicate that Margie had been drinking. It ran thus:- "The (first floor) room was sublet to Margaret on 2nd September 1948 It was let to her and her "husband". Two months ago (i.e. approx September 11th 1949) Margie told me the man was not her husband. They had a quarrel and I turned the man out. On 10th November at 11.30pm Margie came into my living-room and sat there for about 15 minutes. *She appeared quite normal."* (My italics) Between this line and the next line however, the words, *"but she had been drinking"* had been inserted.

The statement continued, "She left the house and returned about five minutes later. At 12.05am my daughter shouted, ' Get the keys to Margie's room! ` The cat was outside on the window sill. The window was closed. She was a happy person and was often under the influence of drink".

Apart from the inserted words - which were clearly added later - nowhere else in the statement did Mrs. Kravitz mention Margie having had any alcohol that particular night. Nor did Evelyn, who had been talking with Margie from 9.10pm, make any mention in her statement of her having drunk any alcohol. Indeed, she specifically stated that there was nothing unusual about Margie that night. Even the constable who examined the scene made no mention of any trace of alcohol or empty bottles in the room. And of course, the pathologist's report did not reveal any alcohol in the body.

There were many questions which perhaps could have been asked at the inquest but which were not. For example: Who informed Margie's sister that she was under the influence of alcohol before her death? Who altered, or who persuaded Miriam Kravitz to alter, her statement? Why did Margie go out for five minutes immediately before her death? Where did she go?. Who, if anyone, did she meet? Why did it take Evelyn almost an hour to arrive at Olive Street when it was only five minutes walk away? And why was the cat put out on the windowsill?

Surely if Margie did not want Tiddles, or anyone in the house, to be harmed by the gas (as seems likely from the precautions she took with the coats and roll of newspaper) would she not have put it on the landing where it would be safe, rather than precariously balanced outside on the window ledge?. And even if the "house rules" forbade this, would she really care at this desperate stage about violating such rules?

The "suicide note" was written in pencil on the back of a title page of a Western paperback. It simply said, "Please don't class this as disturbance of mind. I'm just fed up. Terry knows why. She has tried everything and Pinkie agrees. God help Tony. Look after" (here the name was indecipherable but was probably "Tiddles".)

The word "why" was underlined twice. The note was unsigned.

On the other side of the page, near the top was the printed title of the book, "*The Flying Cowboys*". The remainder of the page was blank apart from the following list, also in pencil, which appeared to be an inventory made by a male:-

Ring" (the next word struck out) "Gold and (word indecipherable).

> *2 coat hangers.*
> *Front stud.*
> *Razor.*
> *Shaving Cream.*
> *Hair Oil.*
> *4lbs Sugar.*
> *Sweet Coupons*
> *Ointment.*
> *1 Pack cards.*
> *1 Photograph.*
> *1 girl...money from Germany.*

Below this list were written the words, " F' rom (sic) Matt and you have till 2-clock. Terry is going Home today." These two short sentences and the preceding list did not appear to be in the same handwriting as the "suicide note".

Who were "Terry" and "Pinkie" and "Tony" and "Matt"? Had they been traced they may have been able to shed some light on Margie's sudden death - particularly "Terry", who apparently knew "why" she was so fed up. Liverpool City Police however apparently did not consider her death important enough to bother tracing them. Their identities remain unknown.

On 14th November, Chief Inspector Balmer finally managed to cajole Dowling into signing a prepared statement, stating that he "definitely" saw Kelly leaving the *Globe* in Cases street on March 19th at 7.30pm.

The statement ran: "On Saturday March 19th I was at the front door of No.15 Cases Street. It was between 7.30pm and 8.00pm because I'd had my Tea and I always go for Tea at 7.00pm until 7.30pm. And I had been at the door for a few minutes when I saw George Kelly come out of the *Globe* public house, 17 Cases Street, which is next door to us. He came out of the public house and I saw him walk towards Ranelagh Street and he turned to the left and out of my sight. I do not remember what he was dressed in. I do not work on a Sunday. And either on the following Monday or Tuesday I again saw Kelly. It would be about 4.00pm. He passed our cafe and he stopped and spoke to me. He said, ` What do you think Paddy, I've been questioned about the Cameo job`. I said, ` Don't be silly, everyone in that district has been questioned`. *My mind went back* to the time I had last seen him, which was between 7.30pm and 8.00pm on the previous Saturday, but I don't think I mentioned that to him. He then walked away. I've seen him on many occasions since but the Cameo affair has never been mentioned." (My italics)

Armed with this statement, significantly containing like Corrie's and Ellis's, his own cliched phrase, "my mind went back", a buoyant Balmer wrote a self-congratulatory report to Smith, pointing out the statement's value in breaking Kelly's alibi:-

"At 4.30pm on November 14th, I interviewed Patrick Dowling, a member of the Corps of Commissioners, living at 56 Scarisbrick Crescent, Liverpool 11, and at present engaged as a doorman at the cafe 15 Cases Street. Dowling is an ex-sergeant major of the army and a man of unblemished character. As I understand that Kelly is going to deny that he was anywhere within that vicinity, this witness's evidence will be valuable."

Smith was accordingly very pleased with his Chief Inspector's work. But, he reminded him, "We still don't have a corroborative witness Bert."

With Margie's death, although convenient to him in many ways, Balmer was only too aware of his desperate need to find another corroborative witness. In the event he didn't have to wait long.

Chapter Twenty-one

November 1949 - January 1950.

> *"Agree to a short Armistice with the Truth."*
> *- Lord Byron*

By November, the forty one year-old convict, Robert Graham, who had in September given Balmer a statement about Johnson admitting to the murder, was back in Walton. He had been remanded in custody on a charge of receiving.

According to a report made by Balmer at the time, Graham, on the 21st of November after appearing at Preston magistrates court, asked a detective to contact the Liverpool C.I.D. as he had some information about the Cameo murders. (1). The detective didn't hesitate. He knew Graham must be genuine because he had given valuable information to the Preston police many times. He therefore telephoned the Liverpool police and was told the officer in charge of the case was Detective Chief Inspector Balmer. When Balmer subsequently interviewed Graham at Walton later that day he, according to Balmer's report, told him he was a cleaner in the hospital wing, and because Kelly and Connolly weren't allowed to exercise together, he exercised with them separately on alternate days. Both of them had confessed their parts in the murder to him, he told Balmer.

After several more visits to Graham at Walton and later at Strangeways, Manchester, Balmer stated that he had obtained a full signed statement from him.

The report continued: "Graham said, 'I want to tell you something about the Cameo cinema murders, if you want to hear it'. He then went on to say, 'On Monday last, the 14th of November, I was in the hospital at Walton prison. Charles Connolly was inside for the murder at the Cameo cinema, and George Kelly is also in the hospital. They are not allowed to exercise together and I do exercise with each of them on alternate days. On Tuesday last I was on exercise with Connolly. We were walking around together and he started telling me what he was in for. That was in the morning, In the afternoon we exercised again, and the subject we talked about again was the murder. He asked me how I thought he would go on. I said, 'I don't know enough about your part to say' He replied, 'Well I had nothing to do with the murder other than being with the same company, with the fellow who did it.' I said, 'How do you mean?' And he said, 'I was with Kelly in the pub about half-seven. A girl named Jacqueline Dickson and a fellow named Stuttering Northam was there too'."

Balmer's report went on to say that Connolly told Graham he didn't shoot anyone and that when he went with Kelly he didn't know there was going to be any shooting. Connolly allegedly then said, "Will you be seeing Kelly tomorrow?" and Graham said, "I don't know Kelly." To which Connolly replied, "Well you'll get to know him. He's on bottom O.C."

The Inspector's report continued, "When leaving Graham he asked if I would see him again in case there were any other items which he had forgotten. At 11.20am on the 23rd of November I again saw him at Liverpool Prison and he made the following statement. 'I wanted to see you to see if you had written down what I told you last time. That is this, on the Tuesday afternoon when I saw Connolly he also said to me 'if we can get at those two, Dickson and Stuttering Northam, we're alright. Half of my relations are in the Peanut gang, and there are some more of the gang in here. If they can get hold of those two they'll make it so they can't give evidence. Kelly's brothers are looking for them too, and if they find them it will be the same'."

On the 26th of November Graham, according to Balmer, told him that on his way from exercise he'd said to Connolly, "How are things?" and Connolly had replied, "Oh alright. The wife's got a photograph of Jacqueline, and her address in Birkenhead so they'll soon get hold of her." Graham said he was then taken away and didn't speak to him anymore.

During these prison visits, said the report, Graham also signed statements saying that Kelly had confessed to him that he had shot the two men; of how many witnesses he had; of how it was "queer" how he came to be arrested because he had gone down to Dale Street to see "an Inspector" about a totally different matter; and of how he was in his "own pub" five minutes after committing the murders; of how the police couldn't break his alibi "in a thousand years", and of how his life hung on that five minutes.

On the 28th November at Strangeways, said Balmer, he again interviewed Graham. Then after stating that he had reiterated his willingness to give evidence, he said, "although Graham has a long list of convictions, he has made a very interesting statement." His report rather officiously ended, "I suggest that the file now be sent to Mr Bishop (prosecuting solicitor) for his information."

Contrary to Balmer's report however, the truth was quite different. For although Graham had indeed signed the statement, it was neither spontaneous nor genuine. It had been dictated by Balmer after extensive coaching. The initial meeting between them had not been instigated by Graham on the 21st of November but by Balmer two days earlier on the 19th. (2) Graham had not initially offered any statement simply because he didn't know anything about the case. Between September and his arrest in November he had been working on a trawler out of Fleetwood. And although he did exercise at the same times as Kelly and Connolly, they each preferred to walk around with fellow Liverpool prisoners, regarding him as a simple "woollyback" from the sticks.

The false statement came about because Balmer, desperately searching for a corroborative witness, discovered that Graham was back in Walton. He visited him there on Saturday November the 19th and asked if he was prepared to do a deal by giving evidence against Kelly and Connolly, as he had against Johnson.

Having secured Graham's agreement to co-operate in principle, his next priority was to distance himself from any future charges of procurement or inducement. He hadn't forgotten the roasting he and his colleagues had received from Heilbron and the D.P.P. over the inducements to Donald Johnson, which had resulted in the latter's acquittal. He therefore told Graham that when he made a remand appearance in two days time at Preston magistrates, he was to ask to speak to the Liverpool police about the Cameo murders. The message he told Johnson, would automatically come to him as the officer in charge of the case. Then there would be a valid reason to visit him at Walton for as often as was necessary, to get his statement right.

On the following Monday November the 21st, a message was duly received at C.I.D. Central from a Detective Gregory of Preston saying that a remand prisoner wished to speak to the Liverpool police about the Cameo murders.

Later that day when Balmer, accompanied by Farragher, visited Graham at Walton, he asked if Kelly or Connolly had actually told him anything. "Well not really", he replied. "What, nothing?" said Farragher. "Well what are you wasting our fucking time for?" Unruffled, Graham quietly replied, "Well, Kelly just says he's innocent. He keep's saying that to everyone, and that he's got loads of witnesses who can prove it. But Connolly, he won't even talk about it. I tried to approach him and get him to talk about it but he's a bit of a snob. D'you know what he said to me? He said, 'if you don't mind I'd prefer to walk on my own', and then walked away from me."

Balmer, his mind racing ahead, said, "Don't worry about that, so long as you're prepared to sign a statement and give evidence in the witness box"

"Well, I don't know about that", said Graham, anxious to gain the maximum benefit from the deal. "A mean it could be very risky. I could be knifed in here or get my head kicked in or something, couldn't I? You know what I mean like, false evidence." He then added threateningly, "Oh I'm not really sure about this."

Balmer reassured him he would come to no harm if he co-operated. "We'll have you transferred to Strangeways before their trial starts", he promised. But Graham wasn't obliging so readily. "Well", he said, "there's the other matter of this charge I'm up on. I mean, with my form I'm expecting quite a long stretch."

"Look", said Balmer, "we know these two bastards done this murder but we just need a bit more evidence to get them convicted. You help us to win this case and I guarantee you, not only will you get a light sentence, you'll get extra remission too. You help us and I give you my word you'll be out in no time." This didn't sound so bad a deal. So with nothing to lose and everything to gain, Graham finally agreed to sign a statement which would be prepared for him. Balmer couldn't believe his good fortune. Only seven days after the inquest on Norwegian Margie he had found the ideal corroborative witness - much better than Margie would ever have been

During the following weeks Balmer and Farragher visited Graham on two further occasions, and when he was transferred to Strangeways on the 28th November, twice further. Their last visit of the 9th of January 1950 resulted in the final version of Graham's lengthy statement. His story of how the two men had confessed to him their parts in the murders was now word perfect. He had been a most willing and able pupil.

Not trusting to Graham's statement alone, Balmer continued to build a most damning case against the two men - particularly Kelly. At one stage, he had six prostitutes agreeing to say they had seen Kelly with Dickson around Lime Street. Smith however, suspecting that he had obtained their co-operation by threats, told him to forget it The police case, he said, was already over-reliant on unsavoury characters and prostitutes. Balmer, by overdoing it might ruin the whole case. Furthermore, he said, prostitutes were notoriously unreliable. They would be discredited and torn to shreds by a clever K.C. - especially a woman like Rose Heilbron, whom he'd heard had been engaged to defend Kelly.

After reading the newspaper reports of the committal proceedings, Johnnie Skelly, called at Livermore's office and told him about the incident in Charlie Mathews's the day after the murder.

It was he who was in the pub that day, he said. And neither his son Jimmy nor George Kelly had been there. "But how do you know they weren't there after you left?", said a cynical Livermore. Because, he replied, according to the papers they were supposed to have been there since 1.00pm but he had been there at that time and hadn't left until about a quarter past.

Livermore, who was Johnnie's local councillor, had known him for several years. Aware of his fondness of a drink, he'd often given him beer money at election time for helping to drum up votes, and for introducing compensation claim clients. Now, looking up from his desk, he insultingly said, "What are you after now Johnnie, a few quid witness expenses?" He then added chidingly, "Look this is no Compo lark. This is serious. A murder case. Way out of your league. Now go away and stop wasting my time."

Disgusted at Livermore's attitude, Johnnie left feeling quite hopeless. There didn't seem much point in taking it any further. If Kelly's mouthpiece didn't believe him, he thought, then what chance would he have with the C.I.D.?

Throughout the long monotonous wintry days of November and December Kelly and Connolly languished in the prison's hospital wing. With the other prisoners roaming freely around the corridors, they often felt like caged animals in a zoo behind the bars of their cells. To make matters worse they were still not allowed to do any work or associate with the other prisoners. The only bright spots on this bleak landscape were the visits from their families and a few friends.

One of the latter was Peter Sherlock, a close friend of Connolly's who lived in Great Newton Street near to the Bullring. He had received two letters from Connolly asking him to visit. But each time he tried he was refused admission at the prison gate. He didn't know why. Perhaps it was because his friend was on a murder charge. Whatever the reason he eventually resigned himself to their refusal. On the 14th of December however, unaware that Connolly's and Kelly's letters were routinely copied to the police, he was visited at home by a detective constable.

Telling him only that he knew he was a friend of Connolly's, the detective asked, since he lived so close to Trowbridge Street, if he knew Kelly? Yes he did. But not to speak to. Had he ever seen Kelly and Connolly in each other's company? No he hadn't. That was a pity, the detective said, because if he could provide a statement saying that the two men knew each other, arrangements could be made for him to visit Connolly as often as he wished.

When it was reported back to Balmer that Sherlock had immediately rejected the proposition, he became very worried. What if news of this blatant attempt to procure false evidence reached the defence solicitors? He would have to cover himself. And the best way would be to strike first and discredit Sherlock. So, in collusion with the detective constable and a uniformed sergeant, he concocted a story to do just that.

The story was that Sherlock had been telephoning the sergeant to get permission to visit Connolly. In response the detective constable called at Sherlock's house and left a message for him to ring the sergeant that evening. When he did so, he said, "Would you be able to fix up for me to see my mate Charlie Connolly. He has written two letters asking me to visit him and the Warder won't let me in because they know me." The sergeant told him he would have to see Chief Inspector Balmer. He called to a suburban police station on the 16th of December but the Inspector advised him to see Connolly's solicitor. Sherlock however, said he'd already seen him and he could not help. Balmer then promised to do what he could and asked Sherlock to call at the C.I.D. Dale Street office the next morning. But early the next morning a message was left at Sherlock's home, telling him not to call at Dale Street because permission could not be obtained. On the following Monday however, Sherlock called to see Balmer and handed him a bullet saying, "I might as well give you this. Connolly was fighting in Lime Street one night after the Cameo. He was fighting another man and when they finished I picked up this bullet and a key. I don't know which of them dropped it but you can guess."

This crudely implausible story was type-written and filed as a report. And in order to consolidate the discrediting of Connolly's friend (and a potentially damaging defence witness), a handwritten note at the top of the page said that Sherlock was an informant of the sergeant's.

In the event Sherlock, who was unaware of the report, did not tell anyone about the detective's corrupt offer. But just in case he did, the filed report, and the word of three police officers, would surely be enough to spike any accusation he might make against the C.I.D. Yet despite Sherlock's alleged incriminating "evidence" against Connolly, the matter was never pursued by the police. Nor was the so-called report ever offered in evidence. Indeed it was never mentioned again.

Four days later on Tuesday the 20th of December, the two accused men were visited by their solicitors and told who would be representing them at the assizes. Connolly was to be defended by Basil Neild K.C., who, in addition to being the Conservative Member of Parliament for Chester, was also the Recorder of Salford.

When Kelly learned that a woman, Rose Heilbron K.C., was to defend him he thought he'd come off worst. "Hey Charlie", his voice echoed along the corridor that night, "I'm not happy with this at all. Why couldn't I have a fella, like you've got? Whoever heard of a judy defending anyone?"

"I don't know so much", Connolly's voice echoed back, "I believe she's great. She defended that Johnson fella a few months ago, yer know. Got him off with it as well. Can't be that bad can she?"

A few days later Kelly was to actually meet his barrister when, accompanied by Livermore, she visited him for a briefing session. After she'd left he felt more hopeful than he'd ever been since his arrest. He could somehow sense that she believed in his innocence, and got the feeling she would do her very best for him.

That evening the sound of his voice, imitating Al Jolson, could be heard reverberating around the hospital wing, *"Rosie you are my posy. You are my heart's bouquet. Come on out into the moonlight, there's something sweet love I wanna say..."* He'd added another song to his repertoire, and this one he would wishfully sing almost every night from now on.

On the 10th of January 1950, with only two days remaining before the trial commenced, Balmer finally solved the problem of Thomella's inconclusive statement.

Calling at *the Leigh Arms* with two other detectives in an unmarked car at 5.25pm, he asked if Thomella would accompany them down to C.I.D. Central. He wanted him to look at some mugshots of people he thought might also be involved in the murders. Thomella protested at first, saying that he was due to open up any minute. But Balmer persuaded him, saying it would only take about twenty minutes.

It was dark and raining as the police car, its windows steamed up, travelled down London Road. Balmer, sitting in the back with Thomella, suddenly produced a piece of paper. "Oh by the way Fred", he said innocuously, "before I forget. You know the statement you made in October? Well unfortunately we've mislaid the signed original. But it's not important really. Luckily we kept a typed copy. I wonder would you mind signing it again for me?"

"Sure", said the unsuspecting Thomella. "Just there at the bottom of the page", said Balmer. Then, with a flattering reference to Thomella's twenty-three years police service, he added, "You know the drill Fred."

Thomella hadn't bothered to read the statement before signing it. And even if he had tried to do so it would have been impossible in the darkened car. But he had no reason to distrust his former colleagues. Statements did get lost and mislaid, he knew that from his own experience. What he didn't know however was that he had signed a crucially altered statement. For where he had originally stated, "*I cannot say whether or not* he (Kelly) was in the house between those times", his statement now read, "I am quite *definite* that Kelly was not in the house between 9.00pm and 9.50pm on the night of March the 19th". (My italics) (3)

By the use of the word "definite" the statement clearly bore Balmer's hallmark. And in order to establish it as superseding Thomella's earlier statement of October the 4th, he had written at the top of the page, "London Road. 5.30pm January 10th 1950."

Later when the hapless Thomella left Dale Street to make his own way back home in the rain, Balmer stretched out behind his desk and allowed himself a broad smile. All in all, a good day's work. Tom Smith and the Chief Constable would be really pleased. They now had a virtually air-tight case.

(1) Balmer's report. Merseyside Police files.
(2) Sworn on oath by Graham at first trial. On this point he had no reason to lie.
(3) Thomella's statements of October 4th 1949 and 10th January 1950. Merseyside Police files

Chapter Twenty - two

"Two and Two equals Five."
- George Orwell

The trial opened on the 12th January 1950 in No 1 Assize Court at St. George's Hall before Mr. Justice Oliver, who nineteen years earlier, as Roland Oliver KC., had led for the defence in the famous Wallace murder case in this same courtroom. (1)

Situated at the northern end of the famous Lime Street and surrounded by the Old Sessions House, the Museum, Walker Art Gallery and the vast William Brown and Picton libraries, the neo-classical nineteenth century building was the centre- piece of the city's civic and cultural quarter. In its shadows, the prostitute Maggie May of sea shanty fame had allegedly plied her trade

Housing as it did, the Liverpool Assizes, the building's imposing architectural grandeur was most appropriate to the legal *cause celebre* which was to be played out there during the next thirteen days. And, ironically, one of the main characters in the drama which was to unfold was also a Lime Street prostitute, whose name would become synonymous with the Cameo case - twenty three year-old Jacqueline Dickson.

By 10.00am the public gallery was filled by members of the public who had camped out all night in order to secure a place. Hundreds more congregated outside on St. George's Plateau, hoping to gain admission, but were moved on by the police.

The Prosecution was led by William Gorman KC., assisted by Mr. Glyn Blackledge. Gorman regularly presided over the city's Quarter Sessions in the Sessions House across the road in Islington. Indeed only a few months earlier he had dismissed Skelly's appeal against the six- month prison sentence imposed at the magistrates court the previous May. (Kelly had meanwhile been arrested for the Cameo murder and his appeal was not proceeded with). (2)

Kelly was defended by the 35 year-old Rose Heilbron KC.,

who had won Johnson's acquittal the previous June. Born in Liverpool this first class honours law graduate and daughter of a Liverpool hotelier was already gaining recognition in legal circles as a brilliant advocate. Having taken silk the previous year, it was her first murder trial since being called to the bar ten years earlier, and the first time a woman had led in a capital case. (3) Her junior was Mr. R.S. Trotter.

Representing Connolly was Basil Neild KC., assisted by Gordon Clover who had appeared for Connolly during the Committal hearing.

This glittering array of legal talent was provided for the accused men on legal aid.

When Ian McCaulay, the Clerk of the Court, declared, "Bring up Charles Connolly and George Kelly", the two well groomed, smartly dressed, young men entered the dock between three prison warders. Connolly was wearing a brown double-breasted suit, white shirt and blue tie, and Kelly, a smartly-cut grey suit, white shirt and American style blue tie. In reply to the charge of murdering Leonard Thomas both men replied in strong clear voices, "Not Guilty."

Another eleven minutes elapsed whilst the jury of ten men and two women were empanelled, during which time Kelly, ignoring the warders reproving gestures, defiantly strolled across the dock to converse with his solicitor Livermore.

In his opening address for the Crown, Gorman dramatically announced that he would be submitting startling new evidence which had come to light since the men had been committed for trial the previous October. This concerned, he said, confessions which were alleged to have been made by both Kelly and Connolly to a go-between, a man named Robert Graham, whilst on remand in the hospital wing of Walton prison.

Forty-one year -old Graham had a criminal record and psychiatric history. He was awaiting trial for receiving stolen property having just finished a twelve month sentence for defrauding the wives of prisoners by obtaining money from them on the pretence of being able to facilitate goods and favours for their husbands in prison. Nonetheless, he was a godsend to the prosecution. The late introduction of his testimony would provide the vital independent corroborative evidence to that of the "part-accomplices", Dickson and Northam.

Outlining the case against the two accused, previously made at the Committal Court and thoroughly ventilated in both Liverpool evening newspapers, Gorman told the jury that Kelly and Connolly set out on that Saturday night wilfully intending to commit robbery with violence. And notwithstanding that Connolly waited outside the cinema, he was nonetheless there to help Kelly. - " to warn him, to give him assistance, to prevent surprise, to be near enough to help him if necessary. He was therefore in law aiding and abetting. It is our submission", he went on, "that although Kelly shot and murdered Leonard Thomas, Connolly - who took part in this nefarious and deadly scheme to give such help as was necessary - is also guilty, although it was not his hand that shot."

Recounting to the jury the events of the night of March 19th, Gorman said that the Cameo was a one-time Methodist Church which had been converted to a cinema. It's main entrance was in Webster Road off the main Smithdown Road, and there was a side exit door opening into Bird Street, a small street at the side of the building. It was the normal practice, he said, for the cashier to take the money from the pay box to the manager's office at about 9.30pm. each evening.

On the night of the murder, Mrs. Jackman, had put the takings of some £50 into a cash bag and taken it to the manager's office, where the manager and assistant manager were counting the confectionery takings. After delivering the money, Jackman and ice-cream girl, Valerie June Thornhill, left the office and joined Supervisor, Mona Watkins, in the nearby staff-room. All three then heard a series of loud bangs. Mrs. Watkins first rushed to the Projection room. But although nothing was amiss there, she did notice the clock said 9.35 pm.

Meanwhile, said Gorman, Griffin the fireman, who had been putting up posters outside, had come up the spiral staircase. These staff members, now congregated outside the manager's office, saw the wooden partition in which the office door was set., rattling. It was as if someone inside was trying to get out. There were then two shots at the lock and a gunman came out brandishing a gun, telling them to "Stand back". He had something like a black scarf covering the lower part of his face and was wearing a brown tweed overcoat and a brown trilby hat, pulled down all around. He also wore black shoes and seemed to have dark eyes and dark hair. The man, continued Gorman , ran down the spiral staircase, out of the cinema into Bird Street and then along Garrick Street towards Smithdown Road.

Telling the jury that the Bird Street exit was a double door with a push bar across it on the inside, Gorman described how the usherette Phyllis Stevens, upon hearing the shots, ran to this door, where she was usually posted, and saw the gunman trying to get out. "She got a good view of him", he said, because, *"he was unable to open that door as quickly as he might have done, and while he was fumbling with the door and the bar* she got a good look at him". (My italics)

Gorman had apparently forgotten, or didn't know, the prosecution evidence given at the Committal court, that Kelly had actually entered the cinema through this door a few minutes earlier.

Continuing, Gorman said that Mrs. Watkins entered the office and saw Mr. Thomas and Mr. Catterall lying on the floor both badly wounded or maybe dead. Catterall was lying behind the door. Also lying on the floor was the rim of the inside of the door's lock and there was money scattered around. Mrs. Watkins, seeing pools of blood, and "everything in a frightful state", shouted for help.

Gorman then related how Griffin had chased after the gunman as far as Garrick Street and returned to phone the police, but discovering that the telephone wires had been cut, again went outside where he saw a policeman and the Simpson's, who got Mrs. Jones to dial 999.

The call to the police was recorded at precisely 9.45pm. Taking this fact with the statements of Mrs. Jackman and usherette Phyllis Stevens, the prosecution submitted the time of the shootings was 9.35pm.

In addition to the door lock on the floor, said Gorman, the police had also found six 9 mm cartridges, a damaged cartridge case, two bullet cores and a damaged bullet core. All were of German origin and had been fired from the same weapon, a self-loading P38 automatic pistol, the type of which was standard issue to German Officers in the war.

One bullet was recovered from the body of Leonard Thomas, said Gorman. Catterall, although suffering additional exit wounds had been shot twice - in the right breast and in the back, the first bullet going straight through his raised hand and on though his breast. It was later found in the wainscoting. Only one bullet was found in his body. Despite being scattered over the office floor, no money had actually been stolen, he added.

On October 14th, two weeks after Kelly and Connolly had been charged, and almost eight months after the murder, Gorman said the police, acting on certain information, recovered from a sewer off Brownlow Hill, a bullet the same size and general type as the ammunition found in the bodies of the dead men and those traced by reason of the cartridge cases. "The significance of that bullet will appear later", he said promisingly. He then proceeded to present the Crown's case against the two accused.

Dickson and Northam came to Liverpool from Birkenhead on the night of March 19th, arriving at the *Beehive* public house in Mount Pleasant at about 7.30pm. Northam was carrying his overcoat over his arm. Connolly was already there drinking alone in the passageway. Dickson introduced Connolly, whom she had known for three or four years, to Northam. Kelly, whom she had also known for four or five years, arrived about fifteen minutes later.

Kelly asked if he could borrow Northam's overcoat, tried it on and said it was "a smashing fit." This was the overcoat, said Gorman, which would later be identified as that worn by the gunman at the Cameo. (4)

All four then began discussing various "jobs". Connolly suggested breaking into a warehouse in Islington but somebody said it was alarmed. Kelly suggested robbing a stall at the fun fair in New Brighton. Connolly then asked Dickson to lure a taxi-driver and police informer named Harry, who was "loaded", up a side street so they could "roll" him. Dickson refused. Connolly then mentioned a "smashing job" at the Cameo cinema in Webster Road, adding that a gun or a dummy gun would be needed. Kelly, said, "I have got just the thing" and pulled out a gun from his back pocket. He said it was a 38. "As he was placing the shells in the gun he was swearing because it was not easy getting them in", said Gorman.

Dickson told him to put the gun away in case he was seen but he replied, "I don't care who sees me. My name's Kelly." He then put a cartridge in the breach of the gun and returned it to his back pocket. Next he tied a handkerchief around his face but it would not fit. A dark heavily-made-up woman then came from the back room and gave him a brown scarf out of a holdall and Kelly said, "This will do fine". Northam was invited by Kelly to go with them but he said he wanted no part of it because he didn't like guns or those who used them.

Kelly, Connolly and Dickson eventually left the *Beehive* between 8.20 and 8.30 pm and went across the road to the No.8 tram stop. But although Dickson waited with them, she had second thoughts when the tram arrived and went back to the pub. The couple then returned to Birkenhead, although it had earlier been agreed that all four would meet at lunch-time the following day in a public house called the *"Star"* in Brownlow Hill, otherwise known as *"Charlie's."*

When Connolly and Kelly arrived at the Cameo - a fourteen minute tram journey according to Gorman - Kelly, went and showed himself in various public houses, without hat or overcoat, in order to establish an alibi. He then returned to Connolly, who had been loitering in the vicinity of the cinema. Then, after the lights went out in the foyer both men went to the side door in Bird Street. Connolly refused to go any further but said he would keep watch outside. Kelly then entered the cinema and committed the murders.

When Kelly dashed out of the cinema minutes later Connolly had gone. Kelly ran towards Smithdown Road, but then doubled-back and quickly made his way to the *Leigh Arms* in Picton Road, where he was seen entering the Buffet at 9.50pm without overcoat or trilby.

In the *Leigh Arms*, said Gorman, Kelly proceeded to make himself as conspicuous as possible; treating a taxi-driver and his lady friend, both of whom he hardly knew, to drinks, and offering to buy the licensee and staff drinks. At one stage the taxi driver asked him had he been in the sun and he replied, "No, I've been having a go." He then boasted, "You can't take liberties with Kelly."

The following morning at 11.15am Detective Chief Inspectors Balmer, Morris, and Detective Sergeant Farragher visited Kelly's girlfriend's home at 67 Cambridge Street, which was five minutes away from the Cameo. When asked to account for his movements the previous night, Kelly told Inspector Balmer he had been with Jimmy Skelly in the *Coach & Horses* public house at opening time but left him and went downtown. He went back at 9.00pm, saw Skelly was drunk so left the pub and caught a tram to the *Leigh Arms* pub in Picton Road at the top of Cambridge Street, *where he stayed till closing time.* (My italics).

At this point Gorman seemed to be unaware of the basic contradiction in his argument. He had first alleged Kelly had deliberately shown himself in various public houses in order to establish an alibi. Now he was asserting, that Kelly had only told Balmer about being in the *Leigh Arms*!

The house, 67 Cambridge Street, was searched, continued Gorman, but no gun, overcoat, trilby or mask was found. The officers then accompanied Kelly to Skelly's house. Skelly did not remember being with Kelly the previous evening. He said Kelly might have been one of the people who brought him home but he was too drunk to remember. The officers then drove Kelly back to Cambridge Street.

Later the same day Skelly and Connolly were in the *Star* public house, on the corner of Clarence Street and Brownlow Hill in the city centre, which was near to Kelly's mother's home. Northam and Dickson arrived at 1.00pm and Kelly arrived shortly afterwards, accompanied by the dark, heavily made-up girl of the previous evening. Connolly, looking pale and frightened, said he wanted to get out of the country and Skelly offered to get him a ship. Kelly called him a yellow bastard for running away instead of keeping watch. He then told them all, "That bastard Balmer was at our house this morning. If I'd still had the gun he wouldn't have stood there so cocksure of himself." He then said to Connolly that he'd probably get a visit from Balmer. And if he did he must say he did not know him. He also told Connolly to get himself an alibi and Connolly said he would fix one up with his wife. Kelly then threatened them all that if they did not keep their mouths shut they would be shut by him or his brothers. Northam asked for his overcoat and Kelly said he would return it the following day.

That evening, in response to a telephone call, the police interviewed Edward Ellis, the manager of the *Spofforth Hotel*, a pub only three minutes away from the Cameo. He told them that Kelly had been in his pub the previous evening at about 9.20pm and had stayed for about three minutes.

On the Monday afternoon of March 21st Northam and Dickson travelled from Birkenhead to Lime Street. Dickson left Northam in Lime Street for about an hour, during which time, he met Kelly at 2.00pm on wasteland opposite the *Adelphi Hotel*. Northam asked for his overcoat and Kelly said he would go and get it. Fifteen minutes later he returned with the overcoat and told Northam he should burn it. He said he would have got rid of it but feared it would be traced back to Northam.

Northam told Kelly he had made an awful mess of the Cameo job but Kelly told him to shut his fucking mouth. And after blaming Connolly for not keeping watch outside, Kelly then described in detail how he committed the murders.

He told Northam that Connolly would not go in the cinema and only went as far as the side door. Complaining that Connolly should have warned him that Catterall was coming up the stairs, Kelly said that when he walked into the manager's office, he saw the bag of money on the table and an old man sitting down. He said he wanted the takings but the man said, "Put that toy away." Kelly told the man it was no toy. The man then said he couldn't have the money because it belonged to the company but he could have some of his own money. He then tried to brush the gun aside. Kelly couldn't be bothered with him any more so he shot him.

Catterall then entered the room and stood by the door with his hands behind his back for a few seconds before moving towards Kelly as if to put his hands around him. Kelly now had the cash bag in his left hand. As Catterall approached Kelly butted him then took the gun out of his pocket and shot him in the chest. Catterall fell to his knees tearing at the shirt on his chest, and tried to tackle Kelly again so he shot him again.

At 2.00pm the following Saturday, March 26th, Dickson met Connolly in *Littlewoods'* cafe. He told her all about the murder and gave her twenty three bullets tied in a handkerchief, telling her to give them to Kelly when she next saw him. On this occasion Connolly told her that he was supposed to be keeping watch outside but had run away when he heard the first shots. He said he was getting out of town and asked her to go with him to London.

A week later Dickson met Kelly in Lime Street, outside the *Palais De Luxe* cinema. She told him she was frightened of a man named Bobby Woolerton so Kelly took her to the *Caledonian* public house, where he bought her whisky. He told her she could have had more if he'd got what he went for at Cameo, and that she shouldn't worry about Woolerton, intimating he had a gun in his pocket. Dickson told him he should get rid of it and he said he would take it to pieces and dispose of it. He then followed her to Central station underground and bought two tickets to Birkenhead. Dickson was afraid of him but he changed his mind and said he was going to see his brother instead.

On Monday, April 4th, continued Gorman, the police received an anonymous letter, now known to be written by Northam and Dickson. It stated that the authors would divulge the killer's name if he/she were not charged as accomplices. Responding to a request contained in the letter, the police put an advert in the Personal Column of the *Liverpool Echo*, giving the required assurance, but there was no response. On May 13th, Dickson was seen by the police and gave them some information about the anonymous letter. She also told them to see Charlie Connolly as he knew all about "the arrangements."

Connolly was taken from his home to the Central C.I.D office in the early hours of May 14th and questioned. Denying any knowledge of the murder or the letter, he said he was working on the night shift on March 19th. The police however, made enquiries and discovered this to be untrue. Some days later Inspector Balmer again interviewed Connolly and told him he had not been at work on that date. Connolly said, "Well I say I was. You say I wasn't. If I wasn't, then I don't know where I was."(5)

Around May 20th, Dickson and Northam left Liverpool and went into hiding because they were terrified and had been threatened. The police launched a nationwide search for Dickson and on September the 29th 1949 she was located in Manchester and brought back to Liverpool Both she and Northam made statements to Inspector Balmer, describing their parts in the planning of the crime and naming Kelly as the murderer and Connolly as his accomplice. Connolly was arrested at 2.30am on September the 30th at his home, and Kelly at 10.45am the same day at C.I.D. Headquarters in Dale Street.

When charged with the murder of Leonard Thomas, both men denied having anything to do with the crime or even knowing each other. But later that day when Kelly was brought into the charge room and saw Connolly, he shouted, "You've never seen me in your life before have you? You don't know me do you?" and Connolly replied "No, I don't". Later that day Kelly was picked out by Dickson on an identity parade, and the following day both Connolly and Kelly were similarly identified by Northam.

On October the 4th, said Gorman, Connolly wrote to Inspector Balmer asking him to visit him at Walton prison. The reason being, that Connolly wanted to make a confession. He later changed his mind however and made a statement relating to something he had allegedly overheard. This statement was regarding something a man named Dennis Barker had told him in the prison van, and what he himself had overheard Kelly saying. That was that Kelly had been with Skelly on the evening of March 19th and that it seemed suspicious that Skelly should go away to sea when he had never been away before. The statement also mentioned that Connolly had heard somebody named Nobby Clarke knew something about the murder. Connolly also told Inspector Balmer that Kelly had an alibi and that he too would have to find one now from his family. When Inspector Balmer asked Connolly to sign this statement he refused.

Gorman went on to state that also on October the 4th Patrick Dowling, a member of the Corps of Commissioners, was interviewed by the police. "This man", said Gorman, "was the doorman at the *Primrose Cafe* in Cases Street. He knew Kelly quite well. He will tell you that he saw Kelly between 7.30 and 8.00pm on March 19th, come out of the Globe Hotel and walk up Cases Street to the corner and turn left towards Lewis's and Renshaw Street. That was also in the direction of the *Beehive* public house."

On October the 10th, continued Gorman, Kelly and Connolly were picked out at identity parades by James Sangster, a store detective at Lewis's department store, as two men whom he had often seen in each other's company around the town. On that occasion, as everyone was leaving the room Kelly had shouted out, threatening Inspector Balmer, "If it's the last thing I do, I'll get you for this Balmer!"

On November the 11th a prostitute, Norwegian Margie, was found dead in her room from coal-gas poisoning. Kelly knew her, and it was believed that she was the "heavily made-up dark-haired girl" in the *Beehive* who had handed him a brown apron to use as a mask.

On November the 21st, said Gorman, Robert Graham, a prisoner in the hospital at Walton prison was interviewed by the police. You will hear Mr. Graham, who has signed a full statement, tell you that over a period of days both Kelly and Connolly confessed to him their respective parts in this murder," he concluded.

Following the lunchtime adjournment Gorman resumed his opening speech. Pointing out that the *Spofforth* pub where Kelly was drinking at 9.20pm., was only three minutes away from the Cameo, he added, "It might take a couple more minutes to get to 67 Cambridge Street where Kelly lived. And to get from the Cameo to the *Leigh Arms* it takes you, walking in a normal way, about eight minutes."

After stating that the time of the shooting was before 9.45 pm, Gorman said that Kelly went into the *Spofforth* at 9.20pm, had a pint and remained three or four minutes. "This is interesting." He went on. "When he was in the *Spofforth* he was not wearing hat or coat. The submission of the prosecution is simple. Kelly could quite easily - had he the desire, and there was ample time to do it - have called at his home in Cambridge Street and picked up his hat and coat." Similarly, he said, Kelly could have called at his house on the eight-minute walk back to the *Leigh Arms*, and disposed of the hat and coat.

The prosecuting counsel's inference was clear: Kelly had deliberately shown himself in the *Leigh Arms* and the *Spofforth* without hat and overcoat, between 9.00pm and 9.20pm He'd then gone to O'Malley's house to don the overcoat and hat, committed the murders then returned to the *Leigh Arms* (where witnesses said he was at 9.45 pm), disposing of the overcoat, hat, gun and mask at O'Malley's on the way.

If that is what actually happened then it would raise a number of serious anomalies. Firstly, If Kelly was intent on establishing an alibi in advance by showing himself without hat or coat in various pubs before the murders, why would he deliberately fail to mention to Balmer the following morning being in the *Spofforth*? Conversely, if it was true that Kelly had not mentioned the *Spofforth* - as the Crown also wished to convince the jury - then he could not have been entering the *Spofforth* or any other local pub for the purpose of establishing his alibi.

Secondly, if it was agreed by the prosecution that Kelly was back in the *Leigh Arms* at 9.45pm (although Kelly and two defence witnesses maintained he was back there at 9.30), and if walking in "a normal way" from the Cameo to the *Leigh Arms* took eight minutes, how could he have ran from the cinema in the opposite direction to his home in Cambridge Street, disposed of hat, gun, mask and overcoat at his home, (which according to Gorman would have taken another three or four minutes) and arrived at the *Leigh Arms* - all in ten minutes?

The Crown had agreed that Kelly's home in Cambridge Street - and every back yard, outbuilding, bombed site and empty house in the area - was thoroughly searched throughout that night and the following morning. Therefore, even if Kelly was back in the *Leigh Arms* as late as 9.50pm, as Gorman suggested, where and how did he dispose of these accoutrements in so short a time? Why did Farragher or Balmer not find any of these items when they searched 67 Cambridge Street the very next morning?.

The biggest anomaly of all however was that, according to the anonymous letter and Northam's and Dickson's statements, Kelly had ran across Botanic park to Edge Lane and caught a 6A tram. If that were true then how could he have been back in the *Leigh Arms* even at 9.50pm .? Either Gorman had got it completely wrong or his two main witnesses were clearly lying.

In relation to this aspect of the prosecution's case a most important fourth consideration arises. Where was the alleged accomplice Connolly, during this time, and how was he occupied whilst Kelly, this brilliant quick-change artist, was touring the local pubs hatless and coatless in order to provide an alibi for himself? Was it not a little strange that Connolly - who would also have faced the death penalty if caught - wasn't at all bothered about an alibi for himself? Indeed, Gorman at one stage suggested that, when he was not loitering outside he cinema, he was probably following Kelly around, waiting outside these pubs, slavishly acting the part of a poor man's valet by dutifully minding his overcoat and hat for him! If this were true, could any accomplice on such a dangerous mission ever have been so disregarding of his own survival? Could there ever have been a more self-sacrificing and moronic partner in crime?

Connolly was not a weak or stupid man. He was not the type to be anybody's lackey. On the contrary, he was a very proud and strongly-principled character. He had a distinguished war record in the Royal Navy, including periods serving in the Indian Ocean hunting German U. Boat wolf packs, and on decoy duty in the Channel on D-Day. He could also boast a brilliant amateur boxing career. If anything, Connolly, a more disciplined character than Kelly, was by temperament and inclination the more natural leader. He did not readily fit the role of stooge. Would such a man therefore render himself so vulnerable on such a dangerous mission? And was it really plausible that this strapping, twelve stone, six - footer, an undefeated winner of sixty amateur fights, would allow the five foot seven Kelly to contemptuously use him in this fashion, call him a yellow bastard and threaten him with violence? Similarly, would Skelly, albeit a street fighter rather than a boxer, have tolerated threats made by the smaller, lighter Kelly in the '*Star*' - who in any case was his friend?

From this opening of the prosecution case, it was clear that the case against Kelly and Connolly was entirely circumstantial. There was not one iota of independent material or forensic evidence; no identification, no murder weapon, no bloodstained overcoat, no trilby, no mask. Moreover, this circumstantial evidence, provided mainly by the two alleged accomplices in the planning of the crime, both with criminal records, was highly questionable.

If Kelly was involved in discussing potential jobs as alleged, was it conceivable that he, a cunning small-time villain, would be so foolish as to pull out a gun, start loading it and childishly tie a handkerchief around his face in a city centre public house on a Saturday night? Would his astute, street-wise character suggest robbing a funfair in New Brighton in March when everybody knew the funfair was closed for the winter? And wasn't it more than coincidental that he just happened to have a gun and ammunition in his pocket when a stick-up was finally agreed on?

Then there was the matter of fingerprints. Not one witness inside the cinema or out, including Northam and Dickson, had testified that the gunman wore gloves. Yet, although Kelly had a criminal record no fingerprints of his were found in the manager's office nor on the spiral staircase or emergency exit door.

Regarding Skelly offering in the *White Star* public house, to get Connolly away to sea. Would this man, who in March had never made a seafaring trip in his life, realistically be in a position to get anyone a ship, much less Connolly, himself an experienced Royal navy and merchant seaman?

The prosecution case also rested on dubious ground in relation to Kelly's alleged point of entry into the cinema via the Bird Street side door. The cinema staff had stated that this was a push bar emergency exit which was always kept closed from the inside. There was no way entry could be effected from the outside unless somebody opened it from the inside. But that was precisely why usherette Phyllis Stevens was stationed there - to stop patrons opening that door to let their friends "bunk in" without paying. Moreover, Gorman himself had stated the reason Stevens had such a good look at the gunman, was because he was fumbling with that door because it was so stiff...*and had been stiff all week.* (My italics)

When the cinema cashier, Mrs. Ellen Jackman, was called and shown the overcoat by Gorman, she said it was "similar" to that worn by the gunman. She was followed by other members of the cinema staff, including the usherette Phyllis Stevens, who arguably had the closest look at the overcoat than anyone. Yet she simply said it "was very much like" the overcoat worn by the gunman. In her evidence Stevens also mentioned that whilst the gunman was trying to open the exit door, despite the difficulty he was having, he significantly kept his left hand firmly in his overcoat pocket, no doubt holding the gun. This fact, together with the location of the wounds on Thomas and Catterall (e.g. Catterall's right hand and right shoulder) would seem to indicate that the gunman was left-handed. Kelly however was right-handed. But Heilbron failed to explore this very important point in her client's favour.

The evidence of the supervisor, Mrs. Watkins, the ice-cream girl, Valerie June Thornhill, and the fireman, twenty-two year-old Patrick Joseph Griffin was essentially a repetition of that given at the Committal court, the consensus being that the fatal shots occurred sometime between 9.35 and 9.40pm. All were all unanimously agreed that the gunman who burst out of the manager's office brandishing the weapon and telling them to stand back, was about five feet eight inches tall wearing a belted brown overcoat with the belt hanging loose, a trilby pulled down over his forehead and a *black silk scarf* which covered his features. (My italics) Yet Dickson and Northam had stated that Kelly in the Beehive had been given by the dark-haired girl, a "brown apron". Indeed, Dickson had specifically stated the colour as, "nigger brown".

Whilst the cinema staff members were giving their evidence there was one person conspicuous by her absence. That was the nineteen year-old usherette, Edna May Ashley. As for the defence they did not even know of her existence because her statement had been withheld from them. She had given the police a statement on the very night of the murder. In it she said she had been sitting in the end seat of the front row of the stalls nearest the aisle when she heard several bangs, then saw a slim man with dark greased hair brushed neatly back, racing down the aisle. According to her statement the man, who was wearing a dark suit and seemed to be carrying a hat in his hand, dashed out into the foyer. She followed him outside and he turned immediately right and ran up Bird Street.

Gorman similarly failed to call a miner named Frederick Ashton, whose statement had also been withheld by the police. He had been sitting in the front stalls with his family and had independently corroborated Edna Ashley's story on the night of the murder.

If these two witnesses had been available to the defence their evidence would have clearly exposed as pure fabrications Northam's, Dickson's and Graham's statements as to what Kelly and Connolly allegedly confessed to them. For it would have shown that the second man had not waited *outside* (where he would have been of no assistance to the killer anyway) as the prosecution - purely to match the contents of the anonymous letter - had alleged, but had been keeping watch inside at the foot of the spiral staircase. Their testimony would have also shown that the second man dashed through the auditorium and out of the main entrance precisely because he could not open the Bird Street emergency exit door. And if he couldn't open that door then how could Kelly have entered through it moments earlier?

Their evidence would have concurred with that of usherette Phyllis Stevens who, when describing the *killer's* getaway *a few moments later*, stated, "The man was pushing the Exit door trying to get out and struggling with the door because it was *stiff and had been stiff all week*". (My italics)

(1) The same courtroom was to double in the 1990s as the Old Bailey, in the films, *Let Him Have It*, and *In The Name of The Father*, about the Craig and Bentley and the Guildford Four capital cases - both of which, ironically, concerned infamous miscarriages of British justice.

(2) As Mr. Justice Gorman twelve years later, he would sentence James Hanratty to death after his conviction for the A6 Murder - a verdict which has also long been regarded as another miscarriage of British justice.

(3) Rose Heilbron was born 19th August 1914. Graduated Liverpool University: 1st Class Honours Degree (LLB.) 1935 followed by LLM. 1937. Called to bar at Grays Inn, 1939. Married Dr. Nathaniel Burstein 1945. Took silk 1949. Recorder of Burnley 1956 -1971. Made High Court judge (only second woman to be made so) and Dame of the British Empire 1974. Conferred with Honorary LLD. by Liverpool University 1975.

(4) The overcoat was never in fact conclusively identified as that worn by the killer at the Cameo. It was apparently not even examined by the forensic laboratory.

(5) Connolly later denied that any further visit by the police took place between May 14th and his arrest but admitted making the alleged remark to Balmer on the 30th September.

Chapter Twenty - three

On the second day of the trial Heilbron successfully objected to he barman at the *Caledonian* being called as a witness. Gorman had wanted him to verify the incident when Kelly was alleged to have taken Dickson there and bought her whisky after the murder. It was agreed however that the barman, Timothy Mulcahey, could only testify that he had been with "a man" on that occasion. He had previously failed to pick out Kelly at an identity parade. That being the case, Heilbron contended that the only purpose in calling him was to prejudice Kelly by innuendo. Winning this minor victory however, she missed the opportunity to score a much greater one. For had Mulcahey been in the witness box, she could have produced Kelly's brother for him to identify. And had he done so the case against Kelly would have been considerably weakened, if not fatally flawed.

Next in the witness box was James Corrie (who was curiously referred to throughout as "Currie"). Described as a private hire operator, he swore that Kelly came in the *Leigh Arms* at 9.50pm, and was flushed and excited. It seemed, said Corrie, that he was trying to make himself conspicuous. Kelly asked him and the lady he was with, to have a drink and said he could have the best in the house. He also invited the manager and staff to have a drink. Due to Kelly's demeanour he asked him if he had been in the sun, to which he replied, "No, I have been having a go. Nobody takes liberties with Kelly."

In reply to Rose Heilbron, Corrie denied that Kelly was inebriated and had said, "I've been having a go on the bevvy." He insisted Kelly had used the words he had testified to. But when Heilbron pointed out that these words were not contained in his deposition at the magistrates court, Corrie said he thought he had mentioned them in his evidence.

However when Corrie had said Kelly entered the pub at 9.50pm, neither Heilbron or the judge thought to ask whether that was the real time or the time *on the clock*.

James Daniel Sangster, the store detective stated that he knew Connolly and Kelly very well and had seen them together on numerous occasions on the blitzed site opposite *Lewis*' and in Harold Davidson's pub in Elliot Street. Kelly had told him on one occasion that he had been interviewed by the police over the Cameo murders, and he had advised him to tell the police anything he knew. When Heilbron put it to him that he had seen Kelly together with Skelly, and another man named Cunningham, but never with Connolly, Sangster replied that he knew Skelly, who was shorter and broader than Connolly. There was no mistaking the two.

Patrick Dowling, the *Primrose Cafe* doorman, said he was sure about seeing Kelly at 7.30pm on the evening of March the 19th coming out of the *Globe* and turning left into Ranelagh Street. Could he not be mistaken, asked Heilbron. No, he was absolutely sure. But he couldn't remember how Kelly was dressed or whether he was wearing an overcoat or a hat. He had told the police, when he heard of Kelly's arrest, he said, because he thought it would be helpful to Kelly. He thought if he was in Cases Street he couldn't be in Wavertree. He agreed however, that when Kelly told him a few days after the murder that he'd been questioned by the police, he didn't mention to him that he had seen him on the Saturday evening. Nor did he speak to him on the Saturday evening. He first told the police in October, he said, but he did not sign a statement until November the 14th. It was Detective Chief Inspector Balmer who took his statement, he said. Although in his evidence he never used the word, his written statement said he "*definitely*" saw Kelly!. (My italics)

Dowling could not be budged from his testimony. Had Heilbron known the precise location of the *Primrose* in relation to the *Globe* however, she might have asked him, how he had recognised Kelly from the back. Going towards Ranelagh Street the *Globe* was the nearest to the street corner. Therefore Dowling, standing outside the *Primrose* No.15 Cases Street, could not have seen Kelly's face when he came out of the *Globe*, No.17, and immediately turned left. The man he saw could have appeared similar to Kelly from the rear but Heilbron could have demonstrated that Dowling's identification was not a positive one - particularly if, as he testified, he hadn't spoken to him.

Other witnesses included Detective Sergeant Ernest Richardson, who said he'd known Kelly and Connolly for several years. He swore he had seen them together in Liverpool city centre on eight or nine occasions. He'd last seem them together about three weeks after the murder. He could not however give any specific dates. He'd never seen Kelly with Skelly.

Constable Nugent, whom Connolly admitted knowing from around the Seaman's Home area in Cleveland Square, testified that he had seen him with Kelly in Lime Street after the murder on September 26th, talking with a woman. When Heilbron suggested he was mistaken, he denied this, saying that the woman actually joked as he passed, "Hello, haven't you retired yet?"

It may seem coincidental but here again we had a detective and a uniformed constable giving the same evidence. The Court however was unaware of the internal Sherlock police "report"!

When Balmer entered the witness box he corroborated the contents of Gorman's lengthy opening speech. As he began to read from his notebook Heilbron immediately protested. But Oliver snapped at her, "He is entitled to refresh his memory." Heilbron agreed but complained that he was reading *verbatim* from it.

Later during cross-examination, first by Basil Neild and then Rose Heilbron, he very adroitly, with only the occasional slip up, told lie after lie. Several times Kelly had to restrain himself from shouting out in protest, but he had been warned by Heilbron that any further protestations from the dock or accusations of lying against the police would prejudice both the judge and jury against him. Connolly had been similarly warned by Basil Neild but he felt no compulsion to protest. Indeed, he was to be much more relaxed, taking the proceedings in his stride. For although very worried about his situation he was confident of being acquitted. His was an attitude of, 'I am innocent so what do I really have to worry about?'

When Balmer was asked if he had been aware that Dickson's and Northam's evidence, as accomplices, required corroboration, the judge interrupted, saying that Neild was asking the Inspector to decide something, which he himself would direct the jury on.

In reply to further questions, Balmer said he first saw Northam on May the 13th or 14th. Asked to be more precise, he consulted his notebook then said it was in the early hours of the 14th, after he had seen Connolly, but it was only, " to pass a word with him." He did not interview him. When asked a similar question about Dickson, Balmer said he first saw her at 11.10pm on the night of the 13th May, and although he didn't take a statement from her, she did say something which he recorded. Between May the 13th and September the 24th he saw her twice and took her statement on the 29th of September. As for Graham, he saw him on November the 19th at Walton prison when Graham told him something. But although he began to take a statement "something happened" (he didn't say what) and he left the statement over till November the 21st. He had only seen Graham twice since then.

This explanation was very astute of Balmer. He had realised that Graham's statement saying he had contacted Balmer on the 19th conflicted with his own report to his superiors which said the 21st. His explanation to Neild therefore, neatly resolved that conflict. The fact remains however that in his report to the Chief Constable, which was not produced in court Balmer had specifically stated that he went to Preston on the 21st of November as a direct result of a message from the Preston police that Graham wished to see him. He had therefore either lied to his Chief Constable or was now lying to the Court. He also lied when stating he had only seen Graham on two occasions since November the 21st. He had in fact seen him at Strangeways twice after the visits to Walton of the 23rd and 26th of November.

Neild, mindful of the "inducement" allegations in the Johnson case, asked Balmer about his methods of obtaining statements - in particular his visit to Connolly at Walton on October the 4th when he had tried to persuade him to turn Kings Evidence. "You agree" he said," that you must not seek to get a signature by any promise, inducement or persuasion?" Balmer agreed. Neild then put it to him that after legal aid was granted it was his duty to deal with the accused through his solicitor. But Balmer disagreed with this. He didn't think he would let the solicitor know. Adding, "If I am sent for by a prisoner I would go and see that prisoner."

Turning to Northam and Dickson, Connolly's counsel asked if Balmer, knowing what an accomplice was, would be interested in whether there was outside evidence to support them. Balmer did not reply but then admitted that there was not one word of evidence that Connolly ever went into the cinema or fired any shot. But when Neild asked if there was any direct evidence, apart from Northam's, Dickson's and Graham's, that Connolly took any part in the planning of the crime, Balmer replied, "That takes a lot of thinking out."

At this point Oliver accused Neild of being vague. "I don't think you have the right", he said, "to ask this witness such a question. These are matters you can make in a speech but I don't think you can ask this question." Suitably chastised, Neild changed direction and asked Balmer if he knew the three main prosecution witnesses were all "convicts." Balmer, aware of the distinction cleverly replied, "They all have convictions."

With reference to the time of Connolly's arrest Balmer was asked if he thought a man would be at his lowest ebb at in the early hours of the morning? "It is invariably my practice", he replied, "if I want to see a man rather badly, to go at the times I'm confident I'll find him in." In answer to further questions from Neild, he denied that, when questioning Connolly in May, he had not mentioned that March the 19th was a Saturday. But when Neild suggested that it would have given Connolly more chance to explain where he was if a particular day had been mentioned, the judge intervened. "He has given an answer to that. It may not be a very good answer but he has given it."

As Neild's cross-examination proceeded, Balmer continued to make denial after denial. Hadn't he shown photographs on May the 14th to Connolly? "I showed no photographs to Connolly whatsoever" was the emphatic reply. And hadn't Connolly picked out Dickson? "That is not so". When Neild said that the photographs shown to Connolly were front face and both profiles, Balmer admitted that police photographs were of that type but insisted he had never shown Connolly any. It was Connolly, he said, who had mentioned Dickson, saying that she knocked around with a Bobby Woolerton who could be found in *Lewis'*.

What Neild didn't know was that Connolly did not have to tell Balmer this. He already knew of Dickson's association with Woolerton through arresting him in 1948 for pimping off her.

Continuing his cross-examination, Neild asked if Balmer had tried to persuade Connolly to turn Kings Evidence? No he hadn't. Hadn't he discussed with Connolly's solicitor, Mr. Maxwell Brown, the charge room incident when Kelly was alleged to have shouted to Connolly, "You don't know me do you...? " Balmer said he might have done. And hadn't he told Maxwell Brown that, *"it stuck out a mile?"* Balmer said he couldn't remember using such an expression. After a short pause the Inspector then denied even discussing the incident with Maxwell Brown. He had realised just in time that he had to deny this because the same phrase was to be used later on by Graham in his evidence, when describing how Connolly told him in Walton about the charge room incident.

After denying trying to persuade Connolly to turn Kings Evidence, Balmer agreed with Neild that he had considered Connolly being a witness rather than an accused. But before Neild could follow up, the judge asked, "Put in the witness box instead of the dock?" "That is so", said Balmer. Neild then asked if he thought Northam and Dickson were themselves involved, and Balmer replied that they were present when the plan was discussed but didn't take part. When Neild again put the question, the judge once more intervened, telling him that he was asking Balmer to decide whether they were accomplices, and that that was a matter for the jury. "Your point", he went on, "is that he was entirely desirous of getting corroborative evidence. Put it that way." Neild then pointedly asked if it was when he was looking for fresh evidence that Graham was discovered. Evading the question, Balmer emphatically stated, "I have looked for fresh evidence since March the 19th, and I am still finding it." That was however, not an answer to the question, and deliberately so. For Balmer realised Neild was trying to make the very real connection between his need of a corroborative witness and the "coincidental" appearance of Graham to fill that role.

In further responses to Neild's persistent probing, Balmer now said he knew at 6.40pm on November the 18th that Graham was in Walton. "I received a message from a detective of Preston Borough police", he went on, "Graham *sent* for the Preston police, and because of that, they in turn sent for me and I went to the prison." (My italics)

Given that a liar has to have a good memory, Balmer, for all his astuteness, was slipping here. Firstly he'd now admitted he had first made contact with Graham at an even earlier date than the 21st of November. Secondly he'd stated that Graham had "sent for" the Preston police, whilst Graham's statement, and his subsequent evidence would say that he was already in Preston, appearing on remand, when he spoke to the Preston police. Fortunately for him however, neither Neild or Heilbron picked up on this.

In a further reply to Neild, Balmer said Graham had signed the statement without any persuasion whatsoever. "Have you ever used persuasion?", he was asked. "I suppose I have used persuasion on many occasions in my life, but not in this particular case" He then added with revealing frankness, "In some cases I would not object to persuading a witness to sign a statement. I see no harm in it."

"Did you get a signature from Dowling by persuasion?", asked a sardonic Neild. "I got his signature by assuring him of protection by the police", said the quick-witted Balmer. But quite why Dowling needed police protection was unclear. It seemed the only purpose of that reply was to further blacken Kelly and Connolly in the eyes of the jury.

When asked if he knew a man named Sherlock, and had he interviewed him?, Balmer said that it was Sherlock who approached him. Did he make a suggestion to him that he could visit the prison? No he did not. Balmer's strategy in getting in first with the concocted report about Sherlock had been an invaluable insurance policy!

Neild then asked about the Johnson case and whether he had interviewed a man named McBride. It was Smith who interviewed him, he said, but agreed McBride did make a statement. "He was a hospital orderly at Walton Gaol", said Neild, just like Graham is a hospital orderly?" Balmer denied this, saying he was simply a prisoner. Was Johnson supposed to have told McBride something which he could give in evidence? "That is what the evidence would have been", he admitted, "but McBride was not called". When the judge said that McBride didn't give evidence so it couldn't be evidence against anybody, Neild said he was attempting to draw the analogy between McBride, a prisoner in the hospital, being called to give evidence, and Graham, who was also a prisoner in the hospital. Oliver however said he couldn't follow the analogy. Neild however was unaware of just how close his analogy was. But how was he or the judge to know that Graham himself had given Balmer a statement in September about Johnson being the murderer.

Coming to Northam, Neild asked Balmer if he had been frightened of being charged? He was frightened, said Balmer, and so was Dickson, but not of being charged. "He (Northam) was never on the list of suspects", he added. Neild then read out the anonymous letter - including the words, 'You will give me you word I won't be charged" - which Balmer said had been written by Northam and Dickson and received by Superintendent Smith. Ignoring Neild's point, the judge said to Balmer, "When Smith showed you that letter had you any idea who had written it?"

"No my lord.", he replied.

Again Balmer was slipping. Although the envelope containing the letter had a word struck out (which Northam said had been a failed attempt at "Superintendent"), it was nonetheless addressed not to Smith, but to "The Inspector." As such Balmer would have received it before Smith. After some prevarication, Balmer finally agreed that the author or authors of the letter were afraid of being charged, and that the promise was put in the *Liverpool Echo* to reassure them they would not be.

Regarding Dickson's alleged reluctance on May the 13th to divulge anything other than Connolly's name, Balmer said she was frightened and told him, "I daren't tell." She then told him of an incident in January when the wife of a man who was up on an assault charge waited outside the court for one of the prosecution witnesses and slashed him across the face with a razor. She told him she was frightened of the same thing happening to her because she had been threatened.

Now apart from nobody being named as the threatener or threateners, this innuendo of Balmer's was intended to make Dickson's fear appear more authentic, thereby further inflaming the jury against the accused men. But if anybody had thought of checking they would have discovered that this incident, for which a woman named Jessie Brady got four years, took place outside Dale Street Magistrates Court on the 13th of January 1949 - the same day Dickson and Northam had been jailed fifty miles away in Brampton, Cumberland. Dickson could therefore not possibly have known about it. Balmer however knew all the details of the case. It was one of his taxi driver informers, called "Harry" whose face Brady had slashed for giving false evidence against her husband. The 'slashing' had required four stiches.

When it came for him to be cross-examined by Rose Heilbron, Balmer continued with his denials. On the Sunday morning after the murder Kelly had not told him everywhere he had been the previous day and night? He had not taken Kelly first to Prescot Street for a cup of tea and to get Skelly's address? " I already knew Skelly's address", he said. Skelly had not confirmed Kelly's story? When he visited the *Coach and Horses* on the Sunday after dropping Kelly off he was not able to verify that Kelly was telling the truth? "It confirmed Skelly's story", he said, "but not Kelly's."

This was of course technically correct because, although the licensee's wife had described Kelly, she did not know him by name. But the description had been sufficient for Balmer to accept it was indeed Kelly at the time.

As his cross-examination continued, Balmer stated that he had spoken to Kelly on many occasions since March the 20th but only once about the Cameo case. That was about April the 20th. Kelly he said, had called on him many times to ask about the progress of the case but he denied offering him £50 to get information about the Cameo. He then agreed with Heilbron that Kelly had given him helpful information on other matters but the information given on the Cameo case had been wrong.

This exchange was puzzling in several respects. Was Heilbron running the risk of branding her client as a police informer - thereby alienating him from his friends in the criminal fraternity - in order to present him to the jury as a person helping the police? Or had Kelly really been giving information? Either way she had presumably made the statement with Kelly's approval. As for Balmer only seeing him once since March the 20th about the murder, had he forgotten the occasion on March the 21st when he'd taken Kelly to the Pier Head and eliminated the overcoat worn by his brother Peter? No he hadn't.

Indeed, it was precisely because he knew Kelly could not deny being in town that he was able to concoct the story of him meeting Northam that particular day in Lime Street when he allegedly told him the details of the murder.

Asked about the interview with Skelly on the Sunday, Balmer said he'd concluded that he knew very little of the previous evening's events. If Kelly had really said he left Skelly in the *Coach and Horses* at opening time and went down town, as Balmer stated, Heilbron wanted to know, why hadn't he checked Kelly's story? "I am of the opinion", he answered irrelevantly, "that my method is the best one."

Unfortunately he was not pressed on this important point. If Kelly had been a genuine suspect, any self-respecting detective would have checked out his movements at the time. But it was not until October, when Dowling casually mentioned seeing Kelly on March 19th in Cases Street, that Balmer acted.

Heilbron asked the Inspector if it would have been fairer to the accused men to hold identity parades before they had appeared in court, but he replied that Northam had no opportunity of seeing Kelly. He was not in the court precincts. There was no way of the defence disputing this. But even the police admitted that Detective Inspector Hector Taylor had brought Northam back from Manchester, at 9.30am on the day of the men's first court appearance, which would have given Northam plenty of time to view Kelly through the cell's "Judas hole" in Cheapside - quite apart from having been shown his mugshot a dozen times.

When Northam entered the witness box on the third day of the trial, he looked around the court apprehensively before taking the oath. At times his muted nervous voice, together with his stammer made his answers inaudible, much to the irritation of Oliver, who told him to speak up as though he were in a pub with his friends.

Replying to Gorman, he said they were plotting jobs in the *Beehive* when Oliver asked if "jobs" meant work. No, said Northam amid courtroom laughter, it meant breaking into places. It was Connolly, he said, who mentioned doing a taxi driver who was a stool pigeon. It was also he who mentioned the Cameo, saying it was a "smasher." Whilst Connolly sitting in the dock, was vigorously shaking his head in denial,

Oliver asked, "what does a smasher mean? Does it mean something that is worth smashing?" Again the court burst into laughter.

As Northam related to Gorman the events which were in his statement, he added that Kelly had told him on March the 21st in Lime Street that Balmer couldn't break his alibi in a thousand years. Some days later, he continued, Dickson gave him 23 shells wrapped in a handkerchief. These had been given to her by Connolly who asked her to give them back to Kelly. He kept six and told her to return the rest to Connolly and tell him to do his own dirty work.. Some time later Dickson took the six shells away. The anonymous letter was written by him, with Dickson's help, about a fortnight after the murder, and he gave the brown overcoat to Balmer about October the 10th.

Cross-examined by Basil Neild, Northam said he was not afraid of being charged as an accessory because he took no part. But, pressed by Neild, he said he thought he might be charged with holding back what he knew. Showing him a facsimile copy of the anonymous letter, Neild asked if he had written, " If I give you my address you might charge me with being an accessory to the killing"? Northam said he had but that was because Dickson thought she might be charged. "But it is your letter", said Neild.
It is the letter of both of us."

Even when Neild quoted the words, "If you put in the personal column of the *Echo*, and give me your word that I won't be charged", Northam still maintained that he wasn't afraid of being charged as an accessory. He wanted to tell the police so he could have protection and give evidence. He was frightened of Kelly, he said, but not the police. When Neild said that he knew very well that however guilty a man may be, if he gives evidence he cannot be charged, he made no reply. "Is the position this", said Neild insinuatingly, "that you gave your evidence-in-chief exactly as it was given, almost word for word, in the police (Committal) court without a single note?"
Yes", he replied.

Did Neild suspect that Northam had been primed with his story of events or was this simply a shot in the dark Whatever the reasons behind this most perceptive question, he did not see the necessity of following it up and Northam was lucky to be let off the hook.

Northam had confirmed the police evidence that Dickson's fla[ ] in Liverpool and his parents Birkenhead home had been searched i[ ] May. Why then, asked Neild, did they not find the overcoat then? "M[ ] father must have been wearing it", was his reply. The truth howeve[ ] was that in May, the police were simply looking for Dickson who ha[ ] skipped bail, and had no reason to be interested in an overcoat - eve[ ] if there had been one at Northam's parents home.

Northam agreed that at the Committal Court he had not mentione[ ] Connolly saying he had to fix an alibi up with his wife. "Had you seen i[ ] the newspaper that Dickson in her evidence was saying that Connoll[ ] was going to get an alibi?", asked Neild. "No", he replied. Then wh[ ] didn't he say that at the committal if it was true? "I must have forgot"[ ] said Northam. When Neild referred to the part of the letter which sai[ ] he didn't think the girl had anything to do with the murder, Northa[ ] denied that Dickson had told him to say that. Why did he say, "When [ ] met her on the Sunday", if he lived with her?, asked Neild. Northa[ ] replied that he didn't want the police to know he was living with he[ ] Why not? "What difference", asked Neild, "does it make to peopl[ ] who are unmarried living together?"

"It makes a difference to me, and I think the police ought not to kno[ ] that." Pressing the point, Neild said he must have a reason, was he abl[ ] to give one?

"No", said Northam.

Was there anything in the letter. Neild wanted to know, to sa[ ] Dickson returned, as he was now saying, to the *Beehive* after fiv[ ] minutes? When Northam insisted that Dickson did go back to th[ ] *Beehive*, Neild said, "Either your letter is untrue or your evidence[ ] How can they both be true?", but Northam simply repeated he didn'[ ] want the police to know they were living together.

Referring to Northam's alleged meeting with Kelly in Lime Stree[ ] on the 21st of March, Neild reminded him that he had said in th[ ] Committal Court that he and Dickson together saw Kelly. He was no[ ] however saying that Dickson left him by *Lewis*'s and he saw Kell[ ] alone. Northam weakly replied, "I don't know why I said 'we'."

Continuing his cross-examination the following day, Neild aske[ ] Northam if anybody had asked him to change his evidence. The answe[ ] he got was totally unexpected. He had been intimating Balmer but Northam caused quite a stir throughout the court when he said. "Yes, Mr. Livermore."

He then went on to make the sensational claim that Kelly's solicitor had offered him money to change his story. A typist from Livermore's office, he said, had called at his address in Manchester just after the committal proceedings. She had taken him by car to Old Swan, where Livermore was sitting in another car outside the *Curzon* cinema in Prescot Road. Livermore offered him £150 to change his story. If he didn't, Livermore told him, he had a signed statement by Kelly saying Northam was at the Cameo with him and he would hand it to the police.

He was told to change his story and tell the police that it was the Sunday and not the previous evening that he was with Kelly. And the pub was not the *Beehive* but the *White Star*. He was to say Kelly only had a dummy gun and although he was bragging about committing the murders, he later started laughing and told everyone he was only joking. Livermore then handed him £35, consisting of twenty pound notes and three white five pound notes, and said, "put that in your pocket." Northam said he gave the fivers back to Livermore and spent the rest of the money.

Looking at him with contempt, Neild said, " Are you aware that Mr. Livermore represents Kelly and is doing so under the *Poor Persons Act*? I put it to you that it is a wicked lie throughout" But Northam insisted it was the truth, although he could not remember what he'd done with the money. "In other words", said Neild, "a solicitor of the Supreme Court threatened you in this way?"

"Yes", said Northam.

Neild then asked if had occurred to him that if he'd said he'd taken the five pound notes they could have been traced and his story could have been proved untrue. "My story is not untrue", he replied.

Neild then asked why he did not go with the police to Livermore's office later that evening, as he said he'd been invited to, to collect the remainder of the £150? "I don't know", he replied.

If he was willing to take a bribe of twenty pounds, said Neild, why not go and collect the remainder? "Because", said Northam, "I would not go. I had no reason." He then added that he wanted to go to the police. So why take the £20, Neild wanted to know. "I just took it", he replied.

During this exchange it emerged, according to Northam, that a sub-editor named Haslam from the *News of the World*, had told him that he'd been approached by Livermore for his address, and that Livermore had said there might be some money in it for Northam. Was this story of the bribe therefore wishful thinking on Northam's part? Or had it been concocted by Balmer, to whom he'd allegedly reported the matter?

Later when replying to a further question about the alleged bribe Northam's answer was inaudible, which prompted the judge to remark " I might just as well not be here as go on like this. Can you tell me what his last answer was?" This brought further laughter from the crowded public gallery, as Neild explained that Northam had said, "Kelly's statement was signed but not signed." A puzzled Oliver then said, "can we move on?"

When Northam said he'd reported the matter to Mr. Balmer, Neild retorted, "I suggest from first to last it is wholly untrue." With a hurtful look, Northam muttered, "It's not untrue." Could he describe the typist who called at his home and drove him to Liverpool, asked Neild. No, "she was just a woman wearing a costume." Neild then remarked how odd it was that he couldn't remember anything about a woman who came to him on such an "extraordinary mission" only two months ago and yet he could recall with regularity the details of events ten months ago.

After questioning Northam on his knowledge of the planning of crimes, Neild took him through his criminal career. Northam then admitted that he was first convicted at the age of 14 and put on probation for stealing. In 1942 he was convicted of shop-breaking and larceny, having 27 other offences taken into consideration. In 1945 he was sent to Borstal for house-breaking and shop-breaking. In 1946 he received 28 days at Birkenhead Sessions for house-breaking. In 1947 he was given a month's imprisonment for taking and driving away a motor car. And in January 1949 he was sentenced to three months at Brampton for receiving stolen property. On the latter occasion he agreed that Dickson was convicted with him.

When Northam denied ever having a gun, Neild asked, "Do you know a man named Rowlands?" Northam said he'd heard of him but wasn't sure whether he'd spoken to him.

This was a reference to a message from a Birkenhead man named Smith, who told Livermore that a man named Rowlands had seen Northam trying to sell a gun in a Birkenhead pub after the murder. Rowlands had however denied telling Smith this, *according to the police*. (My italics)

Neild went on to suggest to Northam that he was telling lies because if somebody else was convicted he would be all right, to which he casually replied, "Not necessarily." At this, the judge said to Neild, "are you suggesting he is a murderer?"

"I cannot do that", he replied. "How can I?"

"I thought you were asking about saving himself from the charge?"

"Yes", said Neild, "from being charged as an accessory, as he himself has indicated."

Before concluding his cross-examination Neild said to Northam that what he was saying about Connolly was wholly untrue in order to save himself. And on the matter of the alleged bribe from Livermore, he said, "I put it to you that it is a wicked lie throughout, and that it is part of your desire to see a conviction to save yourself being an accessory."

When Gorman took the matter up in re-examination the following day and began questioning Northam further, the judge said testily," Mr. Gorman this is not the case the jury are trying. If we are starting trying half a dozen cases I don't think we shall ever finish." But when Gorman persisted Oliver said he'd told him several times he did not want any repetition. Gorman then finally sat down.

During Heilbron's cross-examination Northam said that on March 19th he arrived in Liverpool from Durham at 2.00pm and went to Birkenhead. He and Dickson, *he thought,* went to the pictures and then went back to his home for tea. He then said that Dickson called for him at his home and they both went over to Liverpool in the evening.

The reason for these conflicting statements was not pursued by Heilbron - probably because he had pre-fixed the first with the *caveat,* "I thought."

He was then asked if he knew that at the beginning of May a man named Johnson had been arrested and charged with being an accessory in the Cameo murders *before* he was seen by the police on the 13th of May? Yes, he did but he was not very interested. Wasn't sufficiently interested, Heilbron asked, to even read about it? "I just didn't take much notice", he replied. He agreed he knew Johnson was alleged to have received the gun after the shooting, although according to his evidence, the gun had been thrown in the park lake by Kelly. At this point Gorman intervened to say there was no evidence that Northam had been seen on May the 13th.

To settle the matter Smith was recalled and said Northam was seen by the police on the night of the 13th / 14th of May, and the 23rd of May. Although Northam was allegedly "interviewed" about the Cameo on the occasions in May mentioned by Smith, the truth was that he was simply being spoken to by the police about Dickson's shop theft charges.

After the Chief Superintendent had spoken to him said Northam, it did occur to him to say something but he waited until September before giving a statement to Balmer.

The Liverpool Assizes was not a court of morals so perhaps Heilbron was quite correct in not criticising Northam further. But if his evidence about Kelly and Connolly in the *Beehive* was true, then he was quite prepared in May and June to remain silent whilst an innocent Johnson risked being convicted of accessory to murder.

Northam said he was born in the Brownlow Hill district of Liverpool. He knew the Wavertree district but he did not know where the Cameo cinema was.

In reply to Heilbron. Northam said it "slipped his mind", when he saw Kelly and Connolly leaving the *Beehive*, Kelly with a loaded gun in his pocket, to ask for his overcoat back. It also never occurred to him that, rather than Kelly giving him the overcoat back suggesting it should be burned, it would have been easier for Kelly to have burned it himself. He'd first had discussions with the police about the case in September. He told them, he said, about the overcoat but not that Kelly had given him it back in March. The police had found it after searching his house in October, but he'd already told them about it.

At this stage Northam was asked to try on the overcoat . When he stood in the well of the court and put it on it looked a very tight fit. Had the broader, heavier Kelly been asked to do likewise, it would have been obvious to the jury that it would not fit him. Unfortunately he was never asked.

Northam insisted that it was Connolly who had suggested robbing the Cameo. This was interesting because Graham, later in the proceedings, said Kelly told him the Cameo was his idea.

The judge said to Northam, "If Dickson did not go to lend a hand one could make some sense of the passage in your letter when you say, 'When I met her on the Sunday she had not been with them'. Where should she go on that night except home with you?" When Northam didn't reply, Oliver suggested, "Do you mean she went home with you that night?"

Whether or not the judge was affecting naiveté or deliberately trying to help Northam out of a hole, his observation was not only illogical, it was also irrelevant. He wasn't to know that at base the question was purely academic, since it was not Northam or Dickson who had written the letter but Norwegian Margie.

When Jacqueline Dickson entered the witness box on the fifth day of the trial she was unrecognisable as the scruffy bottle blonde so familiar a sight around Lime Street and it's back streets. With her expensively coiffured hair, now restored to it's original dark brown, and dressed smartly in a trim grey costume set off by a powder blue hat with a feather at the side, the young prostitute looked the epitome of respectability. Groomed, as well as tutored, whilst staying at the flat of W.P. Sergeant Jane Ashmore, the police had certainly done wonders for Dickson's image.

Referring to the incident when Kelly was alleged to have taken her to the *Caledonian* a fortnight after the murder and given her whisky, he said she only went with him because she was frightened of a man named Woolerton who was; "going to batter me." It was on this occasion, she said, that Kelly made the remark about having more money if the Cameo job had been successful, and threatened to cut her face open if she mentioned anything about the Cameo. She also stated he had met Connolly on two occasions since the murder. The first was when he gave her the bullets in a handkerchief, telling her to give them to Kelly when she saw him, and the second when she had tea with him in *Littlewoods'* cafe in Clayton Square, and asked her to go to the "Smoke" with her. When Heilbron asked if she was not concerned about acting as a go-between for two men who had been involved in a murder, she replied, "I was doing them a good turn."

"For a man involved in a brutal murder?", said Heilbron. Unperturbed she haughtily replied, " I would do a good turn for anyone, even for a dog."

Asked why Northam had kept six of the bullets, Dickson said he'd kept them to give to the police. But, said, Heilbron, she'd said in the Committal Court that he had kept them out of curiosity. Dickson made no reply.

During his cross-examination, Basil Neild, asked Dickson: "Who is this man Woolerton whom you say was going to batter you?" But before she could answer the judge told Neild: "If it is something that has nothing to do with this case I won't go into it". He then asked Dickson, "Has Woolerton got anything to do with this case?"

"No sir".

"Is it some private matter?"

"Yes". Addressing Neild the judge said, "Then it has something to do with her private life, and *she does not want to go into it.* But don't think I am trying to stop you". (My italics). Resentful of Oliver's reproval, Neild said, "Your Lordship will forgive my hesitation but I must do everything I can in the interests of my client."

"By all means do everything you think best.", he replied. Neild however said he would not pursue that line of examination any further.

This example of bias and disingenuous leading of the witness which effectively blocked an important and legitimate line of questioning was an unpleasant trait of Mr. Justice Oliver's and a recurring thorn in the side of the defence. Woolerton could well have been the person doing the threatening which the prosecution attributed to Kelly. Dickson had merely agreed that it was a private matter. At no time did she state that she "did not want to go into it". Yet here was the judge putting his own words into the mouth of the prosecution's Star witness?

Dickson had said in the letter she was talking to two people

Brownlow Hill at about 11.00pm. "Who were they?" asked Heilbron. "I cannot answer that", she replied. Given that she had and Northam had admitted that was a lie, Heilbron said, "But there were no two people?"

"No, she replied. She also agreed that it was a lie that she or Northam were drinking in Dale Street at 10.00pm.

Oliver's obstruction of defence counsel was again clearly evident when he now blocked Heilbron. During her cross-examination of Dickson on the dubious authorship of the anonymous letter, she asked, "When it is stated in the letter, `five days ago I seen the man who done the job`, who was the "I"? Dickson trembling and looking pale in the face of this simple question, was lost for words and made no reply. But again coming to the rescue, Oliver intervened, asking her. "Are you feeling unwell? Don't go on giving evidence if you don't feel well. Would you like to have a rest?"

"Yes sir", she gratefully replied.

"I understand she has been very ill", pronounced Oliver. He then excused her from giving any further evidence for the remainder of that day on the spurious ground that, *at his suggestion,* she was unwell. There had been no medical evidence submitted to the court that Dickson either was or had been "very ill."

Heilbron had come close to exposing the lie that Dickson and Northam had written the anonymous letter, only for Dickson to be saved once again by Oliver's unwarranted intervention - which was only slightly more benign than the committal magistrate's crude obstruction when refusing Livermore's repeated requests for Dickson to divulge her address, and refusing to allow the anonymous letter to be introduced as an exhibit.

When Dickson resumed her evidence the following day, she said, in reply to Heilbron, that the dark-haired girl was still there when she returned to the *Beehive,* but she left before her and Northam.

"Did you know at the time where Kelly lived?", asked Heilbron. "I knew where his brother lived."

"You did know Joe Kelly?"

"Yes."

"I am suggesting to you that you did not know George Kelly," said

Counsel. "Oh yes, I did know George Kelly" she defiantly replied.

When Heilbron said Dickson had told the Court she lived in Upper Parliament Street but never gave the house number, she retorted, "I don't intend to give the number" but agreed to write it down.

In a further reply she insisted that she and Northam had written the letter, adding that they wrote the letter just as it came into their minds, and it just set out what they knew. Favourably interjecting once again, Oliver said, "You did not know it would come to anything of this sort? When Dickson answered "No", he helpfully said, "What you put undoubtedly was true."

Returning to her line of questioning from the previous day Heilbron asked, "In the letter you say, 'Five days ago I saw the man who done the job' Who was the "I"?

"That was James Northam".

"And the man who had done the job was Kelly?" Yes. But she could not give any information about Northam seeing Kelly five days before the letter was written. On the 21st of March she had left Northam's company for an hour, according to their statements, which conveniently gave her the opportunity to see Connolly and receive the bullets from him!

Had she talked the letter over with anyone? asked Heilbron. No she had not. Why did the letter say they were in a pub in Dale Street at 10.00pm. when she now said they were in Birkenhead? "We put that because we didn't want the police to trace us."

At this point Oliver again intervened, asking her, "Could you have got witnesses to say you were in a public house in Birkenhead?" "Yes," she relied. Oliver then remarked, "If one substitutes Birkenhead for Dale Street the letter makes sense. You could have proved you were in Birkenhead?"

"Two people saw us."

Annoying as it was to Heilbron that Oliver should rescue Dickson time after time like this, she wasn't going to be deterred so easily. What about the part of the letter about talking to people in Brownlow Hill at 11.00pm?, she asked. Wasn't that also a lie? Dickson brazened this out by replying that it wasn't her who put that in, and that Heilbron "had better ask the witness Northam about that."

"But", she insisted, "you knew he was putting it in?"

"Yes."

"You knew it was false?" Dickson made no reply, and this time even the judge, for a change, had nothing to say.

Pressing her advantage, Heilbron returned to the two people who had supposedly seen her in Brownlow Hill and Dickson was forced to admit there were no two such people. Dickson then said the man in the letter she was scared of was Connolly. But when Heilbron reminded her she had testified yesterday that she wasn't scared of him, she said, "That's right. I was scared that he would make me go away with him."

She was also was frightened of him finding out where she lived because Northam's mother would get to know and the people she lived with knew his mother. Why was she scared of Northam's mother? She wasn't, she was just in love with Northam and didn't want to be separated from him, she said.

This line of questioning and Dickson's cryptic replies were getting Heilbron nowhere so deciding on a frontal attack, she said, "I suggest you never saw Kelly in the *Beehive* that night."

" I did see him", countered Dickson.

"And the rest of your evidence about Kelly is equally untrue?"

"It is all true."

Giving her a disdainful look Heilbron turned to the matter of the anonymous letter. "What did you mean in the passage, "about six weeks ago..."? This was a reference to the passage which stated, "I will give you both their names and some of the bullets he left with me about 6 weeks ago."

Dickson said she didn't think she wrote that part of the letter. "I dictated some of it. You must realise", she said, "this letter was an awful long time back and I don't quite remember everything." But there could be no mistake about a few days or six weeks? "It is badly written", said Dickson., "It might be a two or a six."

At this point Oliver examined the letter with a magnifying glass and told Heilbron, "It is for the jury to decide what it is, but the witness is entitled to say it is two or six."

Here was the judge once again helping out a self confessed liar, for the figure "6" in the letter was clearly distinguishable from a "2".

Moreover the word "weeks", which was clearly spelled out could not be mistaken for "days".

At the conclusion of Dickson's evidence Heilbron said to her, "Having seen that letter do you still say it is true?"

"Yes", she answered defiantly.

Before leaving the witness box, Mr. Justice Oliver, friendly to the end, asked if she was living in Manchester. When she told him she was living in Liverpool he said, in a fatherly tone, "You can go home now. I hope you won't be asked for again."

With a demure glance in his direction she thanked him and went "home" to Detective Sergeant Jane Ashmore's flat.

Chapter Twenty-four

"This Welter of Wickedness."
- Basil Neild, KC, MP.

When Dickson had been allowed to leave the witness box the revious day, Robert Graham was called. Dressed in a green tweed cket and grey flannels, the tall, thin, con man entered the witness box earing a look of bewildered innocence. He said he'd been a prisoner the hospital wing at Walton prison when Kelly and Connolly were here. He exercised with them on alternate days. On November the 4th he was walking around with Connolly when he asked him if he new Kelly. When he said he didn't, Connolly said he was in the bottom bservation cell.

Graham went on to relate how Connolly asked him to ask Kelly ow he was getting on and then said that, apart from being with Kelly n the night, he took no part in the murder. He then told him that he idn't know what made him think of doing a job like that because he ad money to draw from his job, including £15 holiday pay. Referring o the charge-room incident, he said Connolly told him that when Kelly ame in he shouted, "you don't know me, do you. You've never seen he before in your life". Connolly said, "Kelly done a damned fool hing. *It stuck out a mile.*"(My italics.)

Exercising with Kelly the next day, Graham said he passed Connolly's message to him. It was then that Kelly started telling him bout how he carried out the murders, and of how he was back in his wn pub within five minutes. "My life hangs on those five minutes", he aid... Kelly had told him, "*I had decided* to do a taxi driver but we ecided to do the Cameo instead." He also told him that he'd called Connolly a yellow bastard for running away, and that, instead of returning he overcoat to Northam, he should have burned it. (My italics)

This was not what Northam and Dickson had testified. They had oth insisted, even under cross-examination, that it was Connolly's idea o "roll" a taxi driver.

At this stage, Kelly, who had been listening intently, shook his head in disbelief and, ignoring the warders silent remonstrations, walked across the dock and leaned his head through the dock rail to speak to Livermore.

Continuing his evidence, Graham said he was so concerned about the gravity of what he had been told that he informed the Preston police when he appeared on remand there on November the 21st. The same day Mr. Balmer came to see him at Walton. He again saw Balmer two days later and he made a statement.

If he'd had this information which was "too great a responsibility for me to keep secret", asked Heilbron, why did he wait four or five days till his appearance at Preston? Why did he not tell the prison governor immediately? He didn't want to, he said, because he thought he might get into trouble for carrying messages.

In truth the statement was made to Balmer on the 28rd of November, after Graham had allegedly spoken to Kelly and Connolly several times, and had, what would appear, sufficient opportunity to get the full story from them.

In reply to Basil Neild, Graham said he was in prison awaiting trial for receiving stolen property, and had last been convicted in January 1949 of obtaining money under false pretences, for which he had received twelve months. The three offences had involved taking money off women in Lancashire on the pretext of doing favours for their gaoled husbands, including getting tobacco to them. When Neild asked him how many times he had been convicted he said, "Three times I have been in prison." But he had been *convicted* more than three times, said Neild, to which he agreed.

He was released from his last sentence on September the 18th, he said. And from then until November the 9th, he'd been working on a trawler out of Fleetwood and had not been in Liverpool during that time. But he admitted that he was in Walton prison at the time of the Cameo murder, and that other prisoners also knew about it. He arrived at Walton on November the 14th, he said, after being in custody in Preston for five days.

Graham's testimony here begged the question: what was he doing in Liverpool prison in the first place? He was a Preston man, charged with offences committed in Blackpool. Preston prison itself was a local emand prison. Indeed he had been in custody in Preston for five days prior to arriving in Walton. Had Balmer been behind his transfer? Had he been planted in the hospital wing? Unfortunately, none of these questions were put to him.

In cross-examination Heilbron put it to Graham that Kelly had said, "I'm not worried because I'm innocent." But he replied that far from that being the case, Kelly had said, "I'm not worried because I have a lot of brothers and if they find Jackie Dickson she'll never give evidence against me."

Replying to further questions from Heilbron Graham denied that it was possible for Kelly and Connolly to talk to each other through their cell bars. "Absolutely impossible", he emphatically stated. "Where they are situated it is impossible." At this point Kelly leaned across the dock to speak to his junior counsel, Mr. Trotter, and also said something to a warder who was chiding him.

Ignoring Graham's denials, Heilbron went on to suggest that it was not only possible but at night they actually conversed with one another across the corridor. But Graham insisted they couldn't, adding, "If I could describe the position of the cells I could show you how it is impossible."

Re-examined by Gorman, Graham said he got the information he had given the Court about the Cameo murder by the two men who had been charged with it.

Graham's evidence, which had continued after Dickson's resumed evidence, concluded the case for the prosecution which had lasted five and a half days, during which their two main witnesses had admitted lying. Their original statements, that Kelly had ran across the park, throwing the gun in the lake, and caught a tram home, had also been exposed as patently false.

On Thursday the 19th January, the sixth day of the trial, Basil Neild began his opening speech on behalf of Connolly. He was not, he said presenting his client as a faultless citizen. He had been in some trouble with the police but it was relatively minor. Otherwise he was a perfectly decent person and a good husband. The allegations about him consorting with other women were quite untrue. He had joined the Royal Navy at the age of 18 and had served with distinction until 1946, often being in the thick of battle.

The case against him, said Neild, fell into four parts:-

1. The evidence of Northam and Dickson as to the plan in the *Beehive*.

2. Allegations made by those two persons as to utterances made by him or things done by him in the days following March 19th.

3. The statements alleged to have been made by him to the police which were untrue.

4. The evidence of Graham.

he jury had heard 44 witnesses for the prosecution but the first 30 had never even mentioned Connolly, said Neild. Even assuming that the prosecution witnesses were telling the truth, there was no evidence that Connolly entered the cinema or fired any shot. Indeed, both Northam and Dickson had testified that Connolly had ran away after hearing the first shot. And they believed that he wanted to drop out after seeing a loaded weapon. Neild went on to state that Connolly was at a dance hall on the night of the murder, where he had also been on previous Saturday nights, with his wife and sisters Irene and Doris.

During Neild's speech and Connolly's own evidence there was, as there had been during the Crown evidence, numerous references to the police visiting his home at 1.50am on the morning of May the 14th. Mindful of Neild's warning not to alienate the judge and jury by attacking the police, he therefore acquiesced in this, rather than speak out about what he regarded after all as a mere technicality. It wasn't worth getting into the judge and jury's bad books for. The police did after all interview him on the 14th. But they never came to his home in May.

What the naive twenty six year-old Connolly was unaware of however, was the huge distinction between routinely being asked in Lime Street to call at the police station like hundreds of others, and three detectives specifically calling at his home in the early hours of the morning to take him away to be interviewed - and the consequent impression this made on the jury

When he was called by Neild, Connolly walked from the dock, still dressed in his smart brown suit, across the well of the court to the witness box. In reply to Neild's first question, he denied playing any part in the murder or the robbery at the Cameo. He then recounted his movements on the 19th of March, including the daytime visit to *Littlewoods'* cafe, the later visit to *Lewis'* to buy baby Tina a coat, and attending St. Mark's Dance in the evening.

Sangster was wrong to say he'd seen him with Kelly. He did not know Kelly. He knew Constable Nugent from around the Seaman's Employment Exchange but the constable was wrong when he said he had seen him with Kelly on March the 26th. He was not there. He knew Dickson only by sight through seeing her around Lime Street but had never spoken to her. He did not know Northam. He admitted writing the letter to Balmer when he was on remand in Walton but it was not to make a confession, it was to tell of what he'd overheard in the prison van. Balmer had asked him to turn Kings Evidence but he'd told him he didn't tell lies. He had never spoken to Graham about the murder. When in May Balmer asked him where he was on the night of March the 19th Balmer didn't tell him it was a Saturday. He had simply told him that, "around that time" (March) he was working in Bibby's, which he was. Had Balmer told him it was a Saturday, he would not have said that because his shift work did not include Saturdays.

In further replies to Neild, he said he was never at the *Beehive* that night. Was he at the Cameo? "No", he replied, "I don't know where the Cameo cinema is." Asked if he had been in the *White Star* on the Sunday, he said he usually stayed in bed till twelve or one o'clock on a Sunday. As for the allegation that he had told everyone in the *White Star* on the Sunday after the murder, that he was leaving the country, he said he'd been trying to emigrate to Australia for about two years before the murder. He had a brother who was already living there. In answer to the judge, he said he went to the dance that particular night to protect his sister, who had received a black eye the previous week.

When Connolly denied the reason for writing to Balmer was because he wanted to confess his part in the murder, Gorman tried another angle. "In that letter", he said, " Is it not that you are saying quite clearly that Kelly did the murder, and that the man Skelly was with him and he was mistaken for you?" That was not so, said Connolly.

He'd written it simply to tell Balmer what he'd overheard in the prison van, and that all the police officers who'd said they saw him with Kelly might have mistaken him for Skelly, "because he looks a bit like me."

Gorman initially derided Connolly's claims to have been at the Dance. And when his wife Mary was giving evidence he suggested to her that she had got together with her husband to arrange an alibi. She however insisted she was telling the truth.

When Basil Neild rose to re-examine, he asked Connolly's wife if she had a letter in her possession. She then produced a letter which Neild handed to the judge. It bore the date stamp "18th March" on the envelope and the date on the top of the letter, and was addressed to Connolly's sister. In it she had clearly stated to her sister-in-law that she and "Charlie" had been to the Dance the previous week and were going again on Saturday (the 19th). She added that they'd had their photographs taken, "but I don't know what they'll be like till Saturday." The letter also said that she'd entered the crooning competition and "Charlie" had been "made up" because she'd won. It ended with her saying what a good time they'd had at the dance, and that they were now looking forward to going to Bibby's staff dance at Reece's in town on April the 2nd.

This was a damaging setback for the prosecution but, undeterred, Gorman immediately set about trying to build an alternative case to show that Connolly had not arrived at the Dance until about 10.00pm, which would have given him sufficient time to have been at the Cameo.

Connolly's mother and sisters followed his wife into the witness box, as did the sister's friends Betty Dixon, Frances Roberts and Frances Cairns. All swore he was at the Dance between 9.30 and 10.00pm. But another young lady at the dance named Teresa McCormack, who later said she had reluctantly given evidence, testified that she did not see Connolly dancing with his sister until 10.15pm.

When the Dance Organiser, Charles McBain, gave evidence, although a defence witness, he damaged Connolly's case by stating that the Rumba competition, which Connolly said he'd taken part in, did not start till after ten o'clock. He also said that was the first time he'd noticed Connolly in the dance hall. He could remember, he said, because Connolly was *wearing a trilby* and he was going to ask him o take it off. (My italics)

On this matter, McBain may well have been correct in first seeing Connolly 'wearing the trilby' after ten o'clock because it was only when he thought the last waltz had started, and they were getting ready to leave, that Connolly had put on his hat.

The photographer, Thomas Milligan, testified that Connolly did pay him for the photographs but couldn't say whether that was on the 9th or the 26th of March. He agreed with Gorman that he usually arrived at St. Mark's after the pubs closed, which was ten o'clock. He also agreed that Connolly could have collected the photographs from him on the following Saturday if he hadn't been at the dance on the 9th.

In addition to Connolly's family, other defence witnesses included, Michael O'Hanlon, a billiards room attendant at the *Vines* Public house in Lime Street, otherwise know as "The Big House". He testified that Connolly regularly frequented the billiards room and was always alone. He did not know Kelly. James O'Reilly, a doorman at the *Lime Tree Cafe*, likewise said Connolly, whom he'd known for three years, was usually alone when he came to the cafe. He did not know George Kelly.

Father Thomas Frayne then entered the witness box. An " assistant priest" at St. Columbia's Church in Huyton, he testified that Connolly had consulted him twice about emigrating to Australia, once in May 1948 and later in January 1949, both occasions being prior to the murders.

On Monday the 23rd of January Rose Heilbron, in her opening speech on behalf of Kelly, told the jury that the Crown had presented," a remarkable, bewildering, indeed a most fantastic case. You are expected to believe", she said, "that Kelly gave Northam as graphic and detailed account of the murder as a Somerset Maugham short story." Northam and Dickson she said were people quite unworthy of belief. At the approximate time of the murder, 10.40pm Kelly had allegedly dashed from the murder scene to the *Leigh Arms*, where he was drinking at 9.40! But Griffin, the cinema fireman had followed the gunman in the opposite direction. Also, she said, the Crown had asserted that the murderer had entered through the side door but there was a girl on duty to open and close it. No gun, overcoat, bullets, hat or mask had ever been traced to Kelly.

Referring to the bullets allegedly given to Dickson by Connolly Heilbron reminded the jury that Northam was supposed to have kept six of them out of curiosity. It was said they were kept in order to prove the story to be told to the police but Dickson took them out of his pocket and put them down different drains. "It was a curious form of curiosity", she said. And did they jury, she asked, believe one word of Northam's amazing story about lending his overcoat and how he got it back?

When he was finally called to the witness box, a determined looking Kelly took the oath in a loud voice, and when asked had he done the murder he shook his head vigorously and said he had not. At Heilbron's request he then detailed his movements from when he met Skelly on the afternoon of the 19th to the following afternoon when he left the *Leigh Arms* at 2.00pm He had never met Connolly in his life before his arrest, he said, and he did not know Northam or Dickson He hadn't told Graham anything about the murder. He was not in Lime Street on the September 26th when Richardson and Nugent were supposed to have seen him. He was at home all day.

Kelly said he left the *Spofforth Hotel* at about 9.20pm and arrived at the '*Leigh* about five minutes later, where he stayed until closing time. He told Inspector Balmer everywhere he had been on the 19th, including going to the *Spofforth* to look for Doris O'Malley. He denied Skelly had said he supposed Kelly was one of the people who brought him home because he was too drunk to remember. He left Skelly at about 8.30 in the *Coach and Horses*. Despite Heilbron's warning about antagonising the judge and jury, he then said he was prepared to contradict everything Balmer had said about the visit to Skelly's home.

Referring to the charge room incident, he said, "Although I'd never seen Connolly in my life before, I automatically realised he was the man being charged with me because there were no other prisoners there". He didn't deny asking Connolly something but he hadn't said "You've never seen me in your life before have you?"

He denied telling Graham anything about the murder, although he did tell him he was charged with it. His and Connolly's cells were about ten yards from each other, he said, and they talked every night. He also sat next to him in Church. At the identity parade when he was picked out by Sangster, he denied threatening Balmer but admitted saying, "I won't forget you for this Balmer." He'd said that because he was angry at being picked out by Northam and Dickson, whom he didn't know, and then by Sangster whom he did know. "I was boiling at that time because I was charged with a murder I did not commit".

Cross-examined by Gorman, he said he did not mean the remark to Balmer as a threat. He had not adopted the attitude of, "I am Kelly. I am quite different from ordinary people." When Gorman said if he were at the Cameo at 9.35 he could easily have got to the *Leigh Arms* for 9.45, Kelly replied, "I could have done but I didn't."

He denied telling Graham the *Leigh Arms* was his pub. When Gorman asked how Graham could know about him drinking there at 9.45pm, Kelly said he could have got to know through the cleaners. He'd told the cleaners about the case. He denied telling Graham his life depended on five minutes. "My life does not depend on five minutes", he robustly declared, "because I am innocent."

Gorman asked if he was not interested to know what time the murder took place and Kelly again emphatically replied, "I was not interested. I had nothing to do with it." He couldn't explain, he said, why Graham had given evidence against him. He could only suggest that he was in a jam and the best way of getting out of it was to give evidence against him. "I say that", he went on, "because Graham stood in this witness box and told lies against me. There's no other way of looking at it, and I still say that." His voice now rising with emotion, he declared, "I am innocent. I don't know anything about this murder."

When Gorman in his Oxford accent, asked Kelly if the dark, heavily made-up girl was Norwegian Margie, laughter broke out once again. This time Oliver warned he would clear the court if there was any more laughter during the proceedings. Kelly said he knew a Marjory Dawson but didn't know if she was the same woman. Did he know she had committed suicide? asked Gorman. "I don't know", he replied. "She could commit suicide a thousand times for all I know. It is nothing to do with me." Gorman then asked how Graham could know all about

Dickson unless he had told him. "How could I tell him about her if I didn't know her", he retorted. "There are plenty of people in prison who talked to Graham." When Gorman persisted in asking him about Dickson, Kelly angrily protested, "I don't know Dickson. I don't know none of them in this case. I don't know what I'm doing in this hall today!"

Questioned later about Woolerton, Kelly once again erupted. "I deny everything you say", he cried. "I don't know Dickson!. I don't know Northam! I don't know Woolerton ! I don't know any of them!" Aware now of Kelly's excitability, Gorman continued to prod him. How could Northam know everything about how the murder had been committed, he asked, unless Kelly had told him?

By now however, Kelly realised the negative affect his demeanour must be having so he gave his answer in a more relaxed fashion. "I don't know", he replied tellingly. "But Northam seems to be the one who knows all about it; about the lock business and the spiral staircase. He has told the story."

At this point the judge asked Kelly, "Are you saying that he is the murderer?" Avoiding a direct answer, he replied, "All I am saying is that if Northam has done this murder he has blamed two innocent men. I don't know Charles Connolly."

Later in his cross-examination Gorman suggested to Kelly that the charge room incident was to warn Connolly to say he didn't know him. "Why should I say that?", he replied. I could have told him before we ever went to the police station if I'd known him."

At one stage during Gorman's intense cross-examination, Kelly said, " I am sorry for the man who was shot but I didn't shoot him." And Heilbron's warning must have been taken to heart when Gorman asked if Balmer had treated him properly throughout or did he have any complaints about him. Kelly resignedly said, "No, I suppose he was acting on information."

When Kelly left the box, Heilbron called a succession of witnesses, including "Yorkie Bob" and Edna Bore, the barmaid at the *Leigh Arms*. "Yorkie" agreed with Heilbron that he stood with Kelly and Skelly outside the Royal William on March the 19th, before having a drink with them. He left them, he said at about 7.30pm. Seizing on this,

Gorman asked him if Kelly could have been at the *Beehive* some five minutes later, to which he agreed.

Edna Bore said she served Kelly with a drink at 9.45pm in the public bar. He went over towards the dart board and she never saw him after that, because the pub was pretty crowded. Once again however, she unfortunately was not asked whether it was 9.45pm *on the clock*. (My italics) Had she said it was, here again would have been clear proof that Kelly was in the pub at 9.35pm and could not possible have been at the Cameo.

When Thomella, the *Leigh Arms* licensee, was giving evidence he stated that he was not sure whether Kelly was in his pub between 9.00pm and 9.50pm. Gorman then read out the statement he signed in the back of the police car in January, in which he said Kelly was "definitely" not in his house between those times. "You understand the difficulty with this?", he said warningly. Thomella replied that he thought he had used the words, "not to my knowledge" in the statement he made to Mr. Balmer. Was he, a policeman with twenty three years experience, still saying that now, asked Gorman?, brandishing the statement before him. Yes he was. Mr. Justice Oliver then told him, "It was a little rash to say, ' I am quite certain'. It was a categorical statement. You have said he might have been sitting down behind people but you said before you were quite certain he was not there. You see the difference?" Thomella meekly replied, "Yes my lord". He then testified that Kelly was in his pub the following day from about 12.45 till 2.00pm, and was upset because he said he'd been interviewed about the Cameo murder. When Gorman asked why he hadn't told the police that, he said he couldn't remember being asked about Kelly's movements on the Sunday.

The conflict between Thomella's evidence and what was contained in his January statement, had the effect of discrediting all of his testimony. And both Gorman in his closing speech, and Oliver in his summing-up, would ridicule and castigate him for "changing his evidence!" The court however did not have the benefit of seeing Thomella's original statement of October 4th, which would have shown his evidence to be both truthful and consistent. Throughout the licensee's courtroom humiliation Balmer, sitting in the well of the court, remained expressionless. But he was no doubt glad that once again he had got in first.

Skelly, like Graham earlier, had been brought from Walton Prison where he was still serving the six months. But unlike the Crown's witness he was brought up from the cells, and had to make his way through the dock past Kelly and Connolly to enter the witness box. This arrangement made it quite clear to the jury that he was a prisoner.

Corroborating Kelly's evidence about their movements on the 19th of March, he denied that he had told Balmer he didn't remember if Kelly was one of those who brought him home drunk. He had told Balmer that Kelly left him in the *Coach* and Horse at about 9.00pm He knew that because he looked at the clock at 8.55pm. He was helped home by a neighbour, Taffy Roberts, at closing time.

Before continuing his cross-examination, Gorman read out Skelly's extensive record, which included offences of larceny of a bicycle receiving, unlawful wounding and assault on the police. He then asked for emphasis, "Are you not in prison today?", He could hardly do otherwise than agree. In further replies, he said he was amazed that Balmer didn't take his overcoat away for examination since a brown coat was apparently involved. If Kelly said he left him at 8.30pm he was probably right because the clock in the *Coach and Horses* was twenty minutes fast. "You don't set much store by your times do you?" said Gorman sarcastically. "I can't say much about the times", he replied I was getting drunker and drunker." He admitted he had a hangover the following morning when police officers called with Kelly, but he still remembered what had been said.

Skelly said he did not know Northam or Dickson and he was not in the *White Star* the following afternoon. If they said they saw him there they were lying, he said.

Two brothers named Walter and Reginald Bampton said they were in the *Leigh Arms* at 9.30pm on the night in question and saw Kelly in the Bar, and when they left twenty minutes later he was still there. Asked by Gorman how he could fix the time, Walter Bampton said he could fix it by the clock in the *Cambridge*, where they had just left, and the clock in the *Leigh Arms*, both of which were fast. When Reginald Bampton said upon their arrival at the '*Leigh* it was 9.30pm on the clock, Gorman asked, "What do you mean, 'on the clock? Are you guessing the time?". No he wasn't guessing. He knew how fast the pub clocks were, so could gauge the correct time.

Two street photographers named Manson and McKinnon had earlier testified to being in the *Beehive* for practically all of the evening of the 19th of March, and although they knew Kelly, they did not see him there. How could they remember that particular night, Gorman wanted to know? They explained that it was the night before Jump Sunday, when people went around Aintree inspecting the jumps a week before the Grand National, and they were making arrangements to photograph people.

The last two witnesses were Kathleen "Colleen" Dutton aged 19, a waitress at an hotel in Onslow Square London, and her friend Mary Smith, also a waitress. They both testified that in September 1949 they were working in Llandudno. Dutton said that on September the 25th she had received a telephone call and a money order from Kelly. She and her friend came to Liverpool on the 26th and stayed at Kelly's house in Trowbridge Street, arriving at about 2.30pm. They stayed at the house until about 7.30pm when they all went out to the pub. She and her friend then got the midnight train to London. Replying to Gorman, she agreed she was in love with Kelly. But she emphatically refuted his suggestion that she was pregnant by him or had, indeed, ever been intimate with him. When Gorman challenged her that Kelly was in Lime Street at 5.50pm on September the 26th, she said, "He was never out of the house at that time". Smith said that Kelly never left them between 2.30 and 7.30pm. Finally Gorman asked Dutton if she had been told by someone to give this story. With a look of indignation she forcefully replied, " I was not told to say anything, only to tell the truth."

On the ninth day during Basil Neild's closing speech, Gorman made another dramatic disclosure. This time it was a work mate of Walter Bampton's, named Fleming, who had told the police that Bampton told him that he did not see Kelly on the 19th of March until 9.40pm. Brampton had told him that Kelly could have done the murder, as he was out of breath when he saw him. Brought back to the witness box, Brampton vehemently denied the allegation and stated that there were other work colleagues present on that occasion who could disprove what Fleming had said. Brushing this aside Gorman asked Oliver's permission to put Fleming in the witness box, but since there were other work mates present on the occasion who were not being called, Oliver refused, saying if they were all called the case would never end.

In his resumed closing speech, during which he referred to the prosecution case as, "this welter of wickedness", Neild described Dickson as, " a woman of loose morals... for whom one might have more sympathy than censure" Northam, he said had put the blame on Connolly in order to gain immunity. And his account of the alleged Livermore bribery incident was a wicked lie, designed to lay the blame even more strongly elsewhere in order to avoid being charged as an accessory. "When I consider the wickedness of these witnesses", he said, "would it be safe to act on their testimony?"

Heilbron, addressing the jury in her closing speech, again referred to the proceedings as, "this most fantastic case." She went on, "It is suggested for your consideration that on the night of March the 19th 1949 five people congregated in the public part of a well known public house on the busiest night of the week. It is said a plot was hatched. A bulky gun was produced, a handkerchief was tried to see if it would fit as a mask. But the story does not end there. The improbabilities thicken and strengthen. You are taken to another public house and there on a Sunday afternoon these people again foregather, not in some dark corner, not in some secret place, but again in an even more public part of an equally public place..."

Northam and Dickson, she said, were telling lies to protect themselves from prosecution. As for Graham, he could have got his information from the newspaper reports of the committal proceedings. If Kelly confided in him why hadn't he told him where and how he disposed of the mask and the gun and the hat? Why did he only tell things which were *already known to the police?* (My italics)

Kelly had lain in a prison cell, she said, for six weeks protesting his innocence to everyone before Graham arrived. Why should he suddenly unburden his soul to this complete stranger? He had admitted being in the *Spofforth*, she said. Didn't this point to his innocence rather than guilt? If he committed the murder would he go and identify himself to the licensee and admit that he had been only minutes away from where the actual murder was? The police had been engaged on the murder enquiry for six months, and with all the resources at their disposal they had not come up with anyone, apart from Northam and Dickson, who had seen Kelly with a gun. Whether or not she was aware of it Heilbron then went to the very root of the entire case when she remarked, *"Norwegian Margie remains the mystery she started."* (My italics)

In his closing speech, Gorman made great play of the fact that Doris O'Malley had not been called by the defence. "Where oh where is Doris O'Malley?", he dramatically declaimed. "Why hasn't she been called to back up Kelly? She was living with him at the time after all." Although O'Malley, had nothing to contribute, it was nonetheless a very good question.

Was she told that if she gave evidence she would be cross-examined on Kelly's violence towards her, which would make him look even blacker? Or was she told that her reputation as a former prostitute would be revealed? Whatever the reason, she was as Gorman said, conspicuous by her absence.

On the Friday morning of the 27th January, Mr. Justice Oliver began his summing-up…It would prove to be one of the most biased, unfair, and damning against any accused person ever heard in a court of law. (1)

It seemed Oliver, at least, had already made up his mind as to the guilt of the two accused men. Disparaging the evidence called in defence of Connolly he said, that he had admitted he could have been at the Cameo at 9.35pm and still been at the Dance at 10.00pm . He then went on to say that the Dance organiser, McBain, had stated that the Rumba competition would not start before 9.45pm and not after 10.15pm…and he should know. "If you take the average you get ten o'clock and you have two women who have said they didn't see him before the Rumba competition"

Oliver omitted to remind the jury that Connolly had strenuously denied being at the Cameo or even knowing where it was. Nor did he mention that there were four witnesses who had testified that he *was* at the Dance for the Rumba competition. The credibility of these witnesses was scorned by the judge. Referring to Connolly's sister Doris, he said "Just fancy her being asked after more than half a year what happens on a particular evening, which was just the same to her as any other Saturday evening; asked to say when somebody came. If some disaster happened she might, but on that particular evening how could she remember? But she did her best."

When it came to the understandable lack of preciseness by the two photographers McKinnon and Manson, who said they had been in the *Beehive* all night and had never seen Kelly there, Oliver said, "it is terribly difficult to cast you mind back nine or ten months and think what you were doing. You may remember that a particular day was a Saturday but does it necessarily mean that you remember it was the very day?"

This planting of doubt in the minds of the jury was despite the two men having testified on oath that they particularly remembered it was March 19th because it was the evening before Jump Sunday. And that as photographers who earned their living at Aintree, they had met to make arrangements for the following day's event.

Casting further doubt specifically on Manson's evidence of how he fixed the time, Oliver said, He first of all said he judged it, then said he looked at the clock and it was a few minutes before nine. Then he said when he looked at the clock it was 8.45pm, and finally it ends up with, 'I looked at it was about 8.45pm. That is rather like a kaleidoscope of memory".

Once again the judge had cast an entirely unwarranted doubt on the evidence of a crucial defence witness. Given that there had been throughout the trial repeated mention of pub clocks being fast - usually ten minutes - Manson's evidence seemed plausible. In his estimation of the time he was obviously making allowance for the *Beehive* clock being fast.

Referring to Skelly's evidence, he implied that it went without saying it should be rejected. "I have reminded you earlier of his poor record", he said. Adding, with barely concealed derision, "His evidence is what you think it's worth. Neither more nor less."

Then dealing with Kelly allegedly being in Cases Street at 7.30pm he said there was only Skelly's evidence to support Kelly when he denied being there. Having already made clear his contempt for his testimony, the judge then said, "You will give that evidence what weight you think it deserves." As for Kelly's assertion that Balmer took him to Prescot Street to get Skelly's address, he said, "Would you not think a Chief Inspector would know his address? I should imagine everybody knew *his* address."

With a reference to Northam's and Dickson's evidence, Oliver told the jury, "If those were the wrong people that those witnesses picked out, what risks they took - the picking out of people they did not know to be accused of murder. They might have picked out any of 100,000 young men in Liverpool round about the same age, men who were nowhere near Liverpool at the time of the murder. Was it a lucky chance that the two men...picked out were not only in Liverpool that night but that Connolly at the crucial time was at a dance only a mile away, and the other one, Kelly, admitted he was within a few hundred yards of the cinema when the murder was committed..."

As far as is known, Oliver never had an inkling of a conspiracy between Balmer and the three main prosecution witnesses - which included the intensive and prolonged tuition of Northam and Dickson between September the 24th, when they returned from Manchester, and September 29th, when they made their first statements. And it is a truism even today that judges are most reluctant to accept that police officers can be corrupt. But making due allowance for this, could a High Court judge, a former eminent barrister, with years of experience in the courts, trying, prosecuting and defending criminals, and therefore knowing that the police must have checked Connolly's and Kelly's every movement on March 19th, really have been so naive? Did the possibility never once cross his mind that, far from Northam and Dickson "picking out" the two accused, Kelly and Connolly might have been carefully *picked out for them*? And that they were selected precisely *because* they had no alibis for the crucial times.

Whether Oliver's naiveté was assumed or genuine, his prejudice against the accused men knew no limits as he continued his address the jury, "You have got this great chasm. Could it have been true that Northam and Dickson did not know either of the accused? Take their statements given on September 29th. It has never been suggested that anything was added to their statements, *except what you may think very important matters*. Nothing else. They went into the witness box at the police (magistrates) court upon those statements". (My italics).

Here Oliver was at his most disingenuous. Either nothing was added to their statements or some things were. And if "very important matters" were added, as Oliver himself acknowledged, then it was inaccurate, grossly misleading to the jury and most unfair to the accused men, to try to establish at the outset that "nothing else" was added to their statements. It was even more irresponsible to imply to the jury that "very important matters" added to a statement are not really *important* anyway.

If there was any private doubt in the judge's mind about the veracity of Northam and Dickson's evidence, he only had to recall their earlier admissions, under cross-examination, of lying in parts of the anonymous letter, which they both claimed authorship of. Indeed, this self-confessed lying alone entitled the accused men to an acquittal on the grounds that the prosecution evidence was wholly tainted. That is to say, if Northam and Dickson admitted to lying in the letter, which formed the basis of their evidence, then the jury could not be sure that the remainder of their evidence was not also lies. At the very least the accused should have been given the benefit of the doubt. But Oliver never instructed the jury, on that matter, to give them that benefit.

In truth there was a succession of additions to Northam's and Dickson's original statements of September 29th, right up to the committal hearing and beyond. And these "constructive" additions, without exception, each had the effect of building up a more damning case against Kelly and Connolly. The most damaging of these were made in relation to the incriminating overcoat and the equally incriminating meeting in the Star public house the day after the murder. Indeed, a later Home Office report by Sir Frank Newsome, the Permanent Under Secretary, conceded that it was,... "not very satisfactory that Northam's and Dickson's statements to the police were given in instalments. e.g. the important evidence about the borrowing of the coat and the meeting in the *White Star* pub were not mentioned in their original statements."

In Dickson's statement of September 29th, for example, not

only was there no mention of the meeting in the *White Star* but she actually stated, "On the following day witness Northam and I stayed in Birkenhead". Northam's statement agrees that he and Dickson stayed in Birkenhead, *"all* of the next day, 20th March" (My italics).

Again, Dickson's statement ends, "When I saw the accused Kelly in the *Beehive* public house on the 19th March, he was wearing a *dark raincoat* or overcoat, with a belt around it". (My italics)

If this was indeed an overcoat belonging to Northam, and she had witnessed him handing it to Kelly in the *Beehive* passageway, as she later testified, then surely she would have said so in this first statement? Furthermore, if this incident was true, she would have been in no doubt that it was an *overcoat* and that the overcoat was not "dark" but actually medium brown with conspicuous squares, as the cinema eye-witnesses had testified? Northam however, also declared in his *first* statement that, "Kelly's *Mac or coat* was open. I could see a pair of pliers sticking out." (My italics). If, according to this statement, Kelly was already wearing a "Mac" or a coat that looked like a Mac, why would Northam have needed to lend him his overcoat, as he was to later testify? And if Northam did lend Kelly his *own* overcoat, there would be no "or" about it. He would have been *certain* it was an overcoat.

Even if we accept that Kelly took off his "Mac or overcoat" and asked Northam for his more conspicuous garment, what happened to Kelly's own "Mac" or overcoat? Nobody ever explained that. But the prosecution never really had to, because by the time the case reached the Committal Court, the two statements had changed and there was no longer any reference to Kelly's "Mac or coat."

In view of their later statements - that Northam lent his *brown overcoat* to Kelly - why did Northam's and Dickson's original statements both mention the possibility of a "Mac" at all ? Could the reason be that when Kelly was asked by Balmer on the morning after the murder, if he had an overcoat, Kelly had replied, *"No, but I've got a Mac?"* (My italics) And could it be, when the alleged brown murder overcoat finally "emerged" from Northam's house nine days before the committal proceedings, that this was seen by the prosecution as much more valuable to their case, incriminating Kelly, as it did, more directly than a mere "Mac or overcoat"? After all, the " Mac or overcoat" could have been anybody's. But now the prosecution had the *"actual"* overcoat which fitted the cinema witnesses descriptions! Nonetheless, neither the police nor the defence appear to have considered a scientific analysis necessary or sufficiently important to establish that it really was the murder overcoat. Thus the jury were left to dangerously assume without challenge, that this was indeed the murderer's overcoat, simply because Northam, an admitted liar, had said so.

Other passages in both Northam's and Dickson's original statements clearly show how the *real author* of the statements, in his determination to build a stronger case against Kelly and Connolly was guilty of overkill and is thus shown as being too clever by half. That is to say, Dickson says about the anonymous letter in her 29th September statement: *"Northam wrote a letter and sent it to the police*. He felt better after that. *I posted it* in Kingsley Road about half-past four on the Sunday. *It got lipstick on from my pocket"*. (My italics) Northam in his statement of the same date agrees, "I started to write it (the letter) to the Superintendent but couldn't spell it, so I wrote 'Inspector.' I gave it to Jackie to post and it got lipstick on it".

Now despite Dickson's statement cleverly leaving details quite flexible. i.e. "Northam....*sent* it to the police". And, *"I posted it"*, (My italics) nowhere in Northam's statement does he indicate that he was with her when she posted it. How therefore could *he* possibly know there was lipstick on the envelope when she posted the letter? Dickson, moreover, never claimed at any time that the lipstick was put there deliberately as a sort of identification mark. According to her testimony it had got onto the envelope *accidentally* from her pocket. If that were true would even Dickson , in her allegedly agitated state, have observed the lipstick smudge in the split second it took to transfer the envelope from her pocket to the post-box? And if Northam, as he later added to his statement, wrote *and posted* the letter himself, how could lipstick from Dickson's pocket get onto the envelope?

The only other logical explanation is that the reference to the lipstick in their statements was dictated by Balmer. He did after all state in his evidence that it was he who sent the envelope and letter to the Forensic Laboratory at Preston in May 1949, and was told that what he thought was a franking mark on the envelope was actually lipstick Northam's and Dickson's "exclusive" knowledge however, about the lipstick would prove conclusively that they were telling the truth! For, as the judge was to ask the jury, "How could *they* have possibly known about the lipstick unless they had sent the letter"?

There was however, other evidence which clearly indicated that neither Northam or Dickson had anything to do with the writing of the anonymous letter. For at the Committal Court hearing on the 19th of October, Northam's statement, as mentioned above, had completely changed. His deposition given there stated: *"I posted* the letter on the Sunday at about 4-30pm...I *wrote a letter which I posted"*. Dickson's statement had also changed. She now stated that she *and* Northam *wrote* the letter! (My italics)

In the face of so much uncertainty and ambiguity, it should have been clear to a judge of Oliver's experience that, insofar as the purported truth of these statements - and that of Graham - was concerned, the police were the real source of the information contained in them, the "common denominator" throughout being the detective who actually took their statements, the man in charge of the case - Chief Inspector Balmer.   No doubt both Heilbron and Neild suspected this. Indeed Neild at one stage was accused by the judge of being, "willing to wound but afraid to strike", but convention, and the interests of their clients forbade them from directly attacking the police.

Although the hand of Balmer should have been clear as daylight to Oliver, it apparently escaped him because his summing-up continued thus: "Now just consider this members of the jury - a tremendous lot has been made by the defence that they (Northam, Dickson and Graham) could have got a lot of information from the newspapers. Of course they would get some of the details out of the newspapers. They would get the fact of the killing, the shooting and very likely the number of shots. But they would not get any *complete picture* until these court proceedings when the witnesses went into the box..." To support his contention the judge then said, "I am going to take you through Dr Grace's evidence, which was given on October 19th, *three weeks after* Northam and Dickson had given their statements" (my italics)

He then recited in detail the evidence of the expert witness, Dr.

Grace, the Home Office Pathologist, including the telling points that, in Dr. Grace's view, the cinema manager Mr. Thomas, had his arm outstretched when he had been shot and that his assistant, Mr. Catterall was probably on his hands and knees when he had received the fatal bullet wound. "This is what Dr. Grace says in Thomas's case, describing the wounding under the arm and the fatal shot on the chest, `The superficial abrasion under the left arm, I have no doubt, came about by the arm being held up in an attitude of protection`. He described the passage of the bullet and he then examined the body of Catterall. That man's body was found behind the door. The doctor said, 'I form the opinion when the wound was inflicted, probably the man was on his hands and knees when the shot was fired' "

"From there", continued the judge, " I pass to Northam's evidence, And I am going to invite you to consider *how* Northam could possibly have got this information unless he himself were the murderer *or got it from the murderer.*" (My italics) Oliver's clear instruction here to the jury was that Northam was not the murderer so they *must* therefore accept his evidence that Kelly was the murderer. He then stated almost as a matter of *fact*, that there was *no other alternative* for them to consider. (My italics)

But there *was* another alternative. In fairness to Oliver however, even if he wasn't as naive as he appeared to be, he could hardly alert the jury to this other alternative without publicly impugning the police - particularly since neither Rose Heilbron or Basil Neild had suggested it. He could have quite legitimately however, enlightened the jury to the neutral fact that although, as he correctly said, Northam and Dickson's statements were taken almost three weeks before Dr. Grace gave his evidence in the Committal Court, the *police* nonetheless had been in possession of Dr. Grace's findings since the previous March - *six months before* Northam's and Dickson's statements were taken!

The learned judge moreover must have known that the one person who would have carefully studied, indeed, whose *duty* it was to study, the pathologist's report as the officer in charge of the case, was Detective Chief Inspector Balmer - the same officer who had taken Northam's and Dickson's statements. But then, if Oliver had made this observation it would have demolished this crucially telling point against

Kelly !

Oliver continued, " No-one has ever suggested that Northam was himself the murderer." Now although Kelly had never expressly accused Northam of the murder, this remark of Oliver's totally overlooked Kelly's emotional reply to Gorman ,during cross-examination, as to how Northam could have known what happened in the managers office, when Kelly had exclaimed , "He seems to know more about it than anyone else." Again, in order to consolidate the impression to the jury that *only* Kelly could have known what actually took place in the cinema, Oliver went on: *"This is Kelly's statement to Northam*, he went into the manager's office. There was an old fellow sitting down. He said to him, ` I want the takings....the old man tried to brush the gun aside`. Kelly said, `I could not be bothered with him anymore so I shot him`. He then said, ` I put my gun in my pocket and picked up the bag... *the door opened and another man came in* "'. (My italics)

Oliver did not see fit to remind the jury that this was simply what Northam had *alleged* Kelly had told him. By simply telling the jury, "This is Kelly's statement to Northam", as though it were proven fact, with the implication that it had all of the authority of a signed admission, the judge invested Northam's evidence with a totally unwarranted and gravely misleading credibility. Moreover he failed to mention the cinema cashier and the salesgirl Valerie Thornhill, (who was counting money with the two men when the cashier arrived) had both testified that Catterall was in the office with the manager minutes before they heard the shots. Rather than concede that this clearly contradicted what Kelly was supposed to have told Northam, i.e. "The door opened and another man came in", Oliver had a ready explanation for the jury thus: "It was quite properly pointed out to you that when last seen in the room Catterall was with the manager. No doubt the witnesses were right. *But there were rooms to which Catterall might wish to go at any moment"*. (My italics) This was pure speculation on the judge's part, which flew in the face of the evidence of the two women. He was saying in effect, that although the evidence of the cinema staff witnesses was true, they could nonetheless be wrong! But there was not a shred of evidence from anyone in the cinema that night that Catterall had been seen anywhere other than in the manager's office in the minutes immediately preceding the murders.

Resuming his quotation of Northam's evidence, Oliver continued to deal with Kelly's alleged "confession" to him: `"He (Catterall) kept his hands behind his back and said, 'what are you doing here?` And Kelly said the man came towards him and made a grab at the bag...Kelly then said he shot him and Kelly said the man went down and started screaming and tearing at his chest and the man got to his knees.` And remember", emphasised the judge, "the doctor's (Grace's) evidence: `'I should think that the second wound was when he was on his hands and knees.' Then, continuing Kelly's "confession": "... he got on to his hands and knees and tried to tackle Kelly again, and so he shot him again, and he was stretched out by the door. Remember, members of the jury", Oliver again stressed, " 'I had to drag him away to try to open the door'." "He said he thought the man had locked the door so he shot the lock off, and he said, 'I dashed down the spiral staircase and got outside and Connolly was not there. I have seen Balmer and he cannot break my alibi in a thousand years`'".

Not once throughout his reiteration of this crucial evidence of the self-confessed liar Northam, did the judge advise the jury that it was merely alleged that Kelly had made these gravely self-incriminating comments. Not once, throughout this damning passage, did he remind the jury that Kelly had vigorously, denied even knowing Northam, much less confessing to him. And not once did he mention that the police had been fully familiar for several months before Northam's and Dickson's statements were taken , with the manner of the two men's deaths in that cinema office.

When Oliver came to Thomella's evidence, he said, "Member of the jury it is one thing to say, 'I do not know, another thing to say, 'he may have been in but I did not see him', but he has pledged himself *in writing* that, 'Kelly was not in my house at 9.30pm'." (My italics) As for Thomella's testifying that Kelly was in his pub all afternoon, Oliver said, "Do you think anyone would say with certainty that he was there at 12.30pm till two o'clock - a busy landlord seeing lots of people, the house full of people?"

This prejudicial comment was made despite there being no

evidence that the *Leigh Arms* was "full of people" on the Sunday afternoon. On the contrary, Thomella and Kelly had said that it was quiet. In which case the licensee would be more likely to notice anyone in his public house than when it was crowded on a Saturday night. Yet the prosecution and the judge wished the jury to believe that Thomella was "definite" about Kelly *not* being in then.

On the afternoon of the 27th of January, Oliver decided to take the jury to view the interior of the *Beehive* in Mount Pleasant where the crime was alleged to have been planned. Of what benefit this was expected to be nobody said, unless it was to convince them that it looked the sort of seedy place where such a crime would indeed be plotted. The following morning, Saturday the 28th of January, Oliver concluded his summing-up and sent the jury out to consider their verdict.

During the jury's four hours-long deliberation the Clerk of the Court entered the jury room four times for them to pass messages to the judge or to make requests. On one of the occasions they wanted to know if they could find one man guilty or did it have to both? They were told it had to be both. On the fourth occasion, they came back into court. They wanted to know the dates of the searches made at Northam's parents home. There was some delay whilst the shorthand writer was brought back into court.

When Chief Superintendent Smith had given the dates the judge asked if that information helped towards arriving at a decision. The foreman said it did not Whereupon Oliver, said, "Well if there is no chance of agreement it is no use keeping you here any longer." He then dismissed the jury. Kelly and Connolly would be tried again at the next assizes beginning on Monday.

That evening Mr. Justice Oliver told the Clerk of the Court to telephone Chief Superintendent Smith with the following message of condolence: "The judge was anxious that the police should know that had the trial finished *in the way he had anticipated,* he had intended to pay tribute to the admirable work of the police in the case, and for what consolation it was worth he wanted the police to know this." (My italics)

No doubt the police would have been most pleased with his Lordship's commiserations. Kelly and Connolly on the other hand would no doubt have been shattered if they had known that, before he had dismissed the jury, Mr. Justice Oliver had learned that they were eleven to one for an acquittal. (2)

(1) It would only be surpassed for rank prejudice by Lord Goddard in the Craig and Bentley case two years later.

(2) Note made by Mr. Justice Cassels after the second trials. (Home Office)

Chapter Twenty-five

"The law's delay, the insolence of the office."
- William Shakespeare.

On Tuesday the 31st January, the first day of the new Assizes, Rose Heilbron, appeared before Mr. Justice Oliver and asked for permission to, "...mention the case of the King against Kelly and Connolly." Her intention was to request a postponement of the re-trial of the two men, who were not in court, preferably to another town. But she had now heard through the legal grapevine that a decision had been made to try the men separately. This would certainly not be in Kelly's interest. Such a thing, moreover, had never happened before in a murder case where two men were jointly charged.

Heilbron had much to be worried about. Basil Neild had bowed out of the case to contest his Tory parliamentary seat at Chester in the forthcoming General Election. Another judge, in addition to William Gorman, was about to enter the case. Edmund Rowson K.C., the Recorder of Blackpool, was to replace Neild as Connolly's new counsel. And to make matters worse it would appear some sort of deal was being made.

Oliver's thinly veiled chauvinism towards Heilbron throughout the first trial continued unabated, as he dismissively told her: "I suggest your application (for a postponement) should be made in the other court." She responded that she'd been told in the other court by Justice Cassels that she should make the application in this court to him. Affecting exasperation, he chided her: "I am not going to try the case. Will you make your application to Mr. Justice Cassels!" With remarkable stoicism at being given the runaround, Heilbron then dutifully made her way back to the other court.

Addressing an impassive Cassels, she said, "I understand, my Lord, the case is to be retried, and is to be retried separately - that is to say, Kelly is to be tried first." She then made a formal objection on the grounds that, since the prosecution had maintained throughout that the crime was a joint venture, the two men should be tried together. "His Lordship will remember", she reminded him, "the case of Malinowski reported in the *All England Reports*, number 46, volume one, where it is said that if the accused are engaged in a common enterprise it is proper that they should be tried together."

She had done well to unearth this precedent in so short a time. But Cassels was fully aware of the numerous precedents, without having to be quoted the Malinowski case. He could however, when it suited him, be every bit as obdurate and disingenuous as Oliver. "In *that case*", he asked, "did it say that it was *improper* that they should be tried separately?"

"Yes it did my lord," came the unexpected but emphatic reply.

She then went on to argue that the judge (whether Cassels or Oliver) had no jurisdiction to order separate trials -particularly as it was a re-trial. And even if she was wrong on the "jurisdiction" point she maintained that the discretion exercised by the judge had not followed proper procedure. "That is to say", she explained, " it is a judicial discretion which must be exercised at the actual (new) trial. But I understand it has already been decided that there should be separate trials." Responding testily, Cassels said, "Miss Heilbron, I don't know where you got that from." Yet despite his assumed lack of knowledge about the separate trials, Cassels, after offering an abstruse explanation said, "You are entitled to make the application now and I will hear you. I am prepared to treat it as an application, *as if it were made at the trial*." (My italics)

Heilbron however, was not to be so easily mollified...or tricked. She had been referring to the behind-the-scenes decision to hold separate retrials. But Cassels was referring to her application for postponement of the trial which he knew should *also* be made in the presence of the two accused. He seemed to be deliberately causing confusion in order to wriggle out of the impropriety of the decision already having been taken to hold separate trials. Or was he trying to compromise her into making an application for a postponement without the accused being present?

In the event Heilbron fell into the trap. "That brings me to another point my Lord" she said. She then made her request for a postponement

f the trial for two weeks, preferably to another city, on the grounds
at after the daily reporting of the committal proceedings in October,
d the almost verbatim reporting in the local press for the last thirteen
ays, Kelly could not possibly get a fair trial.

Affecting anger at her apparent impertinence, whilst overlooking
e judiciary's own double standards in secretly deciding to have separate
ials, Cassels upbraided her: "In my opinion Miss Heilbron", he said,
his is the wrong course to take, because any such application should
e made *in the presence of the accused persons.*" he then said " I
nderstood that you were going to make application with regard to the
xing of the case (i.e. the commencement date). Now you start by
aking protests against *this separate trial*". (My italics)

Not only was Cassels guilty here of double standards - in that
imself, Oliver, Connolly's counsel and the prosecution had obviously
greed on separate trials in the abscence of the accused men, without
ven consulting Heilbron - he was also implicitly admitting the truth of
er earlier assertion that a decision had indeed been made to try the
en separately - in spite of the Malinowski case law precedent.

In her own defence, Heilbron replied: "I have to do that for this
eason. If the trial was to go on as a *joint* trial...tomorrow, I would
ave no objection. It is only because the trial is going on as a separate
ial."

"That is your point?" asked Cassels.

"Yes", replied Heilbron.

"Tomorrow", she said, "is too soon for the defence to do justice
o this new (separate) case which has been put forward. The conduct
f the defence may well be quite different. A different situation has to
e met, and it is virtually impossible, without great hardship to the
efendant. And the defendant will be prejudiced if this case goes on
omorrow at such short notice, because many considerations have to
e gone into in regard to the defence. For instance", she went on, "the
ne of cross-examination, just to mention one thing, may have to be
ifferent. Obviously, when two persons are cross-examining, as Mr.
asil Neild and myself were, it was easier."

"Tomorrow I have to undertake the cross-examination of the
vitnesses entirely on my own. And, my lord, that is only one point.

There is then another question of witnesses because one man is now absent from the trial - one man who was alleged to be present, both when the crime was planned and when it was committed. In my submission very great hardship would be caused to the defence if this trial went on tomorrow without some real delay. After all, this trial lasted thirteen days and only finished on Saturday afternoon, and this gives very little time for the defence."

Concluding her address Heilbron added, "Another matter which would be of assistance to the defence is if the defence could peruse copy of the transcript of the last trial. I mention that, but it is not as important as the consideration of the conduct of the defence and the preparation of the defence to meet what may very well be different circumstances and a different situation. And for these reasons I apply for a postponement of the trial."

Ignoring the contentious anbd informal decision to try the men separately, Cassels asked, "What is it that you would like? Do you mean a postponement of date or postponement to another Assize" Heilbron replied that she wanted a week or two weeks postponement *and*, if possible, transfer of the trial to another city, or at least to a later Liverpool assize. "Practically verbatim accounts have been given in the local press", she said, "and there can be very few people who do not know about this case locally...and so it would be fairer to the accused if it (the re-trial) could be taken in another place".

When Heilbron sat down Cassels asked who represented the other defendant. He knew only too well who represented Connolly The behind-the-scenes agreement on the separate trials could not have been made without Connolly's counsel. Indeed, the request had actually come from his defence team.

Like Gorman, Edmund Rowson K.C. was conspicuous by his absence in court so Gordon Clover, his junior, stood up. "Have you anything to say about this application?" asked Cassels. Not surprisingly, Clover replied, " I do not support Miss Heilbron's application. I do not feel, without specific instructions, I can say more than that." Glyn Blackledge, Gorman's junior, in an attempt to distance the Prosecution from any conspiracy, stated that he did not wish to say anything with regard to the separate trial aspect. The Prosecution was getting everything it wanted anyway, so why should he rock the boat!

When Cassels again commented that it was irregular for any postponement to be made outside the presence of the accused men - despite the much more important (unofficial) decision to hold separate trials being reached in this way - Blackledge complained that Jacqueline Dickson was suffering from a serious and progressive disease, which was life-threatening. She was waiting to go into hospital, he said, and any delay may be quite serious. He was not however, asked to provide any evidence of this. No disease was specifically named nor did the judge request any medical evidence to substantiate the Crown's statement. And it was never explained why, or to whom, any delay would be quite serious.

Moments later, *despite the accused not being present*, Cassels made his decision, . He saw no reason, he told Heilbron, why the trial should be delayed. "If an extra day is required, I am perfectly willing for the trial to be fixed for Thursday instead of Wednesday. If that is of no assistance, then I think it should be better to bring it in on Wednesday". In effect, he was telling her "You've got one day to prepare the defence of a man on trial for his life. If that is not enough, then too bad, you get nothing!"

Cassels had shown who was boss. This troublesome woman had been effectively put in her place! She was now reduced to pleading, "Can your Lordship not make it Monday? A few days would be a breathing space and give us time hurriedly to do the things that are necessary." Seizing on her use of the word "hurriedly", Cassels, pointing out that the first trial had started on January 12th, wrongly stated that it was last September that the accused men had appeared before the Magistrates. "October 19th", Heilbron corrected him. Ignoring her correction however, he continued, "Tomorrow will be the first of February. You must of course, Miss Heilbron, be familiar with all the facts of the case. It is not as if you have not had your brief for a long time." But Heilbron replied that there was the difficulty of the joint trial.

After further point-scoring against the young female KC, Cassels said, "It is getting a long time away from the incidents that happened. The trial was postponed to the next Assizes, and those Assizes have started today, and there is no reason why the case should not come on in its proper course And it seems to be only right that it should come on at an early stage. And if Thursday is any good to you, by all means have Thursday. But I cannot postpone it beyond Thursday."

A now weary and dispirited Heilbron conceded, "Obviously one day is better than nothing, and if your lordship cannot postpone it beyond Thursday, I must accept it."

"Very well," said the judge, "Thursday. And if you are desirous of making an application on the subject of the trial (i.e. separate trials) then it must be made then."

Cassels had not even considered her most important request, for the trial to be moved to another town because of the widespread prejudice against the two accused men. The lengthy first trial, emotionally exhausting for all concerned - not least Kelly and Connolly - had ended only three days ago. Now Mr. Justice Cassels had ruled that in two days time, the retrials would start. The decision to try the two men separately would be a mere formality. And despite Kelly being the second-named on the indictment, it had already been agreed that he would be tried first. It seemed that British justice was doing somersaults in its determination to nail George Kelly.

Chapter Twenty-six

"It's surprising what the law can do to an innocent man."
- James Hanratty. Hanged 1962.

On the morning of February the 2nd both men stood once again in the dock at St. George's Hall. When Mr. Justice Cassels in the absence of the jury, over-ruled Rose Heilbron's objections and ordered that they undergo separate trials. It would be less complicated for the jury. And the witnesses, he said, would have to be cross-examined once only.

Despite being listed second on the indictment Kelly would be tried first. Meanwhile Connolly was ordered to be sent back to Walton prison.

The trial was virtually a re-run of the first trial. And Kelly this time appeared to be indifferent and emotionally drained, as he sat between two warders impotently watching the same succession of witnesses entering and leaving the witness box.

The lies had come so thick and fast at the first trial that he now seemed inured to them, as Constable Nugent testified he had seen him and Connolly together on several occasions. "But you never said that at the other trial", Heilbron told him. "You stated you had only seen them on the 26th of September." He must have forgotten, said the constable who was on the verge of retirement.

Later when cross-examining Northam about the overcoat, Heilbron asked why the police had not found it during their searches. His dad must have been wearing it, he replied But he couldn't explain why the belt and two buttons were missing off *this* coat.

In his evidence Balmer said that because he was dealing with Kelly he used certain methods during the investigation, one of which was not to tell him if his story at any particular juncture had been borne out. When asked by Heilbron why he hadn't told Kelly in March that he had checked his movements and he didn't think he'd told the truth, he simply said, "That is my method and I have found it works best."

With regard to the lipstick smudge on the anonymous letter, h
said he didn't know it was lipstick until Dickson mentioned it in May.
was only then that he sent it to the Forensic Laboratory and the
confirmed it   This explanation of course conveniently ruled out an
suggestion that he might have told Dickson there was lipstick on th
letter.

Throwing doubt on the prosecution's suggestion that the gun ha
been dumped in Botanic Park lake, Heilbron suggested to Balmer
had been thoroughly drained and nothing had been found. On th
contrary, he insisted, there was nine-feet of mud at the bottom and th
gun could still be there.

In this second trial which lasted six days, Skelly was brought fror
Walton and was actually waiting on the stairs leading from the cells t
the dock but Heilbron decided not to call him. This did not stop Gorma
however, in his closing speech, or the judge in his summing-up, fror
referring to his evidence given at the first trial. Indeed the judge mad
great play of the fact that Kelly, after giving Skelly money on the 19t
of March still had plenty enough to offer drinks all round in the *Leig*
Arms. What this quite had to do with the case, given that no mone
was stolen from the Cameo, only Cassels knew. But, he told the jury
"they might think it a matter for their consideration."

When Kelly gave his evidence on the fourth day of the trial
the strain of the previous thirteen-day trial - the longest so far in Britisl
legal history- appeared to have affected him. He had lost weight an
was irritable and tired. Gorman however, taunted him by showing hin
photographs of the murder scene in the manager's office and repeating
what he had allegedly told Northam "'He fell on his knees tearing at hi
shirt so I shot him again.' Does that remind you of anything Kelly?'
Kelly protested it did not because he was innocent.   Then in a
impassioned outburst, he declared Northam and Dickson were telling
a pack of lies. "I have never shot a man, he almost cried, "I can fac
God with a clear conscience." Then, regarding Northam he said, "If h
was a catholic he would tell the police the truth like I have done. I have
been to Confession and Holy Communion for sixteen weeks, and knel
at the altar rails because I am innocent. That is more than Dickson and

Northam would do!"

Despite Kelly being clearly upset, Gorman then pointed to a man sitting in the well of the court, who was a prison warder, and asked if he recognised him. Yes he did. Did he therefore agree that during one of the lunch-time adjournments in the last trial he had a conversation with his brothers on the stairs leading to the cells? Yes he did. And did he say to his brothers, "Don't forget boys if I go down it's up to you to do something about that Northam?" Yes he did, said Kelly but he didn't mean any harm by it. He meant for his brothers to see Northam and tell him to tell the truth. The effect of this damning exchange however was not lost on the jury.

Asked by the judge about Graham being the go-between for him and Connolly, Kelly said it was unnecessary because they spoke to each other through their cells each night. "How far apart are your cells?", asked Cassels. Correcting the distance he'd given at the first trial, Kelly replied, "about twelve feet. I could show you if I had a pencil and paper." When these were produced he walked out of the witness box, leaned towards the judge's bench and drew a diagram of the location. "I see", said Cassels after perusing it.

In his closing speech, Gorman again capitalised on the conspicuous absence, this time not only of O'Malley, but also Skelly. Where were they?, he asked. The woman who was with Kelly on the murder night, and Skelly, his only alibi witness for the early part of the evening. The judge in his summing up also pointed out to the jury, that Skelly was the only one who could have substantiated Kelly's evidence that he was not in the Beehive between 7.30 and 8.30pm on March the 19th, but the defence for their own reasons had not called him.

The jury therefore only had Kelly's word against that of Northam and Dickson, and Graham. This failure to call Skelly seemed to seal Kelly's fate.

Mr. Justice Cassels went on to tell the jury, in relation to the actual murder, "Only three people knew what went on in the managers office. Two of them are dead. The only remaining person is the killer. Was what Kelly is alleged to have told the three witnesses what really happened? It certainly accorded with the evidence of the pathologist Dr. Grace, who said Catterall was shot whilst on his knees".

Here unfortunately the judge was bending the truth somewhat favour of the prosecution. Grace had actually agreed with Heilbron that Catterall *could* have been standing when he was shot in the back and that he was only speculating.

Cassels failed to tell the jury that although there were only three people actually in the office that night, the police had carefully reconstructed what *most probably* happened. And this could have been told to the witnesses. But then, like Oliver, he had no desire to impugn the police.

Concluding his summing-up Cassels told the jury they had heard that Kelly was a man who used bad language but he said, "The caste to which he belongs are people who probably use forcible language. Don't bear it against him that he *may* have used rather violent language." (My italics) After Gorman's deadly closing speech and a highly damaging summing-up characterised by pronouncement such as that, it wasn't surprising that after only fifty five minutes the jury returned with the verdict. Kelly was Guilty.

When it was announced there were howls and screams from women in the public gallery. But the judge quickly ordered everyone to be quiet.

Standing with his hands tightly clenched around the dock rail and biting his lip, Kelly was asked if he had anything to say before sentence was passed. Clearly shocked, he muttered, "I'm....", but could say no more. The black cap was placed on the head of Cassels, who then said to him, "On that night of March the 19th you committed a cruel and brutal murder, for which the jury have *rightly* found you guilty. A man who uses a gun to assist him in a robbery can expect no mercy". (My italics)

With Kelly now visibly wilting, the judge then solemnly pronounced sentence of death. The warders then tapped Kelly on the shoulder and as if recovering from a daze, he turned and walked smartly to the cell below.

Cassels then commended Northam and Dickson and ordered that they be awarded £20 each from the public purse. He also made a recommendation for Graham's early release

That evening Mr. Justice Cassels penned a terse note for the Home

Secretary, Mr. Chuter Ede, which said:

"Today George Kelly was found guilty of murder and I sentenced him to death. There were no redeeming features in the case."

Chapter Twenty-seven

"No, no" said the Queen. "Sentence first, Verdict afterwards."
- Alice in Wonderland.

That night Kelly did not come back to the hospital wing. He had been sent to the Condemned Cell on "I" Wing, where he would now be watched day and night by two warders until his execution. When Connolly asked a warder what had happened, he silently drew his index finger across his throat and said, "you're next Charlie." Chilled to the bone, he realised for the first time that he was in danger of actually being hanged.

On February the 10th, two days after Kelly's trial had ended Connolly was visited in Walton by his solicitor who introduced his new Counsel, Edmund Rowson KC, the Recorder of Blackpool. Basil Neild, he told him, had to leave the case to fight the General Election.

What Rowson had to say that day deeply shocked him. If he pleaded guilty to robbery, he was told, the murder charge would be dropped. He immediately protested at the suggestion. Why should he plead guilty to anything when he was completely innocent. But Rowson warned him that the same evidence that had been offered against Kelly would be offered against him...and he knew where Kelly now was!

Connolly said he would have to talk it over with his family but was told he could not discuss it with anyone. When he then refused the deal, Rowson, losing his temper shouted, "For God's sake man, I am trying to save your life! Don't you understand, once anyone goes into the condemned cell they never come out!"

It was a very sobering thought. After a few moments Connolly asked, "What about Kelly? How will it affect his appeal?" Rowson told him not to worry as it would not affect Kelly's appeal. "That will be decided on legal matters to do with mis-direction of the jury" Connolly then asked, " Well, how long will I get?", Rowson immediately replied with certainty, "Ten years."

Despite Rowson's warning, Connolly, during a visit the following day, discussed the matter with his mother, who said to him,

"I cannot tell you what to do son, it's your life. But I'd rather have you alive than dead".

On the morning of his trial, February the 13th, he was being escorted down to St. George's Hall in a taxi, when the driver asked one of the warders what time he should come back to pick them up. "With a look of disgust Connolly said to him, "Just come back at half ten. It will be all over by then and I will have been given ten years." The taxi-driver turned to him and grinned, "Some hope!"

When the murder charge was put to Connolly, he pleaded not guilty, as instructed by Rowson. Cassels then ordered the jury to return a formal verdict of Not Guilty. William Gorman, on behalf of the prosecution, then indicated that he would not be proceeding with the second count of murder regarding Catterall. The charge of robbing Leonard Thomas, the Cameo cinema manager of £50.0s.08d was then put to him to which he pleaded guilty. Immediately after that however, a charge of, "Conspiracy to rob with George Kelly and other persons unknown", was put. When he instinctively said "Not guilty," Rowson, sowling at him, said reproachfully, "Connolly!",

"Oh!", he responded, in confusion, "Guilty".

The conspiracy charge had come out of the blue. Rowson had told him he would only have to plead guilty to "robbery." Connolly was still unaware of the significance of his guilty plea to this charge - which he had been tricked into - until prisoners in Walton - and during the next six years in Armley Gaol and Wakefield - began accusing him of turning Kings Evidence against Kelly.

After being told by Cassels that he'd had, "a very narrow escape", Connolly was sentenced to ten years imprisonment on the robbery charge and two years concurrent on the conspiracy one - ten years in all.

As he received his sentence he saw a man rising from his seat in the well of the court as if in slow motion. Beaming, the man raised both hands above his head in a gesture of victory. It was Detective Chief Inspector Balmer.

Outside, on the steps of St. Georges Hall, the Inspector said to Farragher, "Bloody good job Cassels never sent the jury up to the hospital wing to see those cells".

"Never mind that," said the sergeant, "What about the phoney overcoat? What if they'd asked for a forensic on that!"

On the 27th of February, after almost three weeks in the condemned cell, Kelly wrote to Harry Harrison, the street bookie, in a desperate cry for help. Harrison, who had been drinking on March the 19th with Kelly in the *Leigh Arms*, had been subpoenaed as a witness by the defence but in the event had not been called.

> *'Dear Harry'*, he wrote, *'Doris as (sic) been up to see me and she as (sic) give me some very good news, But its no good if these people don't take action about it, Harry I can't believe I am sentenced to Death, I don't know the first thing about this Murder, why these people as (sic) blamed me God only knows. Well there is a lot of people who knows I am innocent of this Crime, But what can we do about it, Tell all the Boys I was asking about them, Please do me a favour, if I get Hung for this Harry please try some day to prove me innocent, I know it will be to (sic) late then, But it will Clear my famlys (sic) Name, also it will get those people in trouble who blamed me for it. There is one thing I can do I can face God with A Clear Conscience so why should I worry,*
>
> *Harry Nobody knows what it his (sic) like to be sentenced to Death, when I know in my own Mind that I am an innocent man, People can only do there (sic) best for me, That Satday(sic) Night I left the Lee (sic) Arms pub, and went down to the Spoford (sic) for a pint just to see if Doris was there, I went in there about 9-15 and stayed there till 9-20. I could not see Doris so I went back to the Lee Arms pub and stayed till 10pm. So Here I am Convicted of Murder The people who Blamed me for this I have never seen them in all my life, also the Man who was Charged with me, I can't understand it. please write me a letter.*
>
>

From George Kelly.
Good Luck.'

Harry Harrison later approached the Home Office on Kelly's behalf but was simply sent a receipt of his letter telling him the contents had been noted.

Chapter Twenty-eight

"Suffer any wrong that may be done to you
rather than come here"
- Charles Dickens

On March 6th in the Court of Criminal Appeal, with Kelly seated in the dock surrounded by prison officers, Rose Heilbron faced the Lord Chief Justice of England, Lord Goddard, and his two colleagues Mr Justice Birkett and Mr Justice Humphreys. What was to follow on that day and four days later on March 10th, was one of the worst examples of judicial chicanery and blatant injustice ever seen in a British high - court.

Heilbron began by relating the arbitrary and unjust decisions of the two trial judges, Oliver and Cassels. But if she was expecting a sympathetic audience her hopes were soon to be dashed.

When she told the Court that Kelly's previous joint trial with Connolly had resulted "in a disagreement of the jury" it was a more than charitable description of the indecent haste with which Mr Justice Oliver had prematurely dismissed that jury from delivering a verdict.

Referring to the ruling to have separate trials she told the Court that her objections had been to no avail. She then went on to make the important point that the first trial had been fully reported in the local newspapers and that a great deal of prejudice had inevitably been engendered against Kelly. Because of this, she told the Court, she had suggested to Cassels that it would be fairer if Kelly's second trial were moved to another city. She had also asked for a postponement of several days. But both these pleas had also been refused.

The application for separate trials, she explained, had been made by Connolly's counsel, Edmund Rowson. Cassels had not only granted this but had also ordered Kelly to be tried first despite Connolly being the first-named on the indictment.

At this point, Mr Justice Humphreys intervened and asked, "What did the Prosecution have to say about it?" Heilbron replied that the id not say anything, adding that it was left to the judge's discretion. Attempting to justify this decision, Lord Goddard then commented, Until it had been decided whether or no there had been a murder by Kelly, Connolly could not have been tried or *convicted* as being an accessory." (My italics).

This was a quite remarkable comment from the highest judge in the land. Firstly, it betrayed his inside knowledge of why separate trials had been ordered and why it had been decided to try Kelly first despite this being the first occurrence in British legal history of two men jointly accused of murder being tried separately, and despite Connolly being the first-named on the indictment. Secondly, this comment clearly showed that getting a conviction was more important to Goddard than the proper administration of justice. Thirdly, if Goddard's comments were genuine, he was displaying a remarkable ignorance of the case and of the criminal law. For Connolly, in both trials, had never been accused, much less "convicted", of being an "accessory" - before of after the murder. Fourthly, even if Goddard's analysis was correct, it nonetheless ignored the ruling of Mr Justice Lynskey in the trial of Johnson the previous June when, over-ruling Rose Heilbron's submission, he declared that Johnson *could* be tried as an "accessory" *before* the actual killer had even been charged or convicted, or indeed, even arrested.

Mr Justice Humphreys again interjected, "The rule is that it is for the Prosecution to decide which indictment shall be tried first." Heilbron agreed. "But", she said, "the matter seems to have come about in such a *peculiar* way". (My italics) Humphreys then asked, "You are not making any point then, that Kelly's case was taken before Connolly's?" Of course she was. And she had said so. But Humphreys, completely missing the point of Connolly being first on the indictment, said, "Then I suggest that is the business of the Prosecution." That was precisely her point, she explained to the 84 year-old Humphreys. The Prosecution, she said, had, "not said one word *in court* as to what their request was." (My italics) The judge had not asked them what they wanted. And they had said they were entirely in the judge's hands. Goddard then rejoined that Cassels had had an opportunity of reading the depositions, or knew something of what had taken place before,

and saw, he (Goddard) should think, that there was a *difference* betwe
the two accused. "He would obviously think", said Goddard, "that t
case against Kelly, who is alleged to be the actual murderer, should
taken first." (My italics)

In law, as had been stated by Gorman and the judge during t
trial, there was no "difference" between the two men, who were join
charged with murder. Humphreys, apart from his failure or unwillingn
to share Heilbron's concern, had been quite correct. Even if t
Prosecution had washed their hands over the issue of the separa
trials, it was still for them to decide who should be tried first. And
they had properly discharged their duty, this would have been Connol
Was this why Heilbron qualified her statement with, "in court?" Did s
suspect, as these three judges must have suspected, that the Prosecuti
had already said enough *out of court* to both Cassels *and* Connoll
counsel in order to get Kelly tried first?

Apart from Goddard glossing over Humphreys prop
interpretation of legal procedure, his own justification for Cassels dubic
decisions and the prosecution's dereliction of duty, he did not ev
follow the precedent he was so eager to justify. For two years later,
the trial judge in the Craig and Bentley case, *he failed* to order separa
trials, when Bentley perhaps could have been charged with a les
offence than Craig. In that case, there was a far greater "differenc
between the two jointly accused. Bentley was actually in police custo
when P.C. Miles was killed. If he, the most senior judge in the land, h
then followed Cassels example perhaps his passing sentence of dea
on Bentley - for which he piously said at the time he had no alternati
- would have been unnecessary. (1)

Heilbron stated her point was simply that the two men could eas
and properly have been tried together because the evidence again
them was substantially the same. She could however be forgiven
not pursuing this point as vigorously as she might otherwise have dc
for she had a much more explosive issue up her sleeve for the thr
learned judges.

After a brief pause to collect her papers, she quietly said s
wished to raise another point. This proved to be a matter of the great
importance, which caught all three judges so completely off guard t

nitially they did not know how to answer it. Indeed, in the early stages of her argument Goddard, despite himself, appeared to be actually supporting her. And as her argument proceeded, it was difficult at times to tell whether the judges were being disingenuous or were genuinely ignorant of the finer points of the law. Whatever the reasons, all three, particularly Goddard, made some quite absurd observations, contradicting themselves several times.

Heilbron's understated but sensational revelation was that one of the jurors who had found Kelly guilty was himself a convicted felon who had served a term of imprisonment. She had, she said, been given this information a few days earlier. If it were true it was her submission that the juror was disqualified from sitting on a jury. And if that were so it might be grounds for the Court to rule that the trial was a nullity.

Clearly disconcerted, the three judges gazed blankly at her as she explained that her information had not been verified, and that she couldn't obtain details of the man's conviction unless the Court ordered the police to divulge the information. Otherwise, she said, they would refuse.

Regaining his composure, and ignoring Heilbron's request for an official order, Goddard calmly said that if she had evidence that the man had a conviction, he supposed someone could be brought to the court to say, "I know that man has been convicted because I was present at his conviction."

"Have you got that evidence?", he asked. She replied that she could not produce anyone who could state they knew the man was convicted. But it could be proved with a certificate of conviction from the police. Despite her earlier request for a police order, Goddard then rather naively asked if she was making an application for an order to the Court? "I think I must", she replied. "Then", he said, "you are applying under Section 10 of the Jurors Act, *which disqualifies a person who has been convicted of a felony?*" (My italics).

In view of the Appeal Court's subsequent judgement, this unguarded comment early in the proceedings showed quite clearly that Goddard was not only familiar with the various Juries Acts (if not their actual names!) but also shared Heilbron's belief that a convicted felon was indeed disqualified from jury service. But that was when he believed her allegation about the juror being a convicted felon would not [be] substantiated.

Heilbron, who had clearly done her homework, confirmed th[at] she was indeed making application for an order. She could have als[o] pointed out to the learned judge that it was the *Juries Act* and not, [as] he had cited, the "Jurors" Act. But she perhaps thought it more prude[nt] not to upset him for he had a fearsome reputation -particularly amon[g] young defence counsel. Instead, she went on to assert, although sh[e] did not yet have the details of the juror's conviction, that if a juryma[n] was disqualified by reason of a criminal conviction, a convicted prison[er] had the right to challenge that his conviction

Heedless of her earlier explanation about the need for the poli[ce] to provide the details, Mr Justice Humphreys asked, "You are not in [a] position to get the facts?" She wasn't sure, she said. But how could sh[e] *prove* a conviction unless the police co-operated. "Have they be[en] applied to?", asked Goddard. "No", she replied.

Again, it appeared that the Lord Cheif Justice was either n[ot] listening to what she had already told the Court or he was once aga[in] affecting naiveté. "When did this knowledge come to you?", he aske[d]. Stating that it was the previous Tuesday or Wednesday, and anticipati[ng] his criticism, she added that she did not initially think there was anythi[ng] in it but realised there was, after going into the matter more deeply wi[th] Mr Trotter her junior.

After the three judges had briefly conferred, Goddard, with bare[ly] concealed condescension, upbraided the young female barrister. "W[e] do not ask you the source of your information", he said, "but you w[ill] recognise that in asking for an adjournment, this is a serious thing. T[he] Court is entitled to ask you, on your responsibility as counsel, wheth[er] the source of your information is such that you have what is more th[an] idle talk."

Here was the criticism Heilbron had anticipated. She was bei[ng] intimidated for truthfully stating she could not be certain the informatio[n] was correct without proof from the police. "I hope your Lordships w[ill] not blame me if it turns out to have no foundation", she pleaded. B[ut] unmoved by her obvious anxiety, Goddard said to prosecuting couns[el] Gorman, "It would be a *great misfortune* if this case had to [be]

djourned." He then asked if there was any reason why a telephone
all could not be made to the Liverpool C.I.D. (My italics)

The Lord Chief Justice did not explain to whom an adjournment
ould be such a "great misfortune." If it meant winning his appeal, it
ertainly would not be to Kelly sitting in the dock under sentence of
eath. Rather it would it be his great fortune!

Gorman informed Goddard that Superintendent Smith, the Head
f Liverpool C.I.D. was in court but had said he had no information to
ffer. Heilbron then mentioned a man's name and handed his written
ame and address to Gorman, who stated the records were in Liverpool
ut the Clerk of Assize was in Manchester and may have the jury list
ith him. With growing exasperation, Goddard said, "The first thing is
 find out whether this man was sworn on the jury, and the second is
hether he is a convicted felon." The point must be properly inquired
to and it could not be done before the following morning, he added.

Gorman, once again making matters appear to be much more
ifficult than they actually were, told the Court, "If this man lives at this
ddress it is outside the Liverpool area and will therefore be in the
ancashire County Police area." In actuality the man who had sat on
e jury lived in Waterloo, about ten miles from Liverpool, and he had
een convicted at Bootle magistrates court, a small borough even nearer
 Liverpool.

Suggesting that the information could be obtained by Friday,
oddard then stated, "It is desirable that the case should stand out until
en." He then formally adjourned the appeal to Friday March the
0th.

Why it was "desirable" that the hearing should be postponed for
ur days as opposed to one or two, Goddard did not say. Such an
nnecessary delay was far from desirable for Kelly, who would now
e taken on a two hundred mile journey back to the condemned cell at
Valton prison to resume his agonising ordeal.

Between Goddard frivolously regarding an adjournment as a
great misfortune" one minute and "desirable" the next, and Gorman
aking a mountain out of a molehill over a simple check on a criminal
ecord, those present that day in the Court of Criminal Appeal could
ave been forgiven for overlooking the real issue, that a man's life was

at stake.

Two days after the adjournment, Detective Chief Superintende Smith submitted a report to the Chief Constable of Liverpool, Charles Martin. It said that at 5.30pm on March the 7th at Bootle, interviewed a man named Arthur Clarkson, aged 49 years of Hy Road, Waterloo. This man had admitted being a member of the ju which, at Liverpool Assizes on February 8th 1950, had convict George Kelly of the murder of Leonard Thomas, the manager of t Cameo cinema. The man also admitted being convicted on 6th Ap 1945 of feloniously receiving a quantity of clothing, knowing it to ha been stolen, and to receiving a sentence of one month's imprisonme In reply to a question from Superintendent Smith, Clarkson had sai "I got my jury Notice so what else could I do?"

Clarkson was never subsequently called before the Court Criminal Appeal, and his name, address and occupation, althoug revealed to the judges, were kept secret. The public, not least Geor Kelly, would no doubt have been shocked to discover that t occupation of the juryman who had helped to convict him was that *cinema manager.* And that he was currently the manager of the *Pala Picture House* in Warbreck Moor, Aintree.

On Friday, March 10th, Kelly was once again escorted handcuffs down to London for the resumption of his appeal. As he s in the dock surrounded by prison warders, he was probably unawa that one of the judges was different from last time. Mr Justi Humphreys, the only one of the three judges to have shown a consideration towards Rose Heilbron, had been replaced by Mr Justi Hillbery. It is difficult to avoid the conclusion that this substitution w a deliberate act designed to remove any last vestige of sympathy f the appellant.

Hillbery was the cruelly insensitive judge who, presiding at t murder trial of Norman Goldthorpe several months later, was to mal national headlines over his treatment of the jury, which he public castigated for daring to request a cup of tea! In that case the jury ha been deliberating in an unheated room at Norfolk Assizes for almo half an hour when they requested some hot tea. On hearing of thi Hillbery had them brought back and berated them in front of a packe urt. Scowling, in the manner of Mr Squeers to the unfortunate retches of Dotheboys Hall, he said, "I understand that you have en asking for cups of tea? In the old days it was the formula that a ry was left without food, fire or drink until they agreed on their verdicts. ave no intention of applying the full rigour of the law but there are no cilities in this building for making tea." After that dressing down, the ry took a mere eight minutes to find the unfortunate Goldthorpe guilty!

When Superintendent Smith's report was disclosed to the Court, orman immediately conceded that the juror had indeed been convicted f receiving at Bootle magistrates Court. He then went on to provide e Court with the details of the conviction. But, in an attempt to excuse e man's presence on the jury, he emphasised that his name was in the ry book and that he had indeed been listed on the panel of jurors. onetheless he still withheld Clarkson's name, address and details of s occupation. And Goddard justified this by stating that since Gorman ad conceded these facts there was no need for these particulars to be ublished.

Was this a move calculated primarily to prevent the public knowing e juror's occupation? For if the Lord Chief Justice advised that there as no need to publish such a contentious person's name or address, en it would certainly be most improper of anyone, including defence ounsel, to reveal his *occupation*.

Rose Heilbron opened by submitting that, not only was the juryman isqualified from sitting on the jury by his conviction of a felony, but at even if he had been subsequently pardoned, he would still have een disqualified from jury service. In support of her argument she then uoted from various legal authorities, in particular Hayes, *Pleas for he Crown (Volume 11)*. She added that further support for her ontention could be found in Bacon's *Abridgement*. But sweeping side her citations, Goddard commented, "This all comes down to the *urors* Act of 1870 doesn't it?" Ignoring the Lord Chief Justice's epeated error of referring to the *Juries Act* as the "Jurors" Act, leilbron replied that she was citing these authorities because they were nore specific than the Act. "I have therefore," she said, " raised the ommon law position."

The three judges sat in silence as Heilbron continued her argument.

Citing as a further example, the case of, " Brown and Crayshaw *(Bulstrode Vol. 11)*", she stated that it had been laid down in early cases that where a juryman had been convicted of felony, conspiracy, perjury or giving a false verdict, such offences, so far as future jury service was concerned, were not absolved even by a free pardon.

Fully aware of the male hostility and legal obduracy she was up against, Heilbron had accordingly prepared her case meticulously. She wasn't leaving any loopholes as she returned to her main weapon, the Juries Act 1870, which she then began to quote from: "Any man who has been or shall be attainted in a treasonable felony or convicted of any infamous crime, unless he has had a free pardon, shall not be qualified to sit on any jury whatsoever." Then, in anticipation of any possible counter arguments, she mentioned the *Civil Rights of Convicts Act (1828)*, which she submitted did not in any way diminish the common law, or the statutory prohibition against a convicted felon sitting on jury.

Goddard, Birkett and Hillbery had listened attentively. Then, with uncharacteristic respect, Goddard asked if she was aware of the *Administration of Justice Act 1938*, which he, even more uncharacteristically, pointed out contained a strong point in her favour. This Act, in relation to a conviction, he advised, "repealed the words referring to Outlawry in Section 10 of the 1870 Act, but left in the others." He did not however, remind Heilbron, if indeed she needed reminding, of what the "others" were. They were *"attainted" "treasonable felony, "* and *"infamous crime "*. He then appeared to concede that, "Parliament apparently recognised that a man who had been, or shall be, convicted shall not be qualified to sit on a jury". But again he did not remind her that the 1938 Act specified the *particular crime,* or *seriousness of offence,* of which a juror should be convicted in order to be disqualified, and that the felony had to be either *treasonable or infamous.* Or that the felon had to be *attainted.*

Were these omissions deliberate?. Was he setting a trap for the young female? It seemed he was perversely playing the part of the crafty Wolf disguised as kindly Grandma, and that she was to be his Little Red Riding Hood.

Heilbron, seemingly grateful for Goddard's unexpected cordiality, et down her guard and engagingly replied, "Apart from anything else it mounts to good sense, otherwise one might have a man convicted of capital crime, reprieved, and having served his sentence, being then free to sit on a jury."

Now however, after kindly Grandma had won the young lady's confidence, "she" betrayed a slight hint of the wolf beneath. "You had better not talk about the sense of it", he warned, "because it means that if a boy of thirteen is convicted of stealing threepenny worth of sweets, he is thereafter forever prohibited from serving on a jury." Then, reverting to his cordial persona, he innocently asked her whether the matter was more than one of challenging the jury. "I have not myself been able to find any authority", he said softly. "Can you say, if a juryman is *not* challenged, whether it renders a trial abortive?"

Despite his assumed civil manner, the Lord Chief Justice was up to one of his tricks again. If there was no precedent for a trial being ruled abortive where a juror had not been challenged *before* the trial commenced, or *during* it, as this juror hadn't been, he might be able to get away with making case law here by ruling that Kelly's trial was not abortive. But he first had to know whether Kelly's counsel knew of any such precedent.

Heilbron replied that she knew of no authority on that particular point. But before Goddard could pounce, she then went on to state, "but there is authority, where it has been held (retrospectively) that if there was *anything* wrong with the composition of the jury the trial was a *nullity*, so that, in that respect, it goes *beyond a matter of challenge to the jury*." (My italics)

This response not only evaded Goddard's trap, it showed his implicit point to be purely academic. Moreover it re-affirmed Heilbron's original argument that if the Appeal Court found that the juror was disqualified - as she believed it should do - then Kelly's trial should be ruled null and void.

Pressing home the advantage, Heilbron then cited a case before Mr Justice Darling in 1917, where that judge held that a person was entitled to be tried before, "twelve men qualified to be jurors." She also quoted a case in 1774 when it was discovered after the trial, that the wrong person had answered as a juror, and another case in 1826 where a son, who was not otherwise qualified, appeared in place of his father. In both cases, she said, new trials were ordered. Thus, she concluded, the legal authorities appeared to indicate that it was much more than a matter of challenging a juror before or during a trial.

Goddard, had under-estimated the brilliant young King's Counsel. She really had done her homework! Like Birkett and Hillbery, he was reduced to impotent silence as she then began to discuss the courses open to the Court if it held, (as she hoped it would) that Kelly's trial was a nullity. She reminded the judges that he had already undergone the ordeal of two trials, and that this was most unusual in a capital case. Recovering however, Goddard immediately retorted that even if she "established her case", the Court, "would not quash the conviction and order the discharge of the prisoner". The case would have to be re-tried.

Here, Goddard, as ever, chose his words carefully. "Established her case", was a vague euphemism for Kelly winning his appeal. And if he did so, even on such a legal technicality - albeit an important one - then he was entitled to have the conviction quashed, particularly after undergoing two previous trials, one in which the jury had "failed to agree." His bias against Kelly was being clearly demonstrated. He was letting everyone know that even if he won his appeal he would not walk free. And to provide a spurious justification for this pre-determined decision he repeated his erroneous assertion that Connolly had pleaded guilty to being, "an accessory after the fact".

Firstly, it was unforgivable that the Lord Chief Justice could be so ignorant of the case as to base his decision on a wrongly attributed criminal charge and conviction to Connolly. Secondly, since the trial judge had departed from legal precedent by ordering separate trials and trying Kelly first, Connolly's guilty pleas to robbery and conspiracy to rob - obtained by deception under severe duress *after Kelly's conviction* - should have had nothing whatever to do with the Appeal Court's consideration of Kelly's appeal. This surely was the legal establishment wanting to have its cake and eat it.

At this point, Heilbron's hopes of an improved, more sympathetic rapport with the three judges must have slumped severely. Somewhat fazed and demoralised by Goddard's prejudicial observation, she failed to point out the inaccuracy and unfairness of it to the Court. Indeed, she gave it legitimacy by conceding that Goddard's introduction of "the other prisoner" into Kelly's appeal, was, "another difficulty". Nonetheless, she quickly picked herself up and, addressed the Court with reference to the other points of Kelly's appeal. But Goddard, again interrupting, told her these had yet to be considered. He was more concerned that there should be no doubt about his ruling, that if her main point about the disqualified juror was upheld and Kelly's second trial then became a nullity, he would have to stand trial for a third time. (2)

For all they had contributed thus far Justices Birkett and Hillbery might as well not have been present. It appeared they were there simply to make up the number. Neither had spoken one word. And certainly no interjections were made which may have contradicted Goddard or which may have been in the slightest sympathetic to Kelly.

Having interrupted Heilbron from making her further points, Goddard invited Gorman to respond to her major submission regarding the disqualified juror. Rising to his feet, the Recorder of Liverpool began by submitting that the juryman had never been "attainted" of felony or convicted of an "infamous" crime, within the meaning of the *1870 Juries Act*. There was a distinction, he argued, between "attainder" and "conviction", and mere conviction did not disqualify a man from service on a jury.

Kelly, listening closely from the dock, was now looking most anxious as Gorman proceeded to define the term, "attainder", stating that the 1870 Act purposely distinguished between "attainder" and "conviction because there was in fact a very real difference.

At this point, Goddard intervened and suggested that Gorman's argument was that, as a distinction was drawn between "attainder" and "conviction", and that "attainder" was abolished by the *Forfeiture Act*, "a *mere* conviction for felony does not disqualify a juryman?" (My italics) After this helpful intervention, which subtly minimised the importance of a convicted juror deciding a man's fate, by prefixing it with "mere", all that Gorman needed to say, and did say, was, "That is so my Lord."

It must have now been dawning on Heilbron that Goddard's

earlier apparent civility towards her had been nothing more than a calculated subterfuge, designed to deceive her into a false sense of security. He had been playing her along. The sly Wolf was now beginning to shed Grandma's clothes!

What Gorman was submitting was that since one could not be "attainted" unless one had been convicted of committing an infamous crime, and that receiving stolen property was not an "infamous crime", such as a "treasonable felony", the juror was not disqualified. In support of his argument he pointed to earlier legislation, the *Larceny Act 1861*, which, he said defined "*infamous crimes*", which did not include the offence of "receiving". "There is a clear distinction", he stated, "between treason and felony, and crimes which are infamous. Receiving goods knowing them to have been stolen, though a felony, is not an infamous crime."

Addressing Gorman, Goddard said, "you say that by the time the Jury (sic) Act 1870 came into force, attainder was then abolished except for anyone then (already) attaint?" Gorman replied, "That is my point." "How do you then account," said Goddard, "for the words in the Act, `*or shall be attainted*?' "

Momentarily caught off guard but confident of Goddard's renowned partiality towards the prosecution, Gorman shrugged this off by stating that this phrase only concerned anyone convicted of an infamous crime, and, as he had already demonstrated, receiving stolen goods, did not fall within that category. Therefore he submitted that the juror, *ipso facto,* was not attainted. According to Gorman, the juror, in order to be "attainted" would have to have been convicted of an "infamous crime" such as treason. Therefore, because the juror had not been *attainted* of any such felony, *and* had not been convicted of a qualifying "*infamous crime*", he was not disqualified from sitting on the jury.

Gorman was muddying the waters in stating the 1870 Act clearly distinguished *between* treason and felony. Receiving stolen property was a felony just as treason was a felony . But neither of the three appeal judges questioned his crucial interpretation. Goddard was conspicuously silent, despite his own earlier interpretation when he had, without qualification, said to Heilbron, "You are applying under Section

10 of the Jurors (sic) Act, *which disqualifies a person who has been convicted of a felony."* (My italics)

Flushed with his unchallenged success, Gorman then re-introduced the "challenge" issue and quoted the *Juries Act 1922* to further support his contention that the convicted juror had been legally entitled to sit on the Cameo jury. This Act, he submitted, " was saying, with the single exception of a vowed woman member of a religious order, every member included in the jurors book, notwithstanding that he might have been disqualified or have grounds for exemption, was liable to serve on a jury." This wording, he said, "...gave (the juror) a right to claim exemption or disqualification, but if he did not do so then he was on the jurors list."

On this point, Gorman was not telling Heilbron or the three judges anything they didn't already know. But the "right", he referred to assumed that either the juror himself, or defence counsel, was *aware* he was disqualified or could claim exemption. In this case however, neither the juror or Kelly's counsel had been aware until *after* the trial, that he was disqualified.

As if to mitigate the convicted man's presence on the jury, Gorman went on to complain that it would be " an "intolerable burden on the registration officer to have to enquire into the offences committed maybe a generation before, by members of the jury," This ostensibly appeared to be a reasonable point, unless one was aware, as Gorman must have been, that police and local authority mechanisms had been in place since before 1922 (notwithstanding the subsequent *Rehabilitation of Offenders Act 1974*) to effectively ensure that no convicted criminal should sit as a juror in a criminal case. So much for the "intolerable burden on the registration officer."

"This particular man", said Gorman, "was in fact on the jurors list and in fact on the panel and, in my submission, *qualified...* notwithstanding the fact that he has this *disqualification.*" (My italics) By this statement, contradictory in itself, he seemed to be saying that if an unqualified juror by some bureaucratic lapse should slip through and have his name in the jurors book then, unless he was challenged at the time, or claimed exemption himself, he was legitimately entitled to serve. Whether they had noticed this clear contradiction in terms or simply ignored it, none of the three appeal judges made any comment.

Rose Heilbron was immediately on her feet and vigorously contending that once a man was disqualified he was prohibited from sitting on a jury. But Goddard, again quickly intervening, disingenuously asked, " There is no penalty for a man sitting who is not qualified, is there?" Increasingly frustrated at the court's over-indulgence of Gorman, she quickly retorted, "There is a penalty for a man *not* sitting who *is* qualified." Goddard's question was not as silly and irrelevant as it appeared. The purpose of it was to insinuate that the matter of a convicted jury member helping to find a man guilty of murder could not be all that serious if the law did not even provide for a penalty against him!

Concentrating on Gorman's point regarding "challenge", Heilbron explained that the possibility of challenging the juror did not arise either before or during the trial, since the information about the convicted juror did not come to the notice of the defence until after Kelly's conviction. Mr Justice Hillbery, speaking for the first time, then suggested that in such circumstances, the inclusion of even a self-confessed convicted criminal on the jury might be lawful.

It was predictable that if and when Hillbery did eventually intervene, it would certainly not be in Heilbron's favour, but even Goddard appeared to have been taken aback by this absurdly biased comment.

Recognising that the Prosecution, not helped by Hillbery's unsound comments, was on weak ground, Goddard declared, "The root of the whole question appears to be whether there is a difference between "attainted" and "convicted." Then addressing Heilbron, he repeated that if her argument was right, "every child brought before a juvenile court and convicted of stealing some sweets, or something of that sort - and many hundreds were convicted every year - was forever afterwards prohibited from serving on a jury." He then lamented, "it will reduce the number of jurymen."

Quite apart from this pathetic suggestion that hundreds of convicted children would seriously deplete the available numbers of future jurors, Goddard was making a most inappropriate analogy. The juror in this murder case was not an errant minor involved in some childish escapade He was a grown adult of 49 years, who had five years earlier been convicted of a serious criminal offence and had served a term of imprisonment.

Heilbron, still giving as good as she was getting, countered, "If my argument is wrong it applies also to serious crime. There is no distinction."

"I agree", said Goddard quite oblivious to her earlier explanation, "but you have the right to challenge". Wearily she repeated that the juror could not be challenged because it was not known until after the trial that he had been convicted. Then, simplifying her case for the benefit of the apparently obtuse Goddard, she said, that for a valid trial the jury should consist of twelve qualified persons, and that in this case the defence had not been able to challenge the juror as they were not aware of his conviction until after the trial. At this point Mr Justice Hillbery again intervened. "Where would this stop", he asked her, " if everyone who discovered a good ground for challenge, which must have prevailed *had it been made*, acted in this way? We should never finish." (My italics)

Devoid of any meaningful intellectual contribution throughout the Hearing, the clearly prejudiced Hillbery was now boorishly insinuating that the defence had been aware of the juror's conviction *before* or *during* the trial and had let it go unchallenged until after the trial in order to win the appeal. Mr Justice Birkett, like Hillbery, also had nothing meaningful to contribute but he had at least maintained his dignity along with his silence. As it was, Hillbery's remarks went unanswered, with Heilbron saying that if this major point failed, she had other points to raise. But before she could do so, Goddard made the remarkable decision to adjourn the Hearing in order to consider this one issue.

When the Court resumed, Goddard intimated that he and his two colleagues had arrived at a decision on the major issue of the juror's disqualification or otherwise. He said it was a point of great importance and that it had been the subject of doubts expressed in some of the leading text books. He then went on to summarise the defence contention that Kelly's second trial had been a mis-trial due to the juror's conviction.

"The Court has come to the conclusion, " he said, "that it is their duty not to give effect to this objection, and they will overrule it. Owing to the importance of the matter however, the Court would later put their reasons in writing. But it was desirable to state now, the reasons why they felt the point was without foundation. In the Court's opinion", he said, "any matter regarding the competence of a juror was now governed by statute and not common-law. Section 10 of the *Juries Act 1870* (at last he had got the name right!) distinguished *attaint* from *conviction*, and this juryman had never been attainted."

Amazingly, the Lord Chief Justice then admitted that although the statute did in fact impose a disqualification on the juror, "in our opinion any matter of disqualification is removed by the Juries Act once the man is on the jurors book" He then concluded the matter by stating that the Court would give its full reasons and the authority from which they were derived at an later date.

It appeared that the court's decision owed more to Gorman's convoluted argument and Hillbery's biased interventions than any legal foundation. Also, the procedure adopted by Goddard halfway through the appeal was most unusual in that he had led the Court in deciding the major point of the appeal before the *full* grounds of the appeal had been heard. This was highly prejudicial to the defence and totally demoralising to Kelly, who had been intently following the proceedings. There was no doubt now: Grandma had fully revealed herself as the big bad Wolf!

Somewhat dispirited, Rose Heilbron began to address the Court on the further grounds of her appeal - the mis-direction of the jury by Mr Justice Cassels. But Goddard, all pretence at cordiality now abandoned, curtly told her that the Court was quite familiar with the facts of the case. He may have been familiar with the facts of the case, but the indomitable young barrister was here to demonstrate the unfair manner in which Kelly's trial had been conducted. And she intended to have her say.

The first point of mis-direction she raised was that Cassels did not remind the jury that the prosecution case had been that Kelly had thrown the gun in the lake in Botanic Park after the murder and jumped a tram car home, and that if this were so he could not, (as they had also alleged), have been at *the Leigh Arms* at 9.45pm, or even 9.50pm. Astonishingly, Goddard's response to this was that it was not for the Prosecution to account for the disappearance of the gun. "The prosecution's case", he declared, "was that this man shot two people and the (trial) judge was not bound to go into every point in the case." This observation contemptuously ignored the fact that nobody expected the Prosecution to account for the gun's disappearance. But it was *they* who had alleged the gun had been thrown into the park lake.

Heilbron may have added that the judge also failed to point out to the jury that the prosecution had abandoned this assertion half-way through the trial and suggested that Kelly simply discarded the hat, overcoat, mask and gun, before returning to *the Leigh Arms* at 9.50pm. In other words the Crown wanted it both ways

Her second point was that Cassels had wrongly instructed the jury that unless they *believed* the photographers, Manson and McKinnon, who were in the *Beehive*, they were to find Kelly guilty. He did not remind the members of the jury that even if they entertained a reasonable doubt about their evidence, they were obliged to give Kelly the benefit of that doubt.

Her third point was that the judge had stressed that the pathologist, Dr. Grace, had stated his impression was that the assistant manager had been shot when he was on his knees (and this of course tallied with Kelly's alleged confession to Northam and Graham). But he had failed to tell the jury that speculation was involved in the pathologist's opinion. He had also testified that Catterall could have been standing when shot.

Fourthly, Heilbron contended that the judge's direction to the jury, that if they *believed* the evidence of the Bampton brothers Kelly could not be guilty, was too limited. The judge failed to also tell the jury that if the Bampton' evidence *raised any doubt*, Kelly was entitled to an acquittal.

In response to this point Goddard pointed out that Cassels had given a *general* direction that if they were left in any doubt, Kelly was entitled to an acquittal. (My italics). "If he had to give such a direction", he went on, "in regard to each individual witness", he wondered how a judge was going to try a murder case. The clear implication of this comment was that, regardless of a man's life being at stake, such scrupulous fairness would have simply taken too long!

Fifthly, Heilbron said that Cassels did not remind the jury of the consistencies between the contents of the anonymous letter -which

Northam and Dickson were supposed to be the authors of - and their sworn testimony. The letter she said, not only contained a number of contradictions in itself, but was very different in material particulars from their evidence. But Goddard said that the trial judge had pointed out that parts of the letter were untrue. "What more could he do?" he asked. She replied that Cassels observations had not helped the jury to come to any conclusion in relation to the credibility of Northam and Dickson. In other words Cassels should have reminded the jury that because both Northam and Dickson were, in relation to the anonymous letter, self-confessed liars, their *overall* credibility should be seriously questioned.

Heilbron might also have pointed out, that the judge failed to order handwriting samples to be taken in order to objectively ascertain whether in fact Northam and Dickson were the real authors of the anonymous letter.

Her sixth point was that Cassels failed to remind the jury that whereas Northam and Dickson had sworn on oath that Kelly had used a brown apron as a mask, several of the cinema staff had testified that the gunman wore a black silk scarf across his face. Goddard's response to this, which completely avoided the point, was to remark," The people at the cinema did not attempt to identify the man. The one thing they swore to was the coat". Heilbron immediately added, "And the mask

"'The judge' should have pointed out this contradiction as to colour for the jury to make up their minds." She might also have added, "and the *material*." Barmaids aprons are not usually made of silk!

She might also have corrected Goddard about the coat: that none of the witnesses had swore it was the actual coat the gunman wore Nor was it forensically proven to be so. And she might have complained about the blatant prejudice shown by the judge towards Kelly when referring to alleged bad language - he told the jury, "You must not judge this man by the amount of language *he used*..." This was despite the fact that there was no evidence that Kelly had used any bad language. Indeed after saying he had "used" bad language, Cassels had amended this to "may" have used.

Heilbron might also have complained about Cassels clear misdirection of the jury when informing them that, according to Graham it was "impossible" for Kelly and Connolly to have communicated with each other in the prison hospital, without also reminding them that Kelly had strongly refuted this and had in fact drawn a diagram of the layout of the cells at his request. She might have protested even more strongly that Cassels - considering the grave importance of this point - did not do the proper thing by ordering the jury to visit Walton Prison to see for themselves. This would have proven Kelly to be telling the truth and clearly have shown Graham to be a liar.

Kelly's counsel may have asked the Court of Criminal Appeal why Cassels felt the need to remind the jury in detail about Kelly borrowing two pounds on the day of the murders, unless it was to plant some vague seeds of suspicion and prejudice in their minds. And why he had told them, that although they were not there to investigate such a matter, "it was a likely subject of speculation that a man who had borrowed two pounds, and had given one pound away, came to be free and easy with money in licensed premises thereafter." She could have legitimately asked Goddard what bearing this totally irrelevant matter had on the brutal murder of two men, when it was admitted no money had been stolen.

Heilbron might also have asked why Cassels saw fit to discredit Kelly even further by making derogatory comments about Skelly, whom Cassels admitted, had not appeared in the trial. What, she may have asked, if not to discredit Kelly's alibi, was the purpose of the judge telling the jury, "Skelly was so frightfully drunk that he proved to be useless to the prosecution, the defence and to himself." Why, she might have asked, if Skelly *had* to be mentioned did Cassels in all fairness not remind the jury that Kelly had stated that Skelly was *not* drunk when he left him in the *Coach and Horses* that fateful night?

She might also have illustrated the bias which had coloured Cassels' entire summing up by quoting his words to Kelly before sentencing him to death. i.e. "...the jury has *rightly* found you guilty." (My italics).

Perhaps Heilbron gave up because she was by now exhausted by the semantics, the verbal manoeuvres and the legal gymnastics to which she and her client had been subjected throughout the hearing. Perhaps she was weary at the basic unfairness exhibited throughout by the octogenarian Goddard. Perhaps she was saddened at the hostility shown

towards her and her client. Perhaps she was appalled when, against a
of her vain hopes kindly, deceptive, Grandma turned out to be the bi
bad Wolf. And perhaps she instinctively knew it was pointless goin
on because Goddard had already made up the Court's mind for it.

Delivering the Court's judgement, the "Wolf" still hadn't full
discarded "Grandma's" clothes! After telling her solicitously that h
meant no disrespect to her and that she had done the best she could, h
told her, "A more hopeless appeal had seldom been before the Court.
Then the "Wolf" finally bared his fangs. "This man", he scowled, "wa
convicted of as cruel and deliberate a murder for the purpose of gain a
can well be imagined. The case against him was that he went into
cinema with an automatic and shot two men there as though they wer
dogs and left them dying on the floor of the cinema, and *took th
money* which he was after. He is a man who, according to the evidenc
at the trial, was accustomed to boast about the violence he would offe
to people who stood in his way. If the jury in this case believed th
evidence which was given - and that is a matter for them - the case wa
proved beyond a peradventure. It was proved *as conclusively* as an
case can be proved, short of actually finding the man with the revolver.
(My italics)

Apart from wrongly stating that Kelly "took the money'
Goddard's pronouncement was rather odd in many other respect
given that the only evidence against Kelly had been circumstantial - an
very dubious circumstantial evidence at that. Was he saying that th
total absence of any material or forensic evidence, the lack of an
identification of Kelly by eye-witnesses and the lack of any murde
weapon traced to him, made no difference at all? Was he really sayin
that the virtual hearsay evidence of two convicted, self-confessed liar
and a mentally ill con man, was "conclusive" evidence of Kelly's guilt
Yes he was. For he then went on to relate, inaccurately, that Dickso
and Northam had testified Kelly had told them of the "ghastly deed'
he was going to do, and that Northam, although a professional thie
was like many professional thieves, averse to the use of firearms. "Thi
man (Northam)," said Goddard, *"having tried to persuade him no
to,* Kelly then went off and *came back to the public house* after h
had committed the deed." (My italics)

Considering Kelly's life was in the balance, this inaccurate and distorted summation was unpardonable. Firstly, by his clever wording, the Lord Chief Justice gave the totally false impression that Kelly in the *Beehive* had told his alleged co-conspirators that he was purposely going off to commit the murders - something which had not even been alleged at the two trials. Secondly, according to Northam's (and Dickson's) own evidence, far from Northam trying to dissuade Kelly, he actually provided him with the murder overcoat. Thirdly, the prosecution had never at any time alleged that Kelly came back to the *Beehive*, after committing the "ghastly deed." The result however, of this skilful blend of conjecture and misrepresentation was to portray Kelly in an even worse light - as a premeditated, cold-blooded killer.

Coming to Graham, the inveterate liar and con man, Goddard said it was his evidence which had, "put the matter (of Kelly's guilt) beyond doubt." Graham, he said, was "undergoing a sentence of imprisonment *or was on remand*." But, "According to that *convict*, Kelly told him exactly what he had done and how he had done it. The question," said Goddard, "was whether the jury believed this evidence, and the Court was not surprised that they did." (My italics).

Despite Goddard's admission that he did not know whether Graham was convicted or on remand he did not hesitate to perjoratively describe even this valuable prosecution "witness" as a "convict". (3)

Graham had been a very plausible witness. And, being charitable, Goddard might, like the judge and the jury, be forgiven for having being taken in by his false testimony. What he could not be forgiven for however, was his stated view that, " It was not the (trial) judge's duty to sift through the evidence...to represent it *fairly* to the jury." (My italics) Surely that was precisely the judge's duty, in order to present to the jury a balanced view of the case and to ensure "fairness" to the accused? But far from criticising Cassels, the Lord Chief Justice eulogised him thus: "I have never read a summing-up which more than answers the qualities I have down as to what a summing-up should be".

Before delivering the *coup-de-grace* to Kelly, Goddard carried out his usual perfunctory consultation by whispering "There's nothing in this is there?" to his two colleagues. Before they even replied he

pronounced to the Court, "The points taken on this prisoner's beh[a]
can only be described as trivial. The Court is of the opinion that there
nothing in any of the points made, and consequently we think the appe
should be dismissed." Then, without as much as a passing glance
the condemned man, he coldly said, "Take the prisoner down."

It is not known whether or not on this occasion Lord Godda[
involuntarily ejaculated, as he usually did when sentencing a man
hang or - before the 1948 Criminal Justice Act - to a flogging with t[
'Cat O' Nine Tails'.

(1) Goddard's decision to ignore the Cameo case precedent and not order separa
trials in the Craig and Bentley case, was the reason given by Home Secreta
Kenneth Clarke in 1992 for refusing Bentley a posthumous pardon. i.e. sin
Bentley was jointly charged, jointly tried and jointly convicted of murder wi
Craig, there was no legal alternative to the death sentence.

(2) Lord Goddard (Re. The 1952 Devlin & Burns murder case) speaking or
House of Lords motion that the Court of Appeal should have the power to ord
a retrial. (Hansard, Lords, 8th May 1952, cols, 745 et seq.) "We declined
consider that evidence (i.e. new evidence about a witness's admitted perju
and another man's admission of guilt), and we declined for very good reason
Matters of this sort have often been before the Court of Criminal Appeal, wl
have always in these circumstances refused to hear such evidence mainly o
the ground that they have no power to order a new trial". The Devlin and Bur
case was two years after Kelly's appeal. If there was no power to order a ne
trial in that case, then Goddard's ruling that even if Kelly won his appeal, I
would have had to stand trial a third time, would appear to have no legal basi
(This power was not given to the re-named Court of Appeal until the Crimin
Justice Act 1967, but has still rarely been used.)

(3) Graham's unimpeachable "evidence" was of course before the profusion o
so-called "cell-mate" confessions during the fifties, sixties and seventies, t[
most notorious, and discredited of which figured in the A6 murder trial, t[
Luton Post- Office murder and the Carl Bridgewater trials.

Chapter Twenty-nine

Why?

Since Northam and Dickson testified he was in the Star public house with Connolly the day after the murder, why was Skelly - who denied knowing them or Connolly - not put on an identity parade?

Why were Kelly and Connolly put on identity parades *after* they had appeared in Court on October 1st.?

Why did Inspector Hector Taylor say he brought Northam back from Manchester on October 1st, when Northam's original statement was dated, "29th September Central Police Office, Dale Street?"

Why was Kelly not asked to try on the overcoat in Court, like Northam?

Why weren't the clothes and shoes Kelly wore on March the 19th tested for bloodstains?

Why wasn't Doris O'Malley, Harry and Ted Harrison and the "Povey's" called as witnesses on Kelly's behalf?

Why was Skelly's neighbour, Taffy Roberts, whom the police accepted was drinking with Skelly in the Coach and Horses up till closing time not called? He could have corroborated Kelly's and Skelly's evidence that Kelly was also there when he was alleged to be in the Beehive with Connolly Dickson and Northam

Why did Mr. Justice Cassels not settle the disputed matter of Kelly and Connolly being able to talk to each other in prison by taking the jury to Walton's hospital wing, or at least ordering an official plan of wing? In the absence of this, the matter was left inconclusive for the ury, who in the event gave the benefit of doubt to the prosecution. This

was crucial, in view of Goddard's announcement at Kelly's appe
that Graham's evidence proved Kelly's guilt.

Why was Graham on remand in Walton when he had bee
arrested and charged at Preston? Why wasn't he remanded to his loc
prison at Preston? Or why was he moved to Walton?

Why did the defence not exploit the fact that none of Kell
fingerprints were found in the Cameo cinema?

Why was the *Coach and Horses* licensee's wife, Liz McDonald
not called by the Defence? She could have proved whether Kelly onl
arrived at 9.00pm and then left, as Balmer testified, or whether he ha
been there earlier and had stayed longer. (In his memoirs in the Liverpoc
Echo November 20th 1967, Balmer said he visited the *Coach & Horse*
later on Sunday March 20th, and that the licensee's wife did not knov
George Kelly. She agreed Skelly came in at 8 to 8.15pm. The onl
other person in Skelly's company "was a stranger." He wore a brow
suit and left about 9.00pm, Skelly stayed till closing time") The "stranger
was undoubtedly Kelly. Had she too been nobbled or was Balme
being merely "technical"? I.e. she did not know Kelly personally? Wh
wasn't this challenged by Heilbron?

Why was Liz McDonald's statement - in which she said Skell
and another man fitting Kelly's description had been in her pub fron
8.00pm - not shown to Defence.?

Why was Kelly not put on an identity parade for her to identif
him as being the man with Skelly in the '*Coach* from 8.00 to 8.45pm
If she had done so he could not possibly have been in the *Beehive* pul
over a mile away at 8.15 - 8.30pm.

Why was no mention made by the Defence of Balmer's an
Kelly's visit to the Pier Head to see Kelly's brother Peter about th
overcoat at 2.00pm on Monday March the 21st? This would have
disproved Prosecution evidence that Kelly was at that time returning

the overcoat to Northam in Lime Street. Home Office papers show that Balmer was with Kelly at the Pier Head at that time.

Why did Dickson deny knowing Balmer before their meeting in Cheapside on the 13th of May 1949? He was the arresting officer on the Woolerton immoral earnings case in 1948 and must have known Dickson. As such he must have interviewed her for a statement. He also must have known that Woolerton's forename was George and not 'Bobby.'

Why didn't Balmer tell the Court Woolerton's real name? Was it because he knew that the jury would know it was a "George" who had been threatening Dickson and this might have caused doubt in Kelly's favour?

If Northam and Dickson were the authors of the anonymous letter, which stated they knew who drove the stolen lorry in Lime Street, why was nobody charged with the killing? In 1957 and 1960 the Home Office admitted this was a valid point but didn't pursue it with Liverpool police - And they didn't answer it.

Why did Northam and Dickson not tell the police, as the letter promised, where Kelly got the gun and ammunition from?

Why wasn't a handwriting expert called to verify that the anonymous letter had indeed been written by Dickson and Northam?

Why did Chief Superintendent Smith and Chief Inspector Balmer state that the anonymous letter was received by Smith when the envelope was addressed to "Inspector"?

Why, if the mud was as deep (9ft) at Botanic Park lake, as Balmer stated, were there no Hazard notices or safety railings around it? Children paddled in this lake. Was this to support his testimony that the murder weapon, "could very well still be there" - thus maintaining credibility for the assertion made in the anonymous letter which he maintained was written by his two main prosecution witnesses?

Why did police withhold the statements of usherette Edna Ashle and Frederick Ashton from the Defence?

Why did Balmer not advise the Court that the taxi-driver's rea name was Corrie and not Currie?

Why was Skelly's wife, a witness to the Sunday morning interview with her husband and Kelly, not called by the Defence? Her evidenc could have disproved Balmer's version of what her husband said abou Kelly.

Why was there no mention in the pathologist's autopsy report c any alcohol in Margie's blood, when Margie's sister said she had onl been persuaded that the handwriting was Margie's because she wa told she had been drinking?

Why did the police tell Margie's sister she had been drinking?

Why did Detective Chief Superintendent. Morris in 1960 (whe Balmer was Assistant Chief Constable) wrongly state in a written repor to the Home Office - following Kelly's brother-in-law's request for th case to be re-opened - that, "Norwegian Margie died *before* th Committal proceedings"? He knew she died almost three week afterwards.

Why did Balmer say in a written report to the Home Office at th same time, "Witness (neighbour Hilda Kelly) said Kelly went toward the Spofforth hotel (during the crucial period) but the note in the suga basin left for him by Doris O'Malley said she was in the *Bramleys* pu which was in the opposite direction to the *Spofforth*"? Balmer kne that the *Spofforth* was also known as the *Bramleys* pub - becaus both were owned by Bramleys brewery.

Why did Balmer in the same report wrongly state that Kelly denie "in evidence" being in the *Spofforth*?

Why was the original statement of Hilda Kelly's, taken by Balmer, not mentioned by the Defence? Why wasn't she called?

Why did Northam and Dickson make their damning statements (all of which were taken by Balmer) "in instalments "over a period of days, constantly adding on each occasion new incriminating evidence against Kelly and Connolly? Even the Home Office criticised this.

Why was a convicted man allowed to slip through the regulations designed to prevent such persons from sitting on a jury? And was it mere coincidence that he happened to be a cinema manager?

Why did Justice Oliver at the first trial dismiss the jury after only four hours, when they had merely said that the answer to their query did not help them? They never said they couldn't agree on a verdict. Was the reason - because the jury had previously asked his advice on the possibility of two different verdicts for the two men - he feared they would bring in Not Guilty verdicts?. And did he discharge them in order to prevent this? This would account for the message he sent to Superintendent Smith after the case. It would also explain a note written by Justice Cassels after the second trial in which he said he understood that the jury in the first trial were eleven to one for a Not Guilty verdict.

Epilogue

Two weeks before his death George Kelly wrote another letter to Harry Harrison. It said:

> '*Dear Harry, Hoping you are keeping well. I suppose you heard the Result of my Appeal, Well what can I do about it. I know every one must be saying I am guilty, but I don't care what they say, I know I am innocent of this crime. Harry if I go for this, well you can always say he was innocent. Doris was telling me you have done all you can for me. Thanks a lot, please tell your Billy I was asking about him, also his wife. As (sic) he still got his Dog, Well I don't know what to do with myself, I am just waiting to see what is going to happen. tell all the Boys I was asking about them, Harry if you can still do anything please try for me. if you want to come up and see me please tell Doris. time is getting very close for me, but I am not worrying, my Mind is Clear, I have never murdered any man in my life Thank God. Well Harry I must Close now hoping you drop me a line soon. Remember me to Fred and his Wife.*
>
> *From George Kelly.* '

On the 27th of March, with one day to go, Sydney Silverman MP., a partner in the firm of Silverman & Livermore, (and later responsible for the abolition of capital punishment) contacted the Home Office saying new evidence had been discovered. Kelly's brother, Joey, also sent a telegram to the Home Secretary and the King requesting a stay because, he said, he could produce a new "witness." It was however, all to no avail. Mr. Chuter Ede, the Labour Home Secretary, who in 1948 had voted against capital punishment, said he could find no grounds for interfering, and that "the law must take its course".

"That evening Colleen Dutton visited Kelly and was given a forget-me-not ring. As she left the prison she said she would keep the ring forever and would always love him. Doris O'Malley told the press she also would always love him. By the following week she was having "jars out" in 67 Cambridge Street with various men friends. At 9.00am on the morning of the execution however, Hilda and Bowie Kelly kept their children off school and they all knelt in prayer in the front parlour.

Kelly's mother, sister Sally and youngest brother Frankie spent the last hours with him on the eve of his execution. Emerging from the prison, Frankie told the press, "Georgie is an innocent man. But he will die with a clear conscience. He told me that just before he goes he's going to sing my Mam's favourite song, " *I Lost the Sunshine and Roses.*"

George Kelly still lies in an unmarked grave at Walton Prison. In 1996 negotiations began with the Home Office to have his body released for re-burial in consecrated ground. Unfortunately however, a mercenary funeral director and a well-known lawyer, both acting on behalf of a member of his family, went public on radio and in the press, which resulted in the Home Office rescinding permission.

Charles Connolly was released from prison in 1956 with full remission for good conduct. His imprisonment and the strain of the case had resulted in the break-up of his marriage. His young daughter had to move to ten different schools because of playground taunts from other children, before finally moving with her mother to Gravesend Kent. On his release however Connolly brought her back to Liverpool, where she grew up to be a nursing sister and captain in the Territorial Army.

Until his death in 1997 he led a honest and industrious life and was never again in trouble with the police. During the 1970s he became a popular, well-known character as a "greeter" in various Liverpool night-spots. A measure of the respect in which he was widely held was generously demonstrated by the four hundred people from all walks of life, including celebrities from the boxing and entertainment worlds, who attended his funeral.

Kelly's young impetuous friend, James Skelly, eventually matured and worked for several years for the city council in various occupations - in one of these actually working for a short period alongside Connolly. He ended up as a foreman in Cammell Laird's shipyard but was forced into retirement following an accident in which he lost an eye. He died in 1993.

At Liverpool Assizes on 27th February 1952, less than two years after the hanging of George Kelly, two young men were sentenced to death for the murder of Mrs. Beatrice Alice Rimmer, a fifty-five year-old widow, at her home No 7 Cranborne Road, off Smithdown Road Wavertree, Liverpool - The next street to the Cameo.

The two men, 20 year-old Edward Devlin and 21 year-old Alfred Burns, both from Manchester, vehemently protested their innocence throughout the eight-day trial, and produced alibi evidence that they were in Salford breaking into a warehouse at the time of the murder.

The motive alleged by the prosecution was robbery yet nothing was stolen from the house. There was no material or forensic evidence against the accused men. No murder weapon was ever found. There were no eye-witnesses to the killing and no identification of Devlin and Burns as the killers. The purely circumstantial evidence against them was given by three witnesses: two prostitutes and a convicted thief and police informer. All three testified that they had been parties to the planning of the crime, and were given immunity from prosecution.

Devlin was defended by Rose Heilbron QC. and the prosecution was led by Basil Neild QC. Appeals were lodged. The main grounds being that after the conviction of the two men, one of the prostitutes had told her friend that another man, the father of her young child, had committed the murder. And further, that another man had confessed to the crime. Lord Goddard however, in summarily dismissing the appeals, ruled that the Court was unable to go into matters such as "mistaken evidence", stating, "We are not a jury. We do not sit here to re-try cases." But the Home Secretary, Sir David Maxwell-Fyffe, took the unusual step of ordering an inquiry. The person he chose to conduct it was a High Court judge from the Isle of Man, assisted by a Scotland Yard Chief Superintendent.

After five days, the Inquiry, which was held *in camera,* concluded that there was no truth in the prostitute's claim, and that the other man's confession to the murder was "pure fabrication."

On the morning of 25th April 1952, whilst a thousand-strong

crowd, including the condemned men's relatives, gathered outside the gates, Devlin and Burns were hanged side by side at Walton Prison.

The police officer in charge of the case was Detective Chief Superintendent Herbert Balmer, by now the Head of Liverpool C.I.D. and later to become Deputy Chief Constable of Liverpool.

Never attaining the rank of Chief Constable because he had never served in another force, Balmer died of cancer in 1970. After his death, veteran criminal lawyer E. Rex Makin, who knew him well, provided this fitting epitaph: "He was a publicity-seeker and a bully. His methods were purely verballing. He was the archetypal detective who believed the best evidence was a cough, whether genuine, forced, induced or voluntary".

In replying to this letter, please write on the envelope:—

Number..7915.. Name.......G. KELLY......

.................................Prison

Hello, Harry

Hoping you are keeping well, I suppose you heard the Result of my Appeal, well what can I do about it, I know

every one must be saying I am Guilty, but I dont care what they say, I know I am innocent of this crime. Harry if I go for this, well you can always say he was innocent, Doris was telling me you have done all you can for me.

No. 243   (21442—3-11-42)

Letter to Harry Harrison from George Kelly after Kelly had lost his appeal. 14 March 1950.

Thanks a lot, please tell your Billy I was asking about him also is wife, as he still got is Dog, well I dont know what to do with my self, I am just waiting to see what is going to happen. Tell all the Boys I was asking about them. Harry if you can still do anything please try for me. if you want to come up and see me please tell Doris. time is getting very close for me, but I am not worrying my Mind is clear

3

I have never Murdered
eny man in my life
Thank God. well Harry I
must Close now hoping
your drop me a line soon.
Remember me to Fred and
his Wife.

From George.
Kelly.

Lime Street; Liverpool's 'Piccadilly'. 1950.

Crowds queued outside St. George's Hall for a seat in the public gallery at the 'Cameo' Trial.

Charles Connolly in the Royal Navy, 1942.

Charles Connolly, age 16 years; Amateur Champion, 1940.

'Greeter' Charles Connolly with Bruce Forsyth.

With American singer Al Martino.

With The Three Degrees.

With British Bantamweight Champion Alan Rudkin.

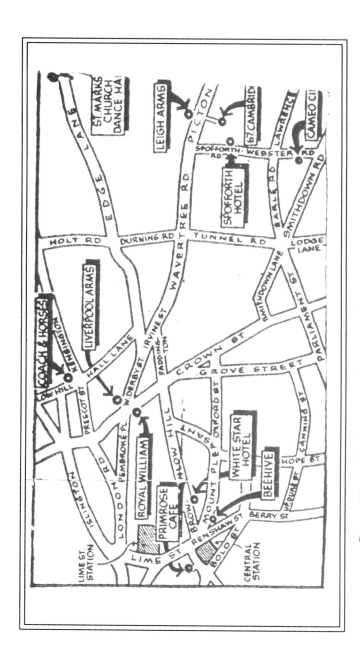

Street Map of 'downtown Liverpool' showing many of the connected locations in the story.

Charles Connolly and his daughter Tina in Liverpool's Lime Street upon his release.

The Cameo Conspiracy

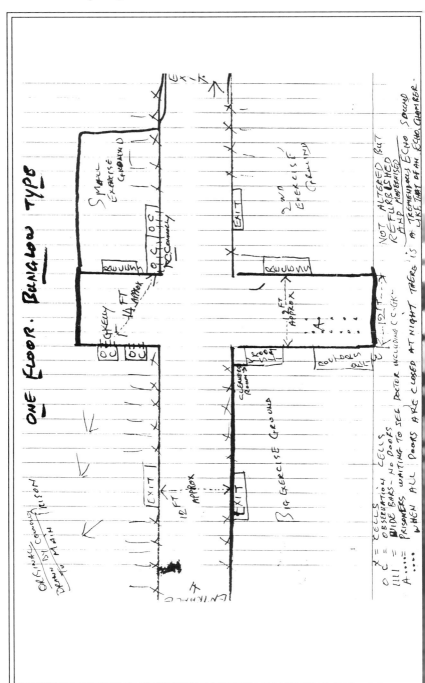

Plan of the Single Storey Hospital Wing at Walton Prison 1949 - 50, and the location of Kelly and Connolly's cells.

This 1949/50 layout was drawn for the author by Charles Connolly in 1996. The wing was refurbished shortly afterwards.

Connolly's cell is in the observation cell at the bottom left hand corner of the small exercise yard area.

Kelly's cell is across the corridor; also in an observation cell, toward the top middle left of the sketch. The stone floor corridors are 12 feet wide, thus making the distance between Kelly and Connolly some 14 feet.

KEY:

C: Ordinary cells with closed doors

O.C.: Observation cells, no doors and wide bars.

Line of dots outside doctors office (bottom of middle corridor on left) represents prisoners waiting to see the Doctor.

Recess: Where 'Slopping out' took place each morning.

Other notes at the bottom of the sketch read:-

'Not altered but refurbished and modernised'

'When all the doors are closed at night there is a tremendous echo sound like that of an Echo Chamber.

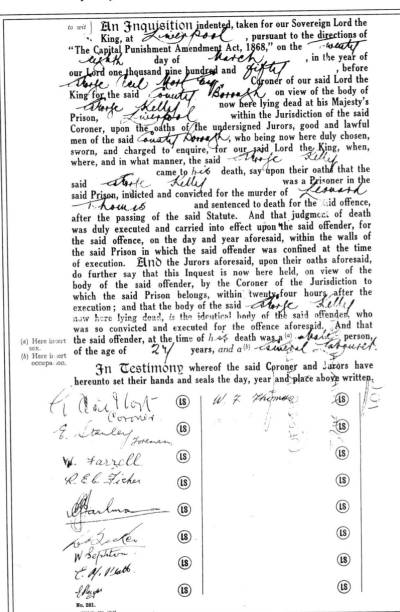

to wit } **An Inquisition** indented, taken for our Sovereign Lord the King, at *Liverpool*, pursuant to the directions of "The Capital Punishment Amendment Act, 1868," on the *twenty eighth* day of *March*, in the year of our Lord one thousand nine hundred and *fifty*, before *George Cecil Mort Esq.* Coroner of our said Lord the King for the said *County Borough* on view of the body of *George Kelly* now here lying dead at his Majesty's Prison, *Liverpool* within the Jurisdiction of the said Coroner, upon the oaths of the undersigned Jurors, good and lawful men of the said *County Borough*, who being now here duly chosen, sworn, and charged to enquire, for our said Lord the King, when, where, and in what manner, the said *George Kelly* came to *his* death, say upon their oaths that the said *George Kelly* was a Prisoner in the said Prison, indicted and convicted for the murder of *Leonard Thomas* and sentenced to death for the said offence, after the passing of the said Statute. And that judgment of death was duly executed and carried into effect upon the said offender, for the said offence, on the day and year aforesaid, within the walls of the said Prison in which the said offender was confined at the time of execution. **And** the Jurors aforesaid, upon their oaths aforesaid, do further say that this Inquest is now here held, on view of the body of the said offender, by the Coroner of the Jurisdiction to which the said Prison belongs, within twenty-four hours after the execution; and that the body of the said *George Kelly* now here lying dead, is the identical body of the said offender, who was so convicted and executed for the offence aforesaid. And that the said offender, at the time of *his* death was a (a) *male* person, of the age of *27* years, and a (b) *general labourer*.

(a) Here insert sex.
(b) Here insert occupation.

In Testimony whereof the said Coroner and Jurors have hereunto set their hands and seals the day, year and place above written.

G. Cecil Mort (LS) Coroner.		*W. F. Thomas* (LS)	
E. Stanley (LS) Foreman.		(LS)	
W. Farrell. (LS)		(LS)	
R. E. C. Fisher (LS)			
[signature] (LS)		(LS)	
[signature] (LS)			
W. Sephton. (LS)			
E. W. Platt. (LS)			
[signature] (LS)		(LS)	

No. 281.
(C72242) 250 12/47

The official confirmation of Kelly's Execution.

Francis Herbert Brisby
being Sworn Says:- I am Principal
Medical officer at this H.M. Prison,
L'pool. This morning I was
present at the Execution of
George Kelly.

There was no hitch in the
arrangements, & everything was
carried out skilfully & decorously.

Death was due to Judicial
Hanging, & was instantaneous.

Francis Herbert Brisby

Sworn before me,

A Cecil Mort—
Coroner.

T.460+1685(3¼290-h719)

CORONER'S DEPOSITIONS.

CITY OF LIVERPOOL, in the County of Lancaster. } To Wit.

DEPOSITIONS of Witnesses produced, sworn and examined this 28ᵗʰ day of March one thousand nine hundred and ~~forty~~ *fifty* before George Cecil Mort, Esquire, Coroner of our Lord the King for the said City touching the death of George Kelly now lying dead at Liverpool aforesaid

Alfred Coombe Wall Richards being sworn says:— I am the Governor of this H.M. Prison, L'pool. The deceased, George Kelly, was received into this Prison on the 1ˢᵗ October 1949. He was 27 years of age, a Casual Labourer, and lived at 3 P.O. Trowbridge Street, L'pool 3. He was tried at the L'pool Assizes Bar commencing on the 30ᵗʰ January 1950, before Mr. Justice Cassels for the murder of Leonard Thomas, and on a plea, a Verdict brought, of 53, Kelwood Drive, L'pool, and being found guilty, he was

A. Cecil Mort.

James Skelly (left) and Charles Connolly . 1992

The Cameo Conspiracy

The triumphant 'murder squad'. Chief Inspector Herbert Balmer is second from the right.

Lusitania - On the 7th May 1915 the Cunard vessel *Lusitania* was torpedoed by a German submarine off the Old Head of Kinsale on the south west coast of Ireland, resulting in the loss of the vessel itself and 1,201 men, women, and children. An act of brutal aggression? Or a cynical plot to bring the United States into the First World War?

More than eighty years on the story of the *Lusitania* continues to be shrouded in mystery and suspicion. What was her real cargo? Why wasn't she protected? Why did she sink so quickly?

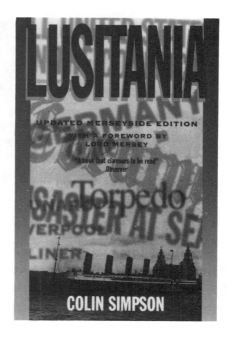

Lord Mersey, the great grandson of the man who chaired the enquiry into the *Lusitania* disaster, (who he calls 'the Old Man'), has been extremely helpful and was kind enough to write a new foreword for this Special Edition.

Containing rare photographs from Germany and elsewhere, it is a truly intriguing and fascinating tale. *'A book that clamours to be read'* - Observer.
'The truth at last' - The Sunday Times.
By Colin Simpson. ISBN 1 9521020 6 4. £9.50.

THETIS
"The Admiralty Regrets..."

The disaster in Liverpool Bay

C. Warren & J. Benson

Thetis - the Admiralty Regrets. The disaster in Liverpool Bay. A minute by minute account of the submarine disaster that cost the lives of 99 men...... Why didn't anyone cut open the submarine? Why was there no urgency in the Admiralty's rescue system? Did the Admiralty **really** regret? Contains previously unpublished photographs and documents.

By C. Warren & J. Benson. Foreword by Derek Arnold, a survivor's son, and postscript by maritime historian David Roberts.

ISBN 1 9521020 8 0.   £9.50.

Life at Levers.
Memories of making
soaps at 'Billy' Lever's
Port Sunlight factory on
Merseyside. The
ordinary people who
worked there talk of
their lives and times
spent in the soapworks.
By David Roberts. ISBN
1 9521020 3 X. £6.99

**Faster Than The Wind - the Liverpool to Holyhead
Telegraph.** A guide to and history of this fascinating
maritime communications system from North Wales
to the busiest port in the world, Liverpool, in the
early 19th century. This book will take the reader on
two journeys. The first is a real journey, to places
with superb views along the North Wales and Wirral
coasts, including full
details of how to find the
substantial remains of the
Liverpool to Holyhead
Telegraph Stations. The
second is a journey into
the workings of such a
telegraph, and into the
experiences of the people

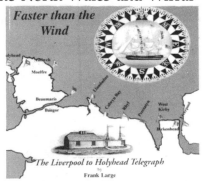

involved in creating and using the signalling system.
By Frank Large. ISBN 1 9521020 9 9. £8.95

Life At Lairds - Memories of working shipyard men at Cammell Lairds world-famous shipyard in Birkenhead. *'The time may not be far off when young people will ask, what did they do, what were they like, those who worked there? This book answers the questions.'* - Sea Breezes.

'A book full of anecdotes and rich in humanity...a piece of social history.' - Liverpool Echo.

By David Roberts. ISBN 0 9521020 1 3 £6.99

Cammell Laird - the golden years. Looks back at the yard's history with particular focus on the 1960s and 70s when Lairds were engaged in the building of the Polaris nuclear submarines.

'Captures life in the prosperous years of the historic Birkenhead shipyard' - Liverpool Echo.

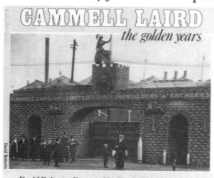

David Roberts - Foreword by Frank Field M.P.

'Puts into perspective...the strikes...the Polaris contract...and those who worked at the yard' - Sea Breezes.

By David Roberts. Foreword by Frank Field MP. ISBN 1 9521020 2 1. £5.99

Off The Cuff - Ex-Merseyside Sergeant Swasie Turner tells the stories of real-life policing on the streets of the area. A book to raise your eyebrows - and sometimes your hair! Foreword by Alison Halford, former Asst. Chief Constable, Merseyside.
By Swasie Turner. ISBN 1 9521020 4 8. £8.99.

If The Cap Fits - The follow-up to the bestselling 'Off The Cuff' brings you more yarns from the sharp end of Merseyside police work. Foreword by Michael Chapman, Executive Producer of TVs 'The Bill'.
By Swasie Turner. ISBN 1 9521020 7 2.. £8.99.

Forgotten Empress by David Zeni.
The fascinating story of the steamship *'Empress of Ireland'* which was lost at sea within two years of the sinking of the *'Titanic'*, and which was an even greater tragedy in terms of passenger fatalities.
Just one year later, the loss of the *'Lusitania'* completed a terrible triangle of maritime disaster.
Of the three, only the *'Empress of Ireland'* remains shrouded in the cloak of history, almost as impenetrable as the fog which caused her loss and the death of 1,012 souls on May 29, 1914.
Contains over 100 photographs. Hardback with full -colour dustjacket. ISBN 1 874448 80 9 £25.00

Schooner Port - Two Centuries of Upper Mersey Sail.

By H. F. Starkey.

Inspired by his father's vivid recollections of working life on a schooner, the author has meticulously researched the story of shipping and shipbuilding on the Upper Mersey, including Runcorn, Widnes & Warrington. 'Schooner Port' contains a wealth of information and makes a very important contribution to our knowledge of the maritime development of

North West Britain. 'Recognised as the only authoritative work on this particular subject' - *Sea Breezes.* 'Packed with hard facts and illustrated with some rare old photographs, this rare book should command a wide readership. - *Liverpool Echo.* 'A wealth of information in both text and appendices...Mr. Starkey's exhaustive research is apparent' - *Marine News.*

£8.95. ISBN 0 9521020 4 6

Videos

Cammell Laird, Old Ships and Hardships - the history and true story of this world-famous shipyard - on video. Contains rare archive footage of famous vessels and comments from the men who built them. £12.99.

All In A Day's Work Vol. 1 - the story of a living, working river - the River Mersey - and the ordinary people that work upon it. Features : Mersey Pilots; Pilot Launch Crews; Shipbuilding and Shiprepairing workers; Dredger crews, and much more. £12.99

Also available -
All In A Day's Work Vol 2 - More stories from the Mersey, on video. Features : Rock Boats; Mersey Ferries; Tugs and Tug management; the Bunker boats and crews; the Vessel Tracking System; New vessels on the river including cruise liners and car ferries, & much more. £12.99